I0754800

Border Studies.
Cultures, Spaces, Orders

Edited by

Prof. Dr. Astrid Fellner, Saarland University

Prof. Dr. Konstanze Jungbluth, European University Viadrina Frankfurt (Oder)

Prof. Dr. Hannes Krämer, University of Duisburg-Essen

Dr. Christian Wille, University of Luxembourg

Volume 1

Christian Wille | Birte Nienaber (eds.)

Border Experiences in Europe

Everyday Life – Working Life – Communication – Languages

The Deutsche Nationalbibliothek lists this publication in the Deutsche Nationalbibliografie; detailed bibliographic data are available on the Internet at http://dnb.d-nb.de

ISBN 978-3-8487-5444-1 (Print)
978-3-8452-9567-1 (ePDF)

British Library Cataloguing-in-Publication Data
A catalogue record for this book is available from the British Library.

ISBN 978-3-8487-5444-1 (Print)
978-3-8452-9567-1 (ePDF)

Library of Congress Cataloging-in-Publication Data
Wille, Christian / Nienaber, Birte
Border Experiences in Europe
Everyday Life – Working Life – Communication – Languages
Christian Wille / Birte Nienaber (eds.)
261 pp.
Includes bibliographic references.

ISBN 978-3-8487-5444-1 (Print)
978-3-8452-9567-1 (ePDF)

1st Edition 2020

Published by
Nomos Verlagsgesellschaft mbH & Co. KG
Waldseestraße 3-5 | 76530 Baden-Baden
www.nomos.de

Production of the printed version:
Nomos Verlagsgesellschaft mbH & Co. KG
Waldseestraße 3-5 | 76530 Baden-Baden

Printed and bound in Germany.

ISBN (Print): 978-3-8487-5444-1
ISBN (ePDF): 978-3-8452-9567-1

DOI: https://doi.org/10.5771/9783845295671

Contents

Border Experiences: Communication and Languages

Borders and border experiences

Christian Wille and Birte Nienaber

Abstract

The idea of a "Europe without borders" has been contested for the last decade and is increasingly overshadowed by rebordering phenomena. This development has sparked debates within border studies on how borders should be thought of and investigated. The introductory article deals with this and reconstructs the formation and differentiation of the bordering approach. Furthermore, the concept of border experiences is determined as an investigative perspective that is interested in everyday cultural arenas of bordering processes. It puts the agency of 'border(lands) residents' in the center and provides insights into everyday cultural border (re)productions. With this in mind, we will present the book articles in the final section.

Keywords

Border studies, bordering, border experiences, Europe without borders, social practice

1. Borders

With the concept of border experiences, this volume aims to strengthen the facet of the concept of the border that is oriented towards everyday cultural realities. This endeavor ties in with the 2016 Association for Borderlands Studies' European Conference, entitled "Differences and discontinuities in a 'Europe without Borders,'" and seeks to raise awareness of the numerous and often-'overlooked' forms of articulation of borders. The background of this is an increasingly questioned epoch, which was discussed in academics until the 2000s as a "borderless world" and is contested in politics today operating under the slogan "Europe without borders." In this volume, Yndigegn speaks about six decades which were politically guided by the idea of a "Europe without borders", but in the past decade, we have increasingly been confronted with a renaissance of borders in Europe. This is reflected in, among other things, the reintroduction of border controls at EU internal borders (Evrard/Nienaber/Sommaribas 2018), the growing

Euroscepticism (Klatt 2018), burgeoning nationalisms (Lamour/Varga 2017) in connection with farther-reaching populism (Brömmel/King/Sicking 2017). These developments, which should be looked at more closely in the context of terrorism, financial crisis, flight, Brexit, Ukraine crisis and many more (Yndigegn in this volume), seem to be the driving force for the fact that the era of "Europe without borders" is already being overshadowed by an epoch of rebordering. The latter has given border studies tangible impulses in recent years with regard to, among other things, a reconsidered concept of the border (Wille 2020).

In Europe, increased attention on borders can already be observed in the area of tension of the 'borderless world' and 'Fortress Europe' of the 1990s, referring also to the simultaneity of globalization dynamics, the fall of the Iron Curtain, on the one hand, and the emergence of new nation states and the stabilization of the EU's external borders, on the other. These seemingly contradictory developments, which have been perpetuated in accentuated form in the recent rebordering tendencies (Yndigegn in this volume), have sensitized us on the concept of the border in such a way that Hess (2018, p. 84) speaks of a *border turn*. This is characterized not only by the heightened interest in and the increased academic involvement in border and migration dynamics, but also in a reorientation of border research, which is oriented on the *practice turn* (Schatzki//Knorr Cetina/Savigny 2001) and implies an understanding of borders, which some authors also refer to as constructivist (Bürkner 2017; Herzog/Sohn 2019). It overcomes the notion of fixed and set borders in favor of the view that borders are the results of social processes (Newman/Paasi 1998; Konrad 2015). This approach is not aimed at the border as an ontological object, but at the processes of the (de-)stabilization of borders–and thus at the forces that create them, as they take place in and through practices or discourses (Newman 2006; Kaiser 2012). In this context, an approach has been adopted across disciplines that provides a catchy term for the notion of border as a social production: the bordering approach, which, with the intention of processualizing, defines the border as a social practice. However, it is not to be understood as an analytical instrument that is applied and makes borders immediately describable and analyzable as de- and rebordering practices. Bordering, according to Yuval-Davis/Wemyss/Cassidy (2019, p. 5), "[...] constitutes a principal organizing mechanism in constructing, maintaining and controlling social and political order." It is therefore a fundamental viewpoint that focuses on border (de)stabilization and/or the mechanisms that are effective and articulated within it.

The implementation of the bordering approach can neither be clearly dated nor attributed to a specific author. It was already being mentioned in the political sciences in the 1990s (Albert/Brock 1996), made productive by human geographers at the turn of the century (van Houtum/van Naerssen 2002) and only later received in other disciplines. The temporally offset reception and ongoing empirical examination of bordering processes has further stimulated and conceptually enhanced the debate on borders. Some authors, for example, address border practices and/or practices of borders as possible operationalizations of the *bordering* approach (Auzanneau/Greco 2018; Wille et al. 2016; Parker/Adler-Nissen 2012; Paasi 1999). In addition, a distinction is to be made between de- und re-bordering processes through which the dynamic and unavoidable interplay of destabilization and stabilization of borders is conceived (Salter 2012; Yuval-Davis/Wemyss/Cassidy 2019, p. 59). The empirical observation of such processes has also shown that border (re)productions – whether in stabilizing or destabilizing form – seldom merge into binary codes, emanate from one actor with a clear agenda and identity or explicitly materialize in a particular place. Rather, the processes of bordering are multifaceted, which is why they are increasingly understood as multiple processes and examined as such (Wille 2020; Gerst et al. 2018). The representatives of critical border studies have largely been responsible for the sensitization of this (Parker et al. 2009; Parker/Vaughan-Williams 2012; Salter 2012; Jones 2019; Brambilla/Jones 2019; Yuval-Davis/Wemyss/Cassidy 2019), and their concerns are based on a rather catchy observation: "the construction of borders [...] must always be done somewhere by someone against some other" (Tyerman 2019, p. 2). Thus they are not only interested in the fact that borders represent social (re-)productions, but rather take a critical-differentiating view of how the multiple processes of bordering (strategically) take place: for example, from whom they emanate, with which interests, effects and who is addressed. In this context, the everyday cultural realities of life become more important as they are now included as sites for bordering processes and assumed to be constitutive of borders (Parker/Vaughan-Williams 2012; Rumford 2012). Addressing everyday cultural realities allows processes of border (de)stabilization to be recognized more broadly, to counteract a simplifying understanding of borders and to inevitably direct the focus onto 'border(lands) residents' as agents of the border. Such an orientation, which is enhanced by everyday cultural arenas, above all challenges cultural border studies and makes discussion possible with the concept of border experiences.

2. *Border experiences*

The concept of border experiences ties in with the idea of the border as a social (re-)production and the insight that processes of bordering are not reserved exclusively for political-institutional actors. Border experiences strengthen the perspective and thus the role and agency of those who 'inhabit' the border, meaning those who are entangled in them and who with their (bodily and sensory) experiences or generation of meaning in and through everyday practices, narratives, representations or objects continuously (re-)produce them. It is an approach that focuses on 'border(lands) residents' and their border experience in order to better understand the modes of action and function, but, above all, the ways in which borders are appropriated and thereby produced. This approach can be understood as a 'humanizing the border' (Brambilla 2015, p. 27), which is discussed and/or practiced by a multitude of authors, each with different focuses (Auzanneau/Greco 2018; Considère/Perrin 2017; Boesen/Schnuer 2017; Brambilla 2015; Amilhat Szary/Giraut 2015; Schulze Wessel 2015; Rumford 2012; Wille 2012; Newman 2007; Rösler/Wendl 1999; Martínez 1994). With this in mind, border experiences is neither a clearly defined concept nor the sovereignty of interpretation of an author or a group of authors. Nevertheless, border experiences can be characterized by the following points as a category, complementary to geopolitical perspectives of borders.

The concept is not just a complementary view *on* the border through the eyes of the 'affected person'; rather, border experiences are developed *through* the border. This methodological approach, which Rumford (2012, p. 895) conceptualizes as "seeing like a border", describes the fundamental issue of following the border in its performative arenas: to where the border takes place as everyday cultural (re-)production. These include moments of representation or meaning production coded in practices, discourses or objects and in which borders are (made) relevant. While Rumford (2012, p. 897) emphasizes that "[i]n aspiring to 'see like a border' we must recognise the constitutive nature of borders in social [...] life", Considère/Perrin (2017, p. 16) focus on possible access points for this: "The border [...] is reflected in perceptions, everyday practices, and constructed ideas." Border experiences stand for such everyday cultural settings and give the border its (sometimes temporary) existence. A vivid example of this is given by Martin in this volume, in which the Franco-Luxembourgish border reproduces itself through an everyday "cut-off point", that cross-border commuters experience on their way to work in Luxembourg: "conversations were interrupted, pages stopped downloading, and there was no signal. Mobile phones were put away in pockets by all those users who had subscriptions to a French network. We have qualified this cut-off point as a real digital border [...]."

Border experiences also imply multiple understandings of borders. This refers to the fact that everyday-culture-oriented considerations exclude neither marginalized nor privileged actors. The concept refers to the entirety of the actors "at, on, or shaping the border" (Rumford 2012, p. 897) and moving in and through the border space (Schulze Wessel 2015, p. 51) and inevitably leads to the insight that "borders [...] mean different things to different people, and work differently on different groups" (Rumford 2012, p. 894). This differentiating view, which Jóźwiak describes in this volume with the statement that "the border is not experienced by everyone in the same way", is based on the multiplicity of border experiences and gives the border multiple and time-changeable existences. In other words, borders are (re-)produced and transformed in a variety of ways, for example by refugees, international managers, tourists, and these ways also include border non-experiences (Rumford 2012, p. 889). This experience is clearly shown by Boesen in this volume with residential migrants, who sometimes have "left Luxembourg without arriving in another country."

Whether and to what extent borders will acquire existences through border experiences or become/(are made) effective in border experiences will remain question to be answered empirically. This question is at the very center of this volume and is being worked on in border crossings – i.e. in the context of (forced) migration, residential migration, travel, commuter and other everyday mobility as well as in language contact situations. In particular, the areas of everyday life, working life, and communication and languages are considered, as well as the border experiences emerging there. These stand for everyday cultural realities in which borders are (made) relevant and thus (re-)produced in and through practices, discourses or objects. The approach of the authors can be summarized in three overlapping questions. *Firstly*, it is a question of to what extent borders are (re-)produced in and through practices, discourses or objects. In addition, awareness of the everyday cultural sites of borders should be raised. The range of such sites is diverse, ranging from (cross-border) recreational practices, shopping and information practices, to those related to (cross-border) employment or relocation, to border control practices or language contact situations. *Secondly*, it asks what social logics are embedded in such (re-)production processes. Questioning from this perspective addresses the creation of meaning of everyday cultural border (re)productions, which can also be discussed as border knowledge (Gerst and Jóźwiak in this volume) or border culture (Álvarez Pérez in this volume). Especially with regard to border regions, the aim here is to better understand the (strategic) use of the border and the local appropriations of the border in and through everyday practices. The use of the border is often based on the pursuit of maximizing individual benefit, but not exclusively, as shown by Wille/Roos in this volume. At the same time, the aim is to uncover the structures of meaning that are constitutive for borders in representations or projections. Several authors comment on this, such as Gerst using the example of a political event on security issues, Boesen through 'moving stories' by residential migrants, Martin with the media practices of cross-border workers, and Álvarez Pérez with border residents. And *thirdly*, this volume asks which effects of the (dis)continuity originate from borders and to what extent they are (made) effective for actors at, on, or in the border. This applies, for example, to Spanish travelers, who – since they too have been able to enter France with simply an ID card – "feel a little more equal to the much-envied citizens of democratic Europe" (Permanyer in House in this volume). However, the potential spaces opening up through borders or border crossings have also been worked out, which, for example, Pigeron-Piroth and Belkacem in this volume understand as a "resource", Martin as a "reservoir of cultural resources" or Dost/Jungbluth/Richter as liminal spaces marked by in-betweenness.

The editors of this volume would like to thank the authors for their diverse and productive examinations of border experiences in Europe. Furthermore, we would like to thank Ulla Connor, who coordinated and communicated with the authors during the book project and always made herself available as a contact person. We also want to mention the editors of the publication series "Border Studies. Cultures, Spaces, Orders", who have included this book as the first volume in the newly established series. Finally, we express our thanks to Beate Bernstein of Nomos Publishing, who patiently and professionally saw the multi-year book project to its end.

References

Albert, Mathias/Brock, Lothar (1996): Debordering the World of States. New Spaces in International Relations. In: New Political Science 18, no. 1, p. 69–106.

Amilhat Szary, Anne-Laure/Giraut, Frédéric (2015): Borderities: The Politics of Contemporary Mobile Borders. In: Amilhat Szary, A.-L./Giraut, F. (eds.), Borderities and the Politics of Contemporary Mobile Borders. Basingstoke: Palgrave, p. 1–22.

Auzanneau, Michelle/Greco, Luca (eds.) (2018): Dessiner les frontières: une approche praxéologique. Lyon: ENS Editions.

Boesen, Elisabeth/Schnuer, Gregor (eds.) (2017): European Borderlands. Living with Barriers and Bridges. London/New York: Routledge.

Brambilla, Chiara (2015): Exploring the Critical Potential of the Borderscapes Concept. In: Geopolitics 20, no. 1, p. 14–34.

Brambilla, Chiara/Jones, Reece (2019): Rethinking borders, violence, and conflict: From sovereign power to borderscapes as sites of struggles. In: Environment and Planning D: Society and Space, DOI: 10.1177/0263775819856352.

Brömmel, Winfried/König, Helmut/Sicking, Manfred (eds.) (2017): Populismus und Extremismus in Europa. Gesellschaftswissenschaftliche und sozialpsychologische Perspektiven. Bielefeld: Transcript.

Bürkner, Hans-Joachim (2017): Bordering, borderscapes, imaginaries: From constructivist to post-structural perspectives. In: Opiłowska, E./Kurcz, Z./Roose, J. (eds.): Advances in Borderlands Studies. Baden-Baden: Nomos, p. 85–107.

Considère, Sylvie/Perrin, Thomas (2017): Introduction générale. La frontière en question, ou comment débusquer les représentations sociales des frontières. In: Considère, S./Perrin, T. (eds.): Frontières et représentations sociales. Questions et perspectives méthodologiques. Paris: l'Harmattan, p. 15–24.

Gerst, Dominik/Klessmann, Maria/Krämer, Hannes/Sienknecht, Mitja/Ulrich, Peter (2018): Komplexe Grenzen. Aktuelle Perspektiven der Grenzforschung (Special issue „Komplexe Grenzen"). In: Berliner Debatte Initial 29, no. 1, p. 3–11.

Evrard, Estelle/Nienaber, Birte/Sommaribas, Adolfo (2018): The Temporary Reintroduction of Border Controls Inside the Schengen Area: Towards a Spatial Perspective. In: Journal of Borderlands Studies, DOI: 10.1080/08865655.2017.1415164.

Herzog, Lawrence A./Sohn, Christophe (2019): The co-mingling of bordering dynamics in the San Diego–Tijuana cross-border metropolis. In: Territory, Politics, Governance 7, no. 2, p. 177–199.

Hess, Sabine (2018): Border as Conflict Zone. Critical Approaches on the Border and Migration Nexus. In: Bachmann-Medick, D./Kugele, J. (eds.): Migration. Changing Concepts, Critical Approaches. Berlin: de Gruyter, p. 83–99.

Jones, Reece (2019): Open Borders: In Defense of Free Movement. University of Georgia Press.

Kaiser, Robert J. (2012): Performativity and the Eventfulness of Bordering Practices. In: Wilson, T. M./Donnan, H. (eds.): A Companion to Border Studies. Chicester: John Wiley & Sons, p. 522–537.

Klatt, Martin (2018): The So-Called 2015 Migration Crisis and Euroscepticism in Border Regions: Facing Re-Bordering Trends in the Danish–German Borderlands. In: Geopolitics, DOI: 10.1080/14650045.2018.1557149.

Konrad, Victor (2015): Towards a Theory of Borders in Motion. In: Journal for Borderlands Studies 30, no. 1, p. 1–17.

Lamour, Christian/Varga, Renáta (2017): The Border as a Resource in Right-wing Populist Discourse: Viktor Orbán and the Diasporas in a Multi-scalar Europe. In: Journal of Borderlands Studies, DOI: 10.1080/08865655.2017.1402200.

Martínez, Oscar J. (1994): Border People. Life and Society in the U.S.–Mexiko Borderlands. Tucson/London: University of Arizona Press.

Newman, David (2007): The Lines that Continue to Separate Us. Borders in Our "Borderless" World. In: Schimanski, J./Wolfe, S. (eds): Border Poetics De-limited. Hannover: Wehrhahn Verlag, p. 27–57.

Newman, David (2006): Borders and Bordering: Towards an Interdisciplinary Dialogue. In: European Journal of Social Theory 9, no. 2, p. 171–186.

Newman, David/Paasi, Anssi (1998): Fences and Neighbours in the Postmodern World: Boundary Narratives in Political Geography. In: Progress in Human Geography 22, no. 2, p. 186–207.

Paasi, Anssi (1999): Boundaries as Social Practice and Discourse: The Finnish-Russian Border. In: Regional Studies 33, no. 7, p. 669–680.

Parker, Noel/Adler-Nissen, Rebecca (2012): Picking and Choosing the 'Souvereign' Border. A Theory of Changing State Bordering Practices. In: Geopolitics 17, no. 4, p. 773–796.

Parker, Noel/Vaughan-Williams, Nick (2012): Critical Border Studies: Broadening and Deepening the ‚Lines in the Sand' Agenda. Geopolitics 17, no. 4, p. 727–733.

Parker, Noel/Bialasiewicz, Luiza/Bulmer, Sarah/Carver, Ben/Durie, Robin/Heathershaw, John/van Houtum, Henk/Kinnvall, Catarina/Kramsch, Olivier/Minca, Claudio/Murray, Alex/Panjek, Aleksander/Rumford, Chris/Schaap, Andrew/Sidaway, James/Vaughan-Williams, Nick/Williams, John (2009): Lines in the Sand? Towards an Agenda for Critical Border Studies. In: Geopolitics 14, no. 3, p. 582–587.

Rösler, Michael/Wendl, Tobias (eds.) (1999): Frontiers and Borderlands. Brussels: Peter Lang.

Rumford, Chris (2012): Towards a Multiperspectival Study of Border. In: Geopolitics 17, no. 4, p. 887–902.

Salter, Marc B. (2012): Theory of the / : The Suture and Critical Border Studies. In: Geopolitics, 17, no. 4, p. 734–755.

Schatzki, Theodore/Knorr Cetina, Karin/Savigny, Eike von (eds.) (2001): The Practice Turn in Contemporary Theory. London/New York: Routledge.

Schulze Wessel, Julia (2015): On Border Subjects: Rethinking the Figure of the Refugee and the Undocumented Migrant. In: Constellations 23, no. 1, p. 46–57.

Tyerman, Thom (2019): Everyday Borders in Calais: The Globally Intimate Injustices of Segregation. Geopolitics, DOI: 10.1080/14650045.2019.1631807.

Van Houtum, Henk/Van Naerssen, Ton (2002): Bordering, ordering and othering. Tijdschrift voor Economische en Sociale Geografie 93, no. 2, p. 125–136.

Wille, Christian (2020): Towards a complexity shift: Aktuelle analytische Trends der Grenzforschung. In: Klessmann, M./Gerst, D./Krämer, H. (eds.): Handbuch Grenzforschung (Border Studies. Cultures, Spaces, Orders). Baden-Baden: Nomos (in press).

Wille, Christian (2012): Grenzgänger und Räume der Grenze. Raumkonstruktionen in der Großregion SaarLorLux. Brussels: Peter Lang.

Wille, Christian/Reckinger, Rachel/Kmec, Sonja/Hesse, Markus (eds.) (2016): Spaces and Identities in Border Regions. Politics – Media – Subjects. Bielefeld: Transcript.

Yuval-Davis, Nira/Wemyss, Georgie/Cassidy, Kathryn (2019): Bordering. Cambridge: Polity Press.

About the authors

Christian Wille | University of Luxembourg | Campus Belval | Maison des Sciences Humaines | UniGR-Center for Border Studies | 11, Porte des Sciences | L-4366 Esch-sur-Alzette | Luxembourg | christian.wille@uni.lu

Wille, Christian (Ph.D.) is a senior researcher at the University of Luxembourg and head of the network UniGR-Center for Border Studies. He has published the books "Spaces and Identities in Border Regions" (2016), "Living Realities and Political Constructions in Border Regions" (2015), and "Cross-border Commuters and Spaces of the Border" (2012). His research areas include cultural border studies, transnational everyday lives, and spatial, identity, praxeological theories.

Birte Nienaber | University of Luxembourg | Campus Belval | Maison des Sciences Humaines | UniGR-Center for Border Studies | 11, Porte des Sciences | L-4366 Esch-sur-Alzette | Luxembourg | birte.nienaber@uni.lu

Nienaber, Birte (Associate Prof. Dr.) is a political geographer specialized in migration, border studies and European regional and rural development. She is experienced with EU-funded activities in the area of migration (e.g. MOVE, DERREG, CEASEVAL, RELOCAL, "Border Studies") and coordinates three national EU contact points (EMN, ESPON and FRANET). Prof. Nienaber is a member of the board of directors of the IMISCOE network and of the steering board of the UniGR-Center for Border Studies. In addition to publishing more than 100 articles and reports, she has also co-edited "Globalization and Europe's Rural Regions" (2015) and "Internationalisierung der Gesellschaft und die Auswirkungen auf die Raumentwicklung" (2015) and has served on the editorial board of "Comparative Migration Studies (CMS)".

The *Europe without borders* discourse and splitting European identities

Carsten Yndigegn

Abstract

The aim of this paper is to trace and scrutinize some of the underlying forces that might contribute to explaining the current skepticism about a policy of debordering Europe. The author therefore discusses why prefiguring a borderless Europe based on European identity has stumbled into misconceived conceptions of the nation, and then presents an explanation of the transformative dynamics that undermine the vision of a borderless Europe. The paper concludes that a borderless Europe will remain a vision as long as the idea of a European identity cannot establish a reliable alternative to its national counterpart, but multiple cosmopolitan forces still keep pushing towards debordering Europe.

Keywords

Borderless Europe, European identity, nationalism, populism, rebordering

1. The end of an epoch?

Regardless of whether it has been a grand delusion or simply the consequence of the end of permissive consensus, we cannot escape the fact that the conceptual framework that forms the basis for the idea of a borderless Europe is being challenged and may already be eroded. The idea of European unification paired with internal debordering has been a key element in the vision for the development of a European Community and the European Union; however, the European construction that has been presented as the outcome of European integration now increasingly seems a controversial goal.

Since the flow of refugees in 2015, exemptions from the Schengen Agreement that used to be rare and based on exceptional situations have been introduced in several European countries, and permanent border control has been reintroduced along several internal Schengen borders. Furthermore, an emerging discourse is that European integration has gone too far in eroding national borders and that "our" nation is better served by leaving the Union. Brexit in the United Kingdom was a radical example, but similar demands have been raised even in core member states (Dennison/Pardijs 2016).

The main drivers in the rebordering discourse that has emerged are critical views on democracy, on mobility and immigration, on the issue of "social Europe", and on the perforation of external borders. All such issues add fuel to the fire that threatens the pragmatic visionary transformation of the European continent after WW2.

In this paper, the theoretical approach to borders is founded on the tradition that was established in the 1990s by a mix of geographers, political scientists, sociologists, and anthropologists (Donnan/Wilson 1994; Kavanagh 1994; Agnew 1996; Paasi 1996; Newman/Paasi 1998). It established a new border paradigm that replaced the classic concept of borders based on the idea that "states establish borders to secure territories which are valuable to them because of their human or natural resources, or because these places have strategic or symbolic importance to the state" (Wilson/Donnan 1998, p. 9). The new border concept focused on people, not spatial and institutional aspects of borders. It envisaged that institutional borders maintain a role in framing mentalities. Borders play a role similar to culture that develops unevenly, which Ogburn (1922) has expressed as a cultural lag in the process of social change: "The thesis is that the various parts of modern culture are not changing at the same rate, some parts are changing much more rapidly than others". (Ogburn quoted in Volti 2004, p. 397). This is formulated exemplarily by John Agnew:

> Borders are artefacts of dominant discursive processes that have led to the fencing off of chunks of territory and people from one another. Such processes can change and as they do, borders live on as residual phenomena that may still capture our imagination but no longer serve any essential purpose. Borders, therefore, are not simply practical phenomena that can be taken as given. They are complex human creations that are perpetually open to question. At an extreme, perhaps, existing borders are the result of processes in the past that are either no longer operative or are increasingly eclipsed by transnational or global pressures. In other words, borders are increasingly redundant, and thinking constrained by them restricts thinking about alternative political, social, and economic possibilities. (Agnew 2008, p. 176)

Furthermore, this paper builds on Etienne Balibar's idea of globalized borders. Balibar proposes that borders have become *polysemic* (Balibar 2004) and *vacillating* (Balibar 1998). On the one hand, they keep on framing nation state sovereignty, and on the other hand, they allow unhindered flow across the borders for some and continue to be a barrier to others. They take on different meanings, for example as passable gateways or barriers, which Balibar terms "*detention zones* and *filtering systems*" (Balibar 2004, p. 111); or as Rumford puts it: "Borders can remain invisible to the many while bordering out the few" (Rumford 2008, p. 38).

According to Balibar, globalized borders have moved from the periphery of a nation, or the "edge of the territory" as he says, "into the middle of political space" (Balibar 2004, p. 109). The reason is that global flows differentiate between the human and the non-human. Material and immaterial entities (traded goods, financial assets) flow freely, whilst the flow of people is regulated by borders that are located in many places.

The aim of this paper is to trace and scrutinize some of the underlying forces that might contribute to explaining the current skepticism about a policy of debordering Europe that has been in effect for six decades. The paper does not pretend to offer a comprehensive view, since it cannot cover the totality of discourse within the EU, and it adopts a one-sided perspective, the perspective taken being from the northern part of Europe. Its focus will be on political attitudes, public discourse and conceptual frames. I will completely refrain from analyzing institutional policy.

The paper is divided into four parts. First, I will discuss the vision of a borderless Europe; then I will discuss why prefiguring a borderless Europe based on European identity has stumbled into misconceived conceptions of the nation and its transformability. The third part will go into more detail, presenting an explanation of the transformative dynamics that seem to so successfully undermine the vision of a borderless Europe; and finally, I will discuss the prospects for a borderless Europe, where the cosmopolitan vision seems outdated, but multiple cosmopolitan forces still keep pushing towards debordering Europe.

2. *The vision of a borderless Europe*

The vision of a borderless Europe, in a broader sense of a unified group of countries cooperating together, has a long history. Europe's past as a continent of warring states (Heffernan 1998; Roche 2010, p. 103–105) has led contemporary thinkers to develop ideas and models for a unified Europe. Figures such as Saint-Simon, Coudenhove-Kalergi and Aristide Briand in particular are leading lights in the history of visions of European identity-building (Delanty 1995; Pagden 2002). However, all visionary proposals have fallen short when confronted with *Realpolitik*.

Since WW2, the vision of a "Europe without borders" has been a main driver in efforts to develop European integration. The founding fathers shared the common experience of the devastating consequences of populism that quickly turned into totalitarianism, and some of them—Konrad Adenauer, Alcide De Gasperi and Robert Schuman—were exposed to severe personal suffering. Furthermore, both De Gasperi and Schumann shared the experience of living in contested border regions and the heritage of military confrontation arising from that. They realized the necessity of putting an end to the vicious circle of war by establishing integrative mechanisms that neutralized the key drivers behind military confrontation, by replacing them with incentives for peaceful cooperation (Martín de la Torre 2014).

The removal of borders for trade, finance and communication has been successful. The "borderlessness" in these areas is not necessarily a European phenomenon. This is exactly what is behind global trade agreements within the framework of the WTO, and the so-called deregulated economy or globalization that have been prevalent over the past thirty years.

Moreover, the idea of debordering found support in cosmopolitan discourse. Ulrich Beck, who builds on Kant's idea of living in one world and being a citizen of the whole world (Beck 2003), perceives the development of cosmopolitanism as inevitable. He proposes that a change from the national to the global perspective is required because of transborder activities or cross-border behavior by national citizens who, as he says, shop, work, love, marry, research, grow up, and are educated internationally. And as he observes, they:

> live and think transnationally, that is, combine multiple loyalties and identities in their lives [and therefore] the paradigm of societies organized within the framework of the nation state inevitably loses contact with reality. (Beck 2000, p. 80)

Therefore, borders are eroded and transnationality negates the borders of the nation state and thereby dissolves the exclusive status of the nation state, which can no longer close its borders to protect its citizens. In Beck's words, cosmopolitanism is an expression of "how far social structures and institutions are becoming transnationalized" (Beck 2003, p. 21). However, such manifestations of freedom have also met with criticism from the political left, and they have been criticized as symptoms of the unlimited expansion of a neo-liberal world order (Della Porta/Tarrow 2005; Della Porta 2006; Volscho/Kelly 2012).

The development of borderless personal mobility has been promising. The more limited idea of free movement for Europe's workforce, as laid out in the Treaty of Rome, has been transformed into an almost universal right of mobility for all European citizens within the European Union. And the signing and implementation of the Schengen Agreement succeeded in giving it a narrower, concrete reality, by removing control posts at physical border crossings, which themselves had been a visual symbol of a national border.

However, the development of a borderless Europe within the fourth of the freedoms of the EU seems to have reached its limits. Three factors indicate that the process towards a borderless Europe is itself reaching its limits: 1) Britain's exit from it, with mobility as a key issue; 2) the reintroduced border controls in parts of the Schengen area; and 3) Euroskeptic right-wing populist movements gaining momentum.

Opening borders and establishing contact and interaction have been the driving components for visions of the development of a transnational European identity. The assumption was that narrow nationalistic feelings and prerogatives would diminish, while cross-border solidarity and recognition of universal needs and rights would thrive.

The opposite happened. The sympathetic idea of European identity ended up being a scapegoat for the consequences of globalization. This leads to questions as to whether the idea of open borders and a European commonality has just been an illusionary vision based on epistemological failures, and whether the realization of a borderless Europe released counterforces with a dynamic power that had not been foreseen in academic theories.

3. *The contested model of European identity*

It is the proposition of this paper that the concept of European identity as a precondition of a borderless Europe has encountered epistemological obstacles that are caused by it having been modelled on an essentialist conception of national identity. To put it simply, this means that national identity is being perceived as something that has developed within a specific historical, territorial and demographic context. From a particular perspective, this can seem to imply that national identity has always existed, and that it is linked to a durable and unchangeable native population within a given territory. However, this is an over-simplification.

There are two positions as regards the relation between concepts of national and European identity. One excludes the transformation from national identity to European identity, and the other conceptually prefigures the possibility of such a transformation, given that the necessary preconditions have been established. I will challenge these positions by invoking Anthony D. Smith and Jürgen Habermas respectively.

Anthony Smith anchors the social construction of national identities in historical memories. He stresses the necessity of a generational continuity that binds together the population, either as a whole or as units, and with the help of shared memories and the collective belief in a destiny common to this group of people (Smith 1992, p. 58).

In a paper from the early 1990s, Anthony Smith claimed that a European identity modelled on the concept of national identity was not possible, because national identity is defined as a product of a common historical legacy, shared traditions and a shared heritage. And this, he claimed, is exactly what Europe lacks:

> There is no European analogue to Bastille or Armistice Day, no European ceremony for the fallen in battle, no European shrine of kings or saints. When it comes to the ritual and ceremony of collective identification, there is no European equivalent of national [...] community. (Smith 1992, p. 73)

Habermas has proposed a strong counter-argument to such historicist naturalization of collective identities. He proposes citizenship as the unifying element in a political construction, but he emphasizes that "the democratic right of self-determination includes, of course, the right to preserve one's own *political* culture, which includes the concrete context of citizen's rights, though it does not include the self-assertion of a privileged *cultural* life form" (Habermas 1992, p. 17). From his point of view, a collective identity is not a cultural or an ethnic identity, but a politically constituted identity. It is not bound to a static historical continuity, but is open to the dynamic possibilities implicit in social change: "Our task is less to reassure ourselves of our common origins in the European Middle Ages than to develop a new political self-confidence commensurate with the role of Europe in the world of the twenty-first century" (Habermas 1992, p. 12).

Drawing on the lessons from the creation of nation states, Habermas notices that it was possible to gradually produce a national consciousness and "solidarity amongst strangers", and he claims that this was in no way different from what would be required today for a European identity to develop. National consciousness was produced gradually "with the help of national historiography, mass communication, and universal conscription. If that artificial form of "solidarity amongst strangers" came about thanks to a historically momentous effort of abstraction from local, dynastic consciousness to a consciousness that was national and democratic, then why should it be impossible to extend this learning process beyond national borders?" (Habermas 1999, p. 58).

Here, Habermas is in line with Benedict Anderson (1991), who demonstrated how a national identity is not restricted to the commonality of a geographically demarcated people, but goes beyond the realm of experience. Anderson proposed the idea of an imagined community, a shared common territory wherein the inhabitants presumed to know each other. In so doing, he showed that the concept of national identity is a social construction and, in this way, he is entirely in line with the epistemological preconditions for a European identity.

For many years, the development of a European identity was a clear strategy of the European Union. The development of a European identity has been furthered by initiatives such as The European Capital of Culture (Sassatelli 2009; Immler/Sakkers 2014; Lähdesmäki 2014) and the Erasmus, now Erasmus+, educational and youth exchange programs (Ambrosi 2013; Striebeck 2013; Van Mol 2013; Mitchell 2015). However, despite the high priority of the EU's policies, identification with Europe has remained low, far behind local and national identifications, and often on a par with identification with the world as a whole. Changing the focus from separate identities to multiple identities has given new insights into the complexity of the formation of European identity (Moreno et al. 1998; Marks/Hooghe 2003; Moreno 2006; cf. Bruter 2008).

For a European identity to develop, Habermas sets four requirements to be fulfilled: a European constitution, a party system built around transnational political interests, the creation of a European public sphere, and the establishment of a common communicative framework based on the teaching of foreign languages in the school system. The EU does have a constitutional framework, but not a European constitution. European political parties are in the making. The European public sphere is developing, while the consciousness of European interdependency is increasing. Finally, the lingua franca, i.e. English, has been established and disseminated in a rapidly spreading process. However, even the most positive evaluation of the progress made can only conclude that the process is still in its infancy.

Still valid is the observation already made by Kohli (2000) that people identify themselves as European only as a multiple identity. As Kohli says, "if identity is conceived of as a multilevel set of attachments, Europe is now a part of it for the majority of its citizens. If, on the other hand, one clings to an exclusionary concept of identity, European attachment is still highly minoritarian" (Kohli 2000, p. 125). European identity has never become a popular project, but remained a project for the elite or the cosmopolitan, and that is precisely what has opened up as its vulnerability in times of renewed nationalism.

4. Restorative dynamics

The resistance to the idea of a united Europe without borders is not new. The European integration project has never been uncontested. The stance taken by the British Prime Minister, Margaret Thatcher, is an exemplary representation of the skepticism about a borderless Europe. In 1988, she gave her Bruges speech, warning against the centralization and bureaucratization of the EU: "We have not successfully rolled back the frontiers of the state in Britain only to see them reimposed at a European level with a European superstate exercising a new dominance from Brussels." (Thatcher 1988).

In her Bruges speech, Margaret Thatcher laid out a principle of minimal integration. With regard to borders, Thatcher admitted that it should be made easier for people to travel across the borders, but at the same time she stated that border controls should be maintained to protect "citizens from crime and stop the movement of drugs, of terrorists and of illegal immigrants" (Thatcher 1988). This is strikingly similar to what is said today by the new right-wing populists. In 2011, ten years after the implementation of the Schengen Treaty, the Danish People's Party negotiated the implementation of a border control camouflaged as customs control with the Danish government (Ministry of Finance 2011). This was proclaimed as a victory on their website, because, as they wrote:

> Denmark is again on track to being safe. … We are setting up physical checkpoints, on the borders with both Germany and Sweden—and at all Danish ports and all Danish airports. In addition to permanently manning the borders with many customs officers—with the police backstage—brand new, fancy equipment will be installed. … It has been a wonderful 10 years for all sorts of suspicious types—gunrunners, drug smugglers, illegal immigrants, criminal burglars—who were free to swoop in across the borders of Denmark in their large, closed vans. That's over now! (Dansk Folkeparti 2011) (translated from the Danish).

Looking more generally at resistance to the open border aspect of European integration, we can say that two major developments have served as obstacles. Internal mobility and external immigration have between them caused social change in Europe and generated grievances that have led to political mobilization and the creation of social movements to promote opposition to the enforced changes. Labor mobility within the EU, continuous immigration from the Middle East, the Caucasus and Africa, combined with the massive influx of asylum seekers, primarily from Syria in 2015, have unleashed reactionary, restorative forces among the populations in the countries affected. The demand for enforced border control is only the visual evidence of the forces that have been set in motion. Underneath, much stronger border work is playing out as a reaction against what has been perceived as national elites becoming disengaged from common people, thereby breaking the bonds that establish national unity and identity.

External border control has been an ongoing policy of the EU, but despite measures taken in the form of the European Neighbourhood Policy (ENP) and Frontex, the external borders, known less than euphemistically as Fortress Europe, have not been watertight. It was, however, only when massive refugee influxes and migration flows found a new path, the so-called Balkan route, that national governments were forced to suspend the Schengen Agreement and reintroduce border controls. This was done either because the immigration of asylum seekers had risen to levels which national immigration frameworks were unable to cope with, as was the case in Sweden, or because the mass influx of asylum seekers allowed right-wing populists to mobilize themselves successfully in its wake.

In the case of Sweden, the end of the open borders policy came suddenly. It used to be the policy of all parties except those on the extreme right, most recently the Sweden Democrats, that Sweden should be a safe haven for refugees from across the world, and that no restrictions should be imposed on the number of asylum seekers that the country could receive. That official policy was based on a welcoming culture of open Swedish hearts, which former Prime Minister Fredrik Reinfeldt has embodied since he took office in 2006. Reinfeldt argued that immigration should be unlimited, because civilizational gains have been caused by an influx of people and ideas from abroad. Furthermore, he argued that Sweden does not belong to certain people just because they have resided in the country for three or four generations, or because they have managed to erect a border (Redaktionen 2006; Nationen 2014). However, in 2015, when Sweden received more asylum seekers per inhabitant than any other European country, immigration became unmanageable and the government suspended the Schengen rules and introduced border controls.

Across the rest of Europe, border policies have been strengthened as well. Europe became divided between those mainly Eastern European countries that refused immigrants, and those who received them in varying degrees. Among the latter, stricter policies towards asylum seekers developed as the governments found themselves faced with the swiftly growing support that right-wing populist parties received when they turned against immigrants. German chancellor Angela Merkel's expression "Wir schaffen das!" reflected the country's administrative ability to handle the refugee crisis but not its political ability to handle the negative reactions among the electorate. Border control was reinstated to stem the tide, but this was too late to close the floodgates of political reaction that had been opened (Hockenos 2017; Hoerner/Hobolt 2017; Mushaben 2017; Sinn 2017; Stelzenmüller 2017).

4.1 The populist tidal wave

All over Europe, parties opposing immigration have gained momentum. Their influence is measurable not only in the support for right-wing populists but is even more evident in the policy changes that have been adopted by mainstream parties.

Right-wing populist movements against asylum seekers as a phenomenon have been seen for decades, but, however annoying, their mobilization has so far not been threatening at the political level. However, this has changed, because a series of disparate trends have merged to form a major stream.

The first such trend is the phenomena relating to the internal development of the EU. There are three main allegations put forward against the EU. The first is the claim that there is a lack of democracy in its decision-making. As has been put forward by scholars studying the EU, this argument is gaining strength mainly because national governments' participation in EU decisions is disconnected from the national political process (Ladrech 2007; Häge 2008; Colombatto 2014; Hobolt/Tilley 2014; cf. Macron 2017).

The second trend lies in the antipathy toward the mobility of workers from Eastern Europe, and so-called 'welfare tourists', who are personally blamed for acting in accordance with arrangements European governments agreed upon at the beginning of the 2000s (Remeur 2013). EU politicians believed that mobility would further the convergence of social welfare, i.e. a more equal distribution of social benefits, but this was a belief that was never accepted by ordinary citizens, because its implementation went hand in hand with austerity policies and social security provisions that were further undermined by neo-liberal deregulation (Guild et al. 2013; Blauberger/Schmidt 2014; Fernandes 2016).

The third and last trend is the emergence of certain forms of criminality taking place in or emerging out of a sphere that is beyond the purely national. This covers both cross-border crime, which is experienced as trafficking, drug dealing, burglaries, economic fraud, etc., but also the development of new forms of criminal behavior within societies. Although the discrepancy between the level of actual crime and perceived crime is huge, the consequences of the perception bias should not be underestimated (Lange et al. 2008; Kersten 2016; Huffington Post 2017; Pfeiffer et al. 2018).

The fourth trend is globalization, which represents a policy of open borders for finance and trade. In her Bruges speech, Margaret Thatcher pointed out that this required politicians to free up markets, widen choice, and reduce government intervention. As she said: "Our aim should not be more and more detailed regulation from the centre: it should be to deregulate and to remove the constraints on trade" (Thatcher 1988). The consequences of these neo-liberal policies have been impossible to overlook. The welfare state and the public sector have been transformed into a competition state (Yeatman 1993; Cerny 1997; Levi-Faur 1998; Lavenex 2007; Evans 2010; Vukov 2016). The labor market has been deregulated and companies have outsourced and been offshored, while at the same time unions have lost their ability to secure the solidarity and the interests of those still working or aspiring to do so (Peters 2008). The precariat (Standing 2011) is one visual example of the outcome of such policies; another is the slide into poverty that has meant the working poor working longer hours for less, and being flexible 24/7 (Fraser et al. 2011; Van Lancker 2011; Walsh/Zacharias-Walsh 2011).

Those exposed to the consequences of these changes, and who are able to compare the present day with the past, might echo Marx and Engels' famous expression about the changes that the bourgeois industrial revolution caused: "All that is solid melts into the air." Those threatened by the constant disappearance of workplaces, witnessing the increased influx of foreign workers, and becoming increasingly uneasy and insecure as they see residential areas and local communities transformed, these people turn towards those who address the phenomena they recognize and who speak about them in a language they understand or use (Inglehart/Norris 2016). Their grievances fuel the rise of right-wing populism and demands to control the borders.

4.2 Profiling right-wing populism

Claus Offe has framed the contemporary rise of right-wing populist movements with concise clarity:

> Populist mobilization relies on the (*vertical*) mobilization of *distrust* (of political elites and intermediary institutions—mendacious media (*Lügenpresse*), academia, experts, civil society associations, also courts)—and the (*horizontal*) spreading of *fear* of outsiders. Migrants/refugees are ideally suited as objects of fearmongering for three reasons:
>
> - *Economic*: they threaten us in the labor and housing markets and live at the expense of our taxes;
> - *Cultural*: allegedly incompatible language, religion, ethnic identity;
> - Failures of state protection: rape, crime, terrorism.
>
> Distrust is particularly effective when the two can be *combined*: elites are to be distrusted because they *fail to protect us* from or are even *actively promoting* (Merkel in September 2015) the access of migrants. (Offe 2017)

If we take this a step further, Ignazi (2003) has delivered a precise diagnosis of the underlying value scheme that guides the grievances of the followers of right-wing populist groups and makes them targets for the mobilization of the new populist right. Ignazi describes how right-wing populist movements are solidly founded on nationalism, and how their political focus is a quest for "harmonious unity":

> The national, local or ethnic *community* must be preserved against any sort of division. Pluralism is extraneous to the extreme right political culture: unity, strength, harmony, nation, state, *ethnos*, *Volk* are the recurrent references. [...] They cannot conceive of a community where people are not "similar" one to another, because differences would entail division. (Ignazi 2003, p. 145)

With this conception, right-wing populists justify closing the borders to protect against the immigration of non-Western people, especially Muslims, because their presence is perceived as a cultural threat to the nation state and the national culture. The right-wing populists also single out the supporters of a multicultural society as traitors. This tactic was first described by Bjørgo (1997), the Norwegian researcher of right-wing extremism. Right-wing populist defamatory and humiliating attacks on the elite, the "swamp" that needed to be drained, has continued until the present day (Norris 2017).

Mondon has shown this in an analysis of the French Front National, which targets as its enemies "globalization (*mondialisme*) and human rights, which threatened to destroy national identities" (2015, p. 398). This is, however, not a form of exceptionalism, as new populist movements founded on this dichotomy have emerged in almost all European countries.

In some European countries, this approach has been even more pronounced. In Hungary and Poland, populist regimes have used their newly obtained power to change constitutions and remold public institutions and other aspects of the political and intellectual framework in order to ensure that the policy changes they have introduced, and their hold on power, become irreversible (Albright/Woodward 2018; Appelbaum 2018).

The most important aspect of right-wing populist movements is not the grievances they exploit to mobilize support or the claims they make, but the fact that the strongest of them have maintained their course now for three decades, and during this period they have morphed from being pariahs to having mainstream respectability. Mondon (2015) has shown this in an exemplary analysis of the French Front National. The party profits from the left's inability to address social changes, and it mobilizes support around a subtle form of racism, which Mondon calls "new racism", which, instead of targeting ethnicity, stresses the incompatibility of cultures (Mondon 2015, p. 402).

Populists perceive themselves as grounded territorially, culturally, and socially in a specific place, and they perceive themselves as having the right of the first-born. Jan-Werner Müller has expressed this with distinct clarity: "Populism, then, is not about a particular social base or a particular set of emotions or particular policies; rather, it is a particular *moralistic imagination of politics*, a way of perceiving the political world which opposes a morally pure and fully unified, but ultimately fictional, people to small minorities who are put outside the authentic people" (Müller 2014, p. 485).

Ostracism, as practiced in ancient Greek society to control the elite, is not a proper populist strategy today. Protection therefore has to be established up front. The rise of right-wing populism has led to a strong claim for the rebordering of Europe on multiple levels, and national governments have in varying degrees adjusted their policies to accommodate the grievances that have fueled the right-wing populist mobilization. Even seemingly liberal intellectuals such as David Goodhart, the former director of the British think tank Demos, blends his voice with those who raise concerns that society is becoming too diverse (Goodhart 2004). In so doing, he becomes a supporter of a restrictive immigration policy from another angle. He simply claims that "the slow disappearance [...] of the rather miraculous, and historically unique, institution of the modern welfare state" (Goodhart 2013, p. 261) is being caused by increased diversity in society, which undermines solidarity, because the welfare state presupposes a "homogenous society with intensely shared values" (Goodhart 2013, p. 262). The propositions of Goodhart find support in recent research. Putnam (2007) in the US, Schmidt-Catran and Spies (2016) in Germany, and Eger (2010) in Sweden all found that solidarity diminishes in communities characterized by immigration and ethnic diversity, and in the European context, that support for welfare has been negatively influenced by immigration.

Increasingly, public discourse is moving toward Goodhart's position. This establishes a paradox for progressives who both want social diversity through open borders and a welfare state. While at first the position of Goodhart was heavily criticized, now there is a multiple echoing of his opinions outside the right-wing populist camp (Skidelsky 2017). Cottakis (2018) calls this the "adoption approach", because the change might reflect subjection to a dominant trend, not a proper and timely reaction to it. It takes over populist positions instead of confronting them. The alternative, the "counter-vision" approach, debunks populists' unsubstantiated promises and presents attractive alternatives. This approach, Cottakis argues, has been used successfully by the French president, Emmanuel Macron (Cottakis 2018).

5. Discussion

The epistemological basis for a justification of debordering the nation state has been addressed in the literature of cosmopolitanism. It offers alternative perspectives to the positions of nationalism and populism, and as Khan has pointed out, its roots are to be found in the German philosopher Kant, who outlined a theory of cosmopolitan law and a universal moral community, "where a violation of rights in one part of the world is felt everywhere" (Kant quoted in Khan 2014, p. 129). According to Khan, the theory of cosmopolitan law "extends the rights citizens enjoy as members of a sovereign state to non-citizens" (Khan 2014, p. 129). From a similar position, Vanessa Barker has criticized the seemingly most liberal Swedish migration policy for being anchored in ethnic nation state principles (Barker 2012; Barker 2017a; Barker 2017b; Barker 2018). Furthermore, it has been argued that despite the launch of the "rights to rights" discourse, and regardless of all proclamations and conventions, universal human rights are still framed by national citizenship and the will of nation states: "The expansion of global human rights will continue to depend on individual countries' citizens' political rights" (Shafir/Brysk 2006, p. 285).

However, as Nobel Prize-winning economist, Robert Shiller, has pointed out, the pressure from those being born at a remove from Western sources of wealth will not accept that such arbitrariness should determine their chances in life, and he foresees that this will drive an intellectual revolution that will "challenge the economic implications of the nation state" (Shiller 2016; cf. Abram et al. 2017).

This is the continuing conflict that will continue to pose a threat to the idea and reality of a borderless Europe. The response to the challenge from a majority of the population might seek support in variants of populism that combine an economically liberal and a national conservative approach with a Euroskeptic position (Decker 2016), or variants that combine a classical social democratic welfare state approach with national conservatism and Euroskepticism.

This conflict will persist as long as the idea of a European identity cannot establish a reliable alternative to its national counterpart. As long as the nation state is seen as the basic protective force in the life of citizens, and an integrated Europe adds to the threat instead of being perceived as a reliable response to global challenges, the obstacles to a debordered Europe will persist.

References

Abram, Simone, et al. (2017): The free movement of people around the world would be Utopian: IUAES World Congress 2013: Evolving Humanity, Emerging Worlds, August 5–10, 2013. In: Identities 24, no. 2, p. 123–155, https://doi.org/10.1080/1070289X.2016.1142879.

Agnew, John (1996): Review of Territories, Boundaries and Consciousness: The Changing Geographies of the Finnish–Russian Border by Anssi Paasi. In: Geografiska Annaler. Series B, Human Geography 78, no. 3, p. 181–182, https://doi.org/10.2307/490833.

Agnew, John (2008): Borders on the mind: re-framing border thinking. In: Ethics & Global Politics 1, no. 4, p. 175–191. https://doi.org/10.3402/egp.v 1i4.1892.

Albright, Madeleine Korbel/Woodward, William (2018): Fascism: a warning. New York: Harper.

Ambrosi, Gioia (2013): The Influence of the ERASMUS Programme on Strengthening a European Identity: Case Studies of Spanish and British Exchange Students. In: Feyen, B./Krzaklewska, E. (eds.): The ERASMUS phenomenon: symbol of a new European generation? Frankfurt am Main: Lang Lang, p. 143–162.

Anderson, Benedict (1991): Imagined Communities: Reflections on the Origin and Spread of Nationalism. London: Verso.

Appelbaum, Anne (2018): A Warning From Europe. The Atlantic Magazine. Boston: The Atlantic.

Balibar, Etienne (1998): The borders of Europe. In: Cheah, P./Robbins, B. (eds.): Cosmopolitics: thinking and feeling beyond the nation. Minneapolis: University of Minnesota Press, p. 216–229.

Balibar, Etienne (2004): We, the people of Europe? Reflections on transnational citizenship. Princeton NJ: Princeton University Press.

Barker, Vanessa (2012): Nordic Exceptionalism revisited: explaining the paradox of a Janus-faced penal regime. In: Theoretical Criminology 17, no. 1, p. 5–25, https://doi.org/10.1177/1362480612468935.

Barker, Vanessa (2017a): Nordic vagabonds: the Roma and the logic of benevolent violence in the Swedish welfare state. In: European Journal of Criminology 14, no. 1, p. 120–139, https://doi.org/10.1177/1477370816640141.

Barker, Vanessa (2017b): Penal power at the border: realigning state and nation. In: Theoretical Criminology 21, no. 4, p. 441–457. https://doi.org/10.1177/1362480617724827.

Barker, Vanessa (2018): Nordic nationalism and penal order: walling the welfare state. London/New York: Routledge.

Beck, Ulrich (2000): The cosmopolitan perspective: sociology of the second age of modernity. In: British Journal of Sociology 51, no. 1, p. 79–105, https://doi.org/10.1111/j.1468-4446.2000.00079.x.

Beck, Ulrich (2003): Rooted Cosmopolitanism: Emerging from a Rivalry of Distinctions. In: Beck, U. et al. (eds.): Global America? The cultural consequences of globalization. Liverpool: Liverpool University Press, p. 15–29.

Bjørgo, Tore (1997): Racist and right-wing violence in Scandinavia: patterns, perpetrators, and responses. Oslo: Tano Aschehoug.

Blauberger, Michael/Schmidt, Susanne K. (2014): Welfare migration? Free movement of EU citizens and access to social benefits. In: Research & Politics 1, no. 3, p. 1–7, https://doi.org/10.1177/2053168014563879.

Bruter, Michael (2008): Legitimacy, Euroscepticism & Identity in the European Union — Problems of Measurement, Modelling & Paradoxical Patterns of Influence. In: Journal of Contemporary European Research 4, no. 4, p. 273–285.

Cerny, Philip G. (1997): Paradoxes of the Competition State: the Dynamics of Political Globalization. In: Government and Opposition 32, no. 2, p. 251–274, https://doi.org/10.1111/j.1477-7053.1997.tb00161.x.

Colombatto, Enrico (2014): The EU and the euro are easy targets in political blame-game. In: United Europe. https://www.united-europe.eu/2014/09/the-eu-and-the-euro-are-easy-targets-in-political-blame-game, 5/22/2018.

Cottakis, Michael (2018): How to tackle populism: Macron vs Kurz. In: EUROPP — European Politics and Policy. https://blogs.lse.ac.uk/europpblog/2018/02/13/how-to-tackle-populism-macron-vs-kurz, 2/13/2018.

Dansk Folkeparti (2011): *Danmarks grænser igen på vej til at blive sikre* [Online]. Copenhagen. https://web.archive.org/web/20110929043317/; https://www.danskfolkeparti.dk/Gr%C3%A6nsekontrol.asp, 11/9/2017.

Decker, Frank (2016): The "Alternative for Germany": Factors Behind its Emergence and Profile of a New Right-wing Populist Party. In: German Politics and Society 34, no. 2, p. 1–16, https://dx.doi.org/10.3167/gps.2016.340201.

Delanty, Gerard (1995): Inventing Europe: Idea, Identity, Reality. London: Macmillan.

Della Porta, Donatella (2006): The Antiglobalisation and the European Union: Critics of Europe. Brussels: European Commission.

Della Porta, Donatella/Tarrow, Sidney (2005): Transnational protest and global activism. Lanham Md.: Rowman & Littlefield.

Dennison, Susi/Pardijs, Dina (2016): The world according to Europe's insurgent parties: Putin, migration and people power. London: European Council on Foreign Relations.

Donnan, Hastings/Wilson, Thomas M. (eds.) (1994): Border Approaches: anthropological perspectives on frontiers. Lanhan MD: University Press of America.

Eger, Maureen A. (2010): Even in Sweden: The Effect of Immigration on Support for Welfare State Spending. In: European Sociological Review 26, no. 2, p. 203–217, https://doi.org/10.1093/esr/jcp017.

Evans, Mark (2010): Cameron's competition state. In: Policy Studies 31, no. 1, p. 95–115, https://doi.org/10.1080/01442870902899871.

Fernandes, Sofia (2016): Access to social benefits for EU mobile citizens: "tourism" or myth? Policy Paper 168. Berlin: Jacques Delors Institut.

Fraser, Neil, et al. (2011): Working poverty in Europe: a comparative approach. Basingstoke: Palgrave Macmillan.

Goodhart, David (2004): Too diverse? In: Prospect 2004, February, p. 1–7. https://www.prospectmagazine.co.uk/magazine/too-diverse-david-goodhart-multiculturalism-britain-immigration-globalisation, 6/24/2016.

Goodhart, David (2013): The British dream: successes and failures of post-war immigration. London: Atlantic Books.

Guild, Elspeth, et al. (eds.) (2013): Social benefits and migration a contested relationship and policy challenge in the EU. Brussels: Centre for European Policy Studies (CEPS)

Habermas, Jürgen (1992): Citizenship and National Identity: some reflections on the Future of Europe. In: Praxis International 12, no. 1, p. 1–19.

Habermas, Jürgen (1999): The European nation-state and the pressures of globalization. In: New Left Review, no. 235, p. 46–59.

Häge, Frank M. (2008): Who Decides in the Council of the European Union? In: JCMS: Journal of Common Market Studies 46, no. 3, p. 533–558, https://doi.org/10.1111/j.1468-5965.2008.00790.x.

Heffernan, Michael (1998): War and the shaping of Europe. In: Graham, B. (ed.): Modern Europe: Place, Culture and Identity. London: Arnold, p. 89–120.

Hobolt, Sara Binzer/Tilley, James (2014): Blaming Europe? Responsibility without accountability in the European Union. Oxford: Oxford University Press.

Hockenos, Paul (2017): East Germans and the far-right AfD: the roots of far-right support in East Germany go far deeper than Merkel's immigration policies. In: International Politics and Society, https://www.ips-journal.eu/regions/europe/article/show/east-germans-and-the-far-right-afd-2315, 10/5/2017.

Hoerner, Julian M./Hobolt, Sara (2017): The AfD succeeded in the German election by mobilising non-voters on the right, https://blogs.lse.ac.uk/europpblog/2017/09/29/the-afd-succeeded-in-the-german-election-by-mobilising-non-voters-on-the-right/?utm_source=feedburner&utm_medium=email&utm_campaign=Feed%253A+Europp+(EUROPP+-+European+Politics+and+Policy+at+LSE), 9/29/2017.

Huffington Post (2017): So entlarvte der Kriminologe Christian Pfeiffer bei Maischberger die Panikmache der AfD. Huffington Post, 11/30/2017.

Ignazi, Piero (2003): The Development of the Extreme Right at the End of the Century. In: Merkl, P. H./Weinberg, L. (eds.): Right-wing extremism in the twenty-first century. London: Frank Cass.

Immler, Nicole L./Sakkers, Hans (2014): (Re)Programming Europe: European Capitals of Culture: rethinking the role of culture. In: Journal of European Studies 44, no. 1, p. 3–29, https://doi.org/10.1177/0047244113515567.

Inglehart, Ronald/Norris, Pippa (2016): Trump, Brexit, and the rise of populism: economic have-nots and cultural backlash. HKS Working Paper No. RWP16-026. Cambridge, MA: Harvard Kennedy School.

Kavanagh, William (1994): Symbolic boundaries and 'real' borders on the Portuguese–Spanish frontier. In: Donnan, H./Wilson, T. M. (eds.): Border Approaches: anthropological perspectives on frontiers. Lanhan MD: University Press of America, p. 75–88.

Kersten, Joachim (2016): Flüchtlingskrise, Männergewalt und „Stranger Danger": Anmerkungen zur Köln-Debatte. In: NK Neue Kriminalpolitik 28, no. 4, p. 367–377, https://doi.org/10.5771/0934-9200-2016-4-367.

Khan, Gulshan (2014): Jürgen Habermas and the Crisis of the European Union. In: Demetriou, K. N. (ed.): The European Union in crisis: explorations in representation and democratic legitimacy. New York: Springer, p. 123–139.

Kohli, Martin (2000): The Battlegrounds of European Identity. In: European Societies 2, no, 2, p. 113–137, https://doi.org/10.1080/146166900412037.

Ladrech, Robert (2007): National Political Parties and European Governance: The Consequences of 'Missing in Action'. In: West European Politics 30, no. 5, p. 945–960, https://doi.org/10.1080/01402380701617365.

Lähdesmäki, Tuuli (2014): Discourses of Europeanness in the reception of the European Capital of Culture events: the case of Pécs 2010. In: European Urban and Regional Studies 21, no. 2, p. 191–205, https://doi.org/10.1177/0969776412448092.

Lange, Hans-Jürgen, et al. (2008): Auf der Suche nach neuer Sicherheit: Fakten, Theorien und Folgen. Wiesbaden: VS Verlag für Sozialwissenschaften.

Lavenex, Sandra (2007): The competition state and highly skilled migration. In: Society 44, no. 2, p. 32–41, https://doi.org/10.1007/BF02819924.

Levi-Faur, David (1998): The competition state as a neomercantilist state: Understanding the restructuring of national and global telecommunications. In: The Journal of Socio-Economics 27, no. 6, p. 665–685, https://doi.org/10.1016/S1053-5357(99)80002-X.

Macron, Emmanuel (2017): Initiative for Europe: speech by Emmanuel Macron, President of the French Republic, 26 September 2017. Paris: Présidence de la République.

Marks, Gary/Hooghe, Liesbet (2003): National Identity and Support for European Integration. Discussion Paper SP IV 2003-202. Berlin: Wissenschaftszentrum Berlin für Sozialforschung (WZB).

Martín de la Torre, Victoria (2014): Europe, a leap into the unknown: a journey back in time to meet the founders of the European Union. Brussels: Peter Lang.

Ministry of Finance (2011): Permanent toldkontrol i Danmark (styrket grænsekontrol) (Permanent Customs Check in Denmark (Strengthened Border Control)). Copenhagen: Ministry of Finance, https://www.eu.dk/da/nyheder/2015/graensekontrol, 11/7/2017.

Mitchell, Kristine (2015): Rethinking the 'Erasmus Effect' on European Identity. In: JCMS: Journal of Common Market Studies 53, no. 2, p. 330–348, https://doi.org/10.1111/jcms.12152.

Mondon, Aurelien (2015): The French secular hypocrisy: the extreme right, the Republic and the battle for hegemony. In: Patterns of Prejudice 49, no. 4, p. 392–413, https://doi.org/10.1080/0031322X.2015.1069063.

Moreno, Luis (2006): Scotland, Catalonia, Europeanization and the 'Moreno Question'. In: Scottish Affairs, 54. https://www.euppublishing.com/doi/10.3366/scot.2006.0002.

Moreno, Luis, et al. (1998): Multiple identities in decentralized Spain: the case of Catalonia. In: Regional & Federal Studies 8, no. 3, p. 65–88, https://doi.org/10.1080/13597569808421060.

Müller, Jan-Werner (2014): 'The people must be extracted from within the people': Reflections on Populism. In: Constellations 21, no. 4, p. 483–493, https://doi.org/10.1111/1467-8675.12126.

Mushaben, Joyce Marie (2017): Angela Merkel's Leadership in the Refugee Crisis. In: Current History 116, no. 788, p. 95–100, http://www.currenthistory.com/Article.php?ID=1393.

Nationen (2014): Fredrik Reinfeldt: Sweden belongs to the immigrants — not the Swedes [Online], https://www.youtube.com/watch?v=d5pPmcYUHVU, 7/8/2016.

Newman, David/Paasi, Anssi (1998): Fences and Neighbours in the postmodern world: boundary narratives in the Postmodern World. In: Progress in Human Geography 22, no. 2, p. 186–207, https://doi.org/10.1191/030913298666039113.

Norris, Pippa (2017): Why populism is a threat to electoral integrity [Online]. London: London School of Economics and political science. https://blogs.lse.ac.uk/europpblog/2017/05/16/why-populism-is-a-threat-to-electoral-integrity, 5/16/2017.

Offe, Claus (2017): Germany: What Happens Next? In: Social Europe https://www.socialeurope.eu/germany-happens-next, 10/3/2017.

Ogburn, William Fielding (1922): Social change with respect to culture and original nature. New York: B.W. Huebsch, Inc.

Paasi, Anssi (1996): Territories, Boundaries and Consciousness: the changing geographies of the Finnish–Russian Border. Chichester: John Wiley & Sons.

Pagden, Anthony (ed.) (2002): The idea of Europe: From antiquity to the European Union. Cambridge: Cambridge University Press.

Peters, John (2008): Labour market deregulation and the decline of labour power in North America and Western Europe. In: Policy and Society 27, no. 1, p. 83–98, https://doi.org/10.1016/j.polsoc.2008.07.007.

Pfeiffer, Christian, et al. (2018): Zur Entwicklung der Gewalt in Deutschland. Schwerpunkte: Jugendliche und Flüchtlinge als Täter und Opfer. Zürich: Zürcher Hochschule für Angewandte Wissenschaften, Institut für Delinquenz und Kriminalprävention.

Putnam, Robert D. (2007): E Pluribus Unum: Diversity and Community in the Twenty-first Century. The 2006 Johan Skytte Prize Lecture. In: Scandinavian Political Studies 30, no. 2, p. 137–174, https://doi.org/10.1111/j.1467-9477.2007.00176.x.

Redaktionen (2006): Reinfeldt: Det ursvenska är blott barbari [Online]. Stockholm: Dagens Nyheter. https://www.dn.se/nyheter/politik/reinfeldt-det-ursvenska-ar-blott-barbari, 7/8/2016.

Remeur, Cécile (2013): Welfare benefits and intra-EU mobility: Library Briefing. Brussels: Library of the European Parliament.

Roche, Maurice (2010): Exploring the sociology of Europe: an analysis of the European social complex. Los Angeles Calif.: SAGE.

Rumford, Chris (2008): Cosmopolitan spaces: Europe, globalization, theory. New York: Routledge.

Sassatelli, Monica (2009): Becoming Europeans: cultural identity and cultural policies. Basingstoke: Palgrave Macmillan.

Schmidt-Catran, Alexander W./Spies, Dennis C. (2016): Immigration and Welfare Support in Germany. In: American Sociological Review 81, no. 2, p. 242–261, https://doi.org/10.1177/0003122416633140.

Shafir, Gershon/Brysk, Alison (2006): The Globalization of Rights: From Citizenship to Human Rights. In: Citizenship Studies 10, no. 3, p. 275–287, https://doi.org/10.1080/13621020600772073.

Shiller, Robert J. (2016): The Coming Anti-National Revolution. In: Project Syndicate https://prosyn.org/4KLfVw6, 9/19/2016.

Sinn, Hans-Werner (2017): Germany's Götterdämmerung. In: Project Syndicate. https://www.project-syndicate.org, 11/26/2017.

Skidelsky, Robert (2017): Inconvenient Truths About Migration. In: Project Syndicate https://prosyn.org/BYoUlm6, 11/22/2017.

Smith, Anthony D. (1992): National identity and the idea of European unity. In: International Affairs 68, no. 1, p. 55–76, https://doi.org/10.2307/2620461

Standing, Guy (2011): The precariat: the new dangerous class. London: Bloomsbury Academic.

Stelzenmüller, Constanze (2017): After the election, Germany's democracy faces its hardest test since 1949. Washington: Brookings Institution Press.

Striebeck, Jennifer (2013): A Matter of Belonging and Trust: The Creation of a European Identity through the ERASMUS Programme? In: Feyen, B./Krzaklewska, E. (eds.): The ERASMUS phenomenon: symbol of a new European generation? Frankfurt M.: Lang-Ed., p. 191–206.

Thatcher, Margaret (1988): Speech to the College of Europe: 'The Bruges Speech', https://www.margaretthatcher.org/document/107332, 7/5/2016.

Van Lancker, Wim (2011): The European world of temporary employment. In: European Societies 14, no. 1, p. 83–111, https://doi.org/10.1080/14616696.2011.638082.

Van Mol, Christof (2013): ERASMUS Student Mobility and the Discovery of New European Horizons. In: Feyen, B./Krzaklewska, E. (eds.): The ERASMUS phenomenon: symbol of a new European generation? Frankfurt M.: Peter Lang, p. 163–174.

Volscho, Thomas W./Kelly, Nathan J. (2012): The Rise of the Super-Rich. In: American Sociological Review 77, no. 5, p. 679–699, https://doi.org/10.1177/0003122412458508.

Volti, Rudi (2004): William F. Ogburn: Social Change with Respect to Culture and Original Nature. In: Technology and Culture 45, no. 2, p. 396–405, https://www.jstor.org/stable/40060750.

Vukov, Visnja (2016): The rise of the Competition State? Transnationalization and state transformations in Europe. In: Comparative European Politics 14, no. 5, p. 523–546, https://doi.org/10.1057/cep.2016.20.

Walsh, John P./Zacharias-Walsh, Anne (2011): Working longer, living less: understanding Marx through the workplace today. In: Kivisto, P. (ed.): Illuminating social life: classical and contemporary theory revisited. Thousand Oaks Calif: Pine Forge Press, p. 5–40.

Wilson, Thomas M./Donnan, Hastings (1998): Nation, state and identity at international borders. In: Wilson, T. M./Donnan, H. (eds.): Border Identities: Nation and State at International Frontiers. Cambridge: Cambridge University Press, p. 1–30.

Yeatman, Anna (1993): Corporate managerialism and the shift from the welfare to the competition state. In: Discourse: Studies in the Cultural Politics of Education 13, no. 2, p. 3–9, https://dx.doi.org/10.1080/0159630930130202.

About the author

Carsten Yndigegn | University of Southern Denmark | Department of Political Science and Public Management | Centre for Border Region Studies | Alsion 2 | 6400 Sønderborg | Denmark | T +45 65501764 | cy@sam.sdu.dk

Carsten Yndigegn holds a Ph.D. in Cultural Studies. He is an Associate Professor Emeritus at the Centre for Border Region Studies in the Department of Political Science and Public Management at the University of Southern Denmark. He has specialized in media and youth studies. His recent research interests have focused on debordering Europe, the development of European identity, and nationalism, populism and Euroskepticism. He was the national project manager for the EU FP7 research project MYPLACE (2011–2015), about how the shadows of totalitarianism and populism in Europe influence young people's social and political participation.

Border Experiences: Everyday Life and Working Life

Cross-border links at the boundaries of the European Union: an ethnography of mobility, work, and citizenship in uncertain times

Ignacy Jóźwiak

Abstract

This chapter explores the role of the state border in the daily life of the inhabitants of the Transcarpathia region in western Ukraine. Based on ethnographic fieldwork, it offers an insight into the region, which has been affected by the "Europeanization" of the border regime on the one hand and by the post-2014 crisis in Ukraine on the other. The study points to the use of the border and cross-border links as well as the changes the patterns for doing so have undergone. In the face of political crisis and economic recession, Ukrainians face greater pressure to migrate, while in the country's western borderlands increased utilization of already existing cross-border links can be observed.

Keywords

State border, borderlands, mobility, ethnography, Ukraine

1. Introduction[1]

This chapter explores the state border as experienced in the daily life of the borderlanders, the inhabitants of the Transcarpathia (*Zakarpatska Oblast*) region in western Ukraine, which borders Romania, Hungary, Slovakia,

---

1 This chapter was prepared under the National Science Center's PRELUDIUM grant number UMO-2015/17/N/HS6/01167. I would also like to express my gratitude to the colleagues who shared their remarks during the early stages of work on the manuscript: Kamila Fiałkowska (University of Warsaw), Karolina S. Follis (Lancaster University), Michał Garapich (University of Warsaw), Anna Romanowicz (Jagiellonian University), Sandra King-Savic (University of St. Gallen), and Gregory Schwartz (University of Bristol). Regardless of the institutional funding and collegial support, the study would not be possible without the help and engagement of the people directly or indirectly mentioned in the text, with whom I was

and Poland. It is based on ethnographic fieldwork focused on dealing with the border: making use of it and familiarization with the border as such as well as with the people and places on the other side. The subject matter is framed in the wider relations between the local inhabitants, the border, and state apparatuses applied at it. I make use of concepts that interpret borders as factors in both overcoming and preserving inequalities on the international, regional, or local levels. The role of borders as factors for negotiation and transgression of the given social order is also developed.

The sites the study is based upon are Uzhhorod (approximately 120,000 inhabitants), Beregovo (approximately 30,000 inhabitants), and Solotvyno (approximately 10,000), which are located at the Slovakian, Hungarian, and Romanian borders respectively, with border checkpoints either in the towns themselves or on their outskirts. Their specificities are also shaped by their ethnic composition (predominantly Ukrainian in Uzhhorod, predominantly Romanian in Solotvyno, and predominantly Hungarian in Beregovo) and linguistic composition (Ukrainian, Hungarian, and mixed with the occasional dominance of Russian). Importantly, what this paper reflects upon is the common knowledge among the inhabitants of the region. For a researcher, this kind of local understanding of the border, its workings, as well as the potential benefits it offers serves as a window on the processes under study. I visited these places in the summers of 2016 and 2017, however, my experience with fieldwork in the region dates back to 2005/2006 and 2009–2011.

The leading idea behind my last visit was to trace the local grassroots responses to national and international political developments. It is reflected in a research question which refers to the way the political and economic situation in Ukraine as well as the neighboring countries' policies influence the local transnational dynamics in the country's westernmost region.

This study represents an ethnographic revisit (Burawoy 2003)[2], covering the sites of Beregovo (studied in 2005/2006, with a focus on ethnic identities in the borderland) and Solotvyno (studied in 2009–2011, with a focus on the state border and its role in the local daily life practices). This approach enables me to grasp changes in the sites and in macro-forces which impact and shape the local and regional realities, and to understand the phenomena being studied better. Uzhhorod had not been the subject of

---

able to get in contact and who shared their time and experiences with me. I am very grateful for that.

2 To quote Micheal Burawoy, "An ethnographic revisit occurs when an ethnographer undertakes participant observation [...] with a view of comparing his or her site with the same one studied at an earlier point in time" (Burawoy 2003, p. 646).

my ethnographic inquiries prior to 2016; nevertheless, as a regional academic and cultural center it served as a location of library queries and academic networking between 2009 and 2011. Including it in my fieldwork could thus also be considered a revisit. Apart from the fieldwork in 2016 and 2017, the chapter refers to my research conducted between 2005 and 2011, as well as my general knowledge deriving from frequent visits to the region over those 11 years. In that manner, I link the locally observed processes with wider phenomena of international political and economic issues and the way they impact the localities. Ethnographic observations provide us with the "links to outside forces" (Tavory/Timmermans 2009, p. 254).

This kind of strategically situated ethnography provides us with connections between people, stories, places, biographies, and their meanings. It enables us to understand "something broadly about the system in ethnographic terms as much as it does in local subjects. It is only local circumstantially" (Marcus 1995, p. 111). My reference to multi-sited ethnography apart from my physical presence in three different locations concerns the level of entanglement of locally observed phenomena in the large-scale processes, rather than connections between these particular places (cf. Marcus 1995). My previous research (Jóźwiak 2014) revealed that living close to the checkpoint, speaking the neighboring country's language, or even having relatives on the other side of the border is not necessarily associated with regular visits or an interest in visiting. It has also pointed to the uncertain, often critical, attitudes of ethnic minorities towards their "external national homelands" (cf. Brubaker 1996), that is, Hungary and Romania. The current study is linked to my earlier work, and broadens previous findings and anticipations with a perspective on more recent uncertain times.

Depending on particular situations, I accompanied my informants in their daily routines at home, at work, or in other surroundings such as cafes or arranged appointments in order to accommodate my inquiry. Participants were approached in informal conversations or semi-structured and unrecorded interviews. Observations and notes in my diary were equally important. This kind of "hanging out" served as an opportunity to participate, accompany, and follow Transcarpathians in their daily activities, as well as an occasion for conversations on the subjects of interest. These subjects are illustrated with the examples of three people whose experiences serve as ethnographic vignettes of the phenomena under study. The research deals with some sensitive issues, such as involvement in greyzone businesses and possession of dual citizenship, which is not recognized in Ukraine. In order to ensure the informants' anonymity, and so as not to accidentally point to other people who could have similar characteristics as my informants, no names (real or pseudonyms) are mentioned throughout the text. Instead, they are referred to with capital letters, related to their order of appearance, and not to their names, surnames, or nicknames.

This chapter presents the voices and stories of those whose lives are affected by the border. It dwells upon the practices of the use of border and cross-border links: migration, seasonal work, daily commuting, and registering cars abroad, alongside the changes in these activities. These transformations are grounded in historical legacies[3], the national and international passport and visa policies, the economic situation in Ukraine, and political developments such as the 2011 amendment to the Hungarian Law on Citizenship. The latter enables the descendants of former Hungarian citizens to acquire Hungarian citizenship regardless of their ethnic identification, which, in practice, favors the inhabitants of the former Hungarian territories.

As it borders Slovakia, Hungary, and Romania, past statehood changes, regional ethnic composition and cross-border kinships translate into livelihood strategies. Local inhabitants often speak the neighboring country's language or have relatives there, which is likely to facilitate their travel, stays there, and search for employment. In the face of the political and economic crisis in Ukraine resulting from the 2014 revolution, the Russian annexation of Crimea and the armed conflict in Donbas, citizens of Ukraine are exposed to increased pressure to migrate or use the state border in other ways. Transcarpathians maintain and make more extensive use of the already existing local cross-border links with Romania, Hungary, and Slovakia. That in turn leads to the general increase in the role of the state border in everyday life. However, I claim that despite the possibilities that the border offers, and the borderlanders' agency when working out strategies to overcome the border as an obstacle, the social inequalities and exclusive mechanisms inherent in their functioning prevail. Obtaining foreign passports, applying for visas, making use of language skills, and cultural competence appear to be widespread practices, but it does not mean that everyone engages in them. As we shall see, not everyone has the necessary networks or wealth, both social and material, to put this subversion of

3 Between 1867 and 1919, Transcarpathia was part of the Kingdom of Hungary within the Hapsburg Empire. In the interwar period (1919–1938), it was a part of Czechoslovakia, being annexed by Hungary in 1938 following the short-lived independence some of its territory enjoyed as part of the republic of Carpathian Ukraine. In 1944, it was incorporated into the Soviet Union as a Transcarpathian District (*Zakarpatska Oblast*) of the Ukrainian Soviet Socialist Republic.

the state border into motion. Thus, border experience is far from being universal to all borderlanders.

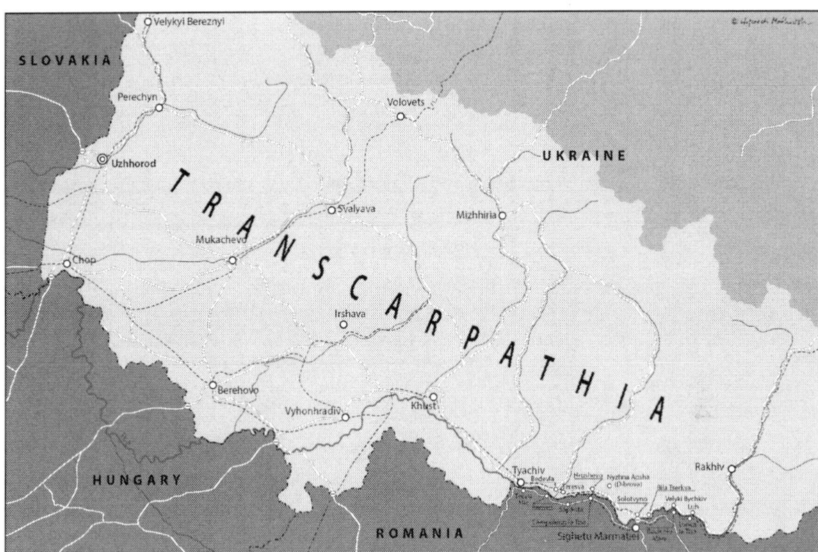

Illustration 1: Map of Transcarpathia

2. *Borders of the borderless: ambivalence and transgression*

The regimentation provided by the state borders and the control over mobility, as well as policies related to it (cf. Feldman 2012; Torpey 2000), structure not only patterns of mobility, but also the horizons of belonging while living "simultaneously on two [or more] sides of the border" (Follis 2012, p. 79). Even if perceived as "absolutely nondemocratic, or 'discretionary' condition[s] of democratic institutions" (Balibar 2004, p. 109), the contradictory nature of state borders creates potential sites for transgression (Green 2010, p. 262) as well as "zones of engagement" (Simonyi/Pisano 2011, p. 224), where different kinds of contact, inclusion, and exclusion are possible. With their selectivity and non-democratic character, state borders preserve global social and economic inequalities on the one hand, while at the same time being exposed to being undermined at the bottom-up level. In the spaces like borderlands where the state is subjected to subversion, the mutual influence of the values, ideas, customs, and shared economic relations on both sides of the state border can also contribute to transnationalism (Donnan/Wilson 1999, p. 4–5). Such is the case with the apparatus of state security, which "contributes to the formation of local and transnational networks" (Simonyi/Pisano 2011, p. 223–224), as individuals reinvent and renegotiate the rules and order as well as their social meanings at the limits of the state.

Reflecting on contradictions characteristic of the functioning of state borders in Europe, Sarah Green (2012) and Ruben Zaiotti (2007a; 2007b) point to their functioning as a combination of surveillance, security, and commercial enterprise. Entrepreneurial aspects of state borders apply to public and private investments along the border and around checkpoints, as well as other profit-generating activities, including grey zones, such as shuttle trade, carrying passengers, and the legal infrastructure (shops, gas stations, open-air markets) that accompany them. There are significant differences between Ukraine and its western neighbors in terms of wages and living standards.

Borders also relate to the region's history of statehood changes over the last 100 years. In this regard, we can speak of the Ukrainian/Hungarian struggle at the symbolic level. The involvement of Hungarian national ideology extends beyond the boundaries of the nation state and meets Ukrainian state-building and pursuit of territorial integrity. This symbolic tug of war is translated into particular policies of single against multiple citizenship. As the latter is tolerated *de facto* (but not *de jure*), Hungary appears as a symbolic winner in this regard. Apart from granting citizenship to around 200,000 Transcarpathians, Hungarian extraterritorial policy also takes the form of subsidies not only for Hungarian-speaking schools and cultural institutions, but also health-care institutions in Transcarpathia regardless of the language of their services. In the framework of "gesture politics", Ukrainian cultural initiatives in the region are also supported (Erőss/Kovaly/Tatrai 2016, p. 22–23). Obtaining Romanian citizenship is also a possibility, but this country's regulations, unlike Hungary's, do not favor Transcarpathia (which unlike the Ukrainian region of Bukovyna—*Chernivetska Oblast*—has never belonged to Romania), and are not as easily applicable as Hungarian ones (cf. Jóźwiak 2014, p. 32–33). The procedure can take years and there is never a guarantee of success. Even for people who identify as Romanians, it is often easier to obtain a Hungarian passport than a Romanian one. This is where the borderlanders enter the scene as actors and agents of negotiation and transgression, as it is up to the local inhabitants to deal with these contradictions, navigate their way through them, and make use of them.

3. *Border locations: sites of inclusion, exclusion, and subversion*

Unlike the neighboring Lviv and Ivano-Frankivsk regions (*Lvivs'ka Oblast'*, *Ivano-Frankivs'ka Oblast'*), which in the course of history were parts of Red Ruthenia, the Polish–Lithuanian Commonwealth, Hapsburg Galicia, and Poland, the territories comprising Transcarpathia from the Middle Ages until the First World War belonged to the Kingdom of Hungary, Hapsburg Austria or the Hungarian part of the Austro-Hungarian empire. After the Treaty of Versailles (1919), they were ceded to Czechoslovakia, and in 1938 were annexed by Hungary, to be ceded to the Soviet Union in 1944 as part of the Yalta agreement. Transcarpathia is characterized by a mixed ethnic composition, since apart from Ukrainians (and people referred to as Rusyns or Ruthenians, whose number is difficult to estimate), it is inhabited by ethnic minorities: Hungarians, Romanians, Roma, Slovaks, Germans, Russians, and other nations of the former USSR. The region has 13 checkpoints and three of the neighboring countries maintain their consulates there: Hungary in Uzhhorod and Beregovo, Slovakia in Uzhhorod, and Romania in Solotvyno. The consulates, apart from their usual task of issuing visas or representing their citizens abroad, also issue citizenship and local border traffic (LBT) documents.

Ukraine as a whole appears affected by the "EU-ropeanization" of the border regime and post-2013 turmoil in Ukraine. However, in Transcarpathia, due to its geographical location, this is particularly visible. Historical legacies expose the region and its inhabitants to the historical and symbolic policies of the neighboring countries, most of all Hungary. The very functioning as well as the social role of the border has changed due to the passport/visa regulations introduced by Ukraine's western neighbors in the context of the EU's enlargement. Thus, even though it is not a member of the EU, Ukraine has been impacted by its policies.

On the other hand, the country as a whole has been facing continuous political and economic crises since Russia's seizure of the Black Sea Crimean Peninsula in 2014 and the armed conflict in the Donbas region. The conflict covers less than 5% of the Ukrainian territory in the east of the country and is occurring 1,500 kilometers from Transcarpathia (the distance between the two regions' administrative centers is 1,534 kilometers), that is, extremely far from Transcarpathia (the westernmost region of Ukraine). Nevertheless, the economic impact of these political and military developments can be sensed throughout the entire country. Ukraine had already been affected by the 2009 global recession; the post-2014 turmoil has added to this situation, and the country has been struck by further recession (cf. Iwański 2015; Yurchenko 2018).

Uzhhorod, the regional administrative, cultural and academic center of *Zakarpatska Oblast*, is a city of approximately 120,000 inhabitants situated on the border with Slovakia, and the checkpoint is located just on the outskirts of the city. The border cuts through a hilly area, so when leaving Uzhhorod in a western direction, one is not exposed to any significant interventions in the landscape until one reaches the border crossing. When one looks in the same direction from the top of one of the city's hills, the boundary line is not visible either. Approached from the Slovakian side, the city appears out of the blue, as there is a hill separating it from the checkpoint. Unlike the territories in nearby Slovakia and—somewhat further away at around 30 kilometers—Hungary, or numerous small towns and villages in Transcarpathia largely inhabited by ethnic Hungarians, the city itself is predominantly of Ukrainian ethnic and linguistic composition. The Ukrainian language dominates the public space in inscriptions and in conversations. Russian and Hungarian can be heard sporadically, while the Slovak language is not present at all.

Arriving in the town of Beregovo from Hungary, one is not exposed to any changes in the landscape or to natural geographical obstacles like rivers or mountain passes. In fact, the area is quite flat apart from the hills in the town, which are visible from Hungary (and in good weather conditions from Romania as well). There is also hardly any difference in the architecture between the countries, which looks pretty much the same in Beregovo and in Hungarian towns of similar size. If it were not for the queue at the checkpoint and the better quality of asphalt roads in Hungary, one might have found it difficult to spot the place where the actual state border is delimited. The use of languages changes slightly, but the majority of communication after crossing to Ukraine is still carried out in Hungarian; however, Ukrainian and, too a much lesser extent, Russian can also be heard. It is slightly different in the case of inscriptions, most of which, unlike in Hungary, are bilingual (Ukrainian and Hungarian). When approaching the city from within Ukraine, one observes gradual changes in both the natural and human landscapes, as well as an increase in the use of the Hungarian language and the number of cars with Hungarian license plates.

Crossing the bridge from the Romanian town and municipal center of Sighetu Marmaţiei (or simply Sighet) to the Ukrainian town of Solotvyno, one can clearly see the river Tisza and the bridge over it, which serve as border landmarks. In the middle of the bridge joining two checkpoints on the two sides of the border, the borderline (officially delimited in the middle of the river) is marked with a red stripe. On the Ukrainian side, the river bank is planted with a line of tall acacia trees, which block out the view of the river but make the boundary even more visible. Thus, for the visitor, the border viewed from Ukraine appears hidden and blurred, as clearly visible trees do not delimit either the official borderline or the publicly accessible space. Here, the use of languages changes slightly after leaving Romania, since in addition to the Romanian language (spoken by the majority of the Solotvynians), one can easily hear Russian, the local *lingua franca* which is not spoken on the Romanian side apart from by visitors from Ukraine. Hungarian and Ukrainian are spoken on both sides of the river but they are much more widespread in Solotvyno than Sighet. Entering Solotvyno from within Ukraine, one passes different villages, some inhabited almost exclusively by ethnic Ukrainians and others also almost exclusively by ethnic Romanians. One thus finds oneself in a multilingual space where Romanian, Russian, Hungarian, and Ukrainian can be heard, often spoken by the same people. This kind of local "ethnic and linguistic map" depicts the way local communities function in bilingual or multilingual conditions, but also as "islands" within the Ukrainian linguistic space. However, one should bear in mind that the ethno-linguistic composition looks similar on both banks of the Tisza, as there are also Ukrainian-speaking villages on the Romanian side.

In Uzhhorod, a careful observer can easily spot the numerous cars with foreign license plates (mostly Slovakian and Polish, but also Czech, Hungarian, Lithuanian, and others). In Beregovo, around half of the cars have Hungarian license plates, and individual ones with Czech, Polish, Slovakian, or German plates can be noticed. In Solotvyno, Ukraine-registered cars are in a minority. Most of them have license plates of, in order of approximate popularity, the Czech Republic, Romania, Slovakia, Hungary, Poland, and other EU member states. These cars, apart from Romanian ones which are mostly driven by the visitors from that country, belong to the local inhabitants. Buying a second-hand car in the EU is at least three times cheaper than in Ukraine, while not registering a car in their country of actual residence enables owners to save even more on taxes and import tariffs. Depending on the vehicle's ownership status and due to some legal gaps, it has to leave Ukrainian territory every five days or once a year. Referring to the owners of these cars as "Ukrainians" or "Ukrainian citizens" would not present us with a full picture of the situation, as many of them also have either Hungarian or Romanian citizenship, and use the respective countries' passport when registering their vehicles. "Foreign" cars (i.e. those registered abroad) driven by the local inhabitants serve as one of the preliminary indicators of local and regional cross-border links. Spotting a car with Czech, Polish, or Slovakian license plates in eastern Hungary or north-western Romania, one may assume that they are driven by Transcarpathians, who in turn might be traveling with Ukrainian, Hungarian, or Romanian passports in their pockets.

In all three locations, job adverts offering work abroad and visa brokers can be easily spotted. As migration patterns from this region will be elaborated elsewhere, here I will just point to the familiarization with the state borders, as well as pragmatic aspects of the citizenship issue, of which international mobility is a part. The number of announcements and the level of professionalization of the intermediaries depend on the size of the town. Local specificities are also relevant, as in Uzhhorod all of the adverts and announcements are in Ukrainian, and they offer work mostly in the Czech Republic and Poland, as well as higher education in Poland and Slovakia. Many adverts and announcements in Beregovo are bilingual (Ukrainian and Hungarian), some of them are only in Hungarian, and some are in Russian. It is in Beregovo that the issue of Hungarian citizenship is most visible, as some advertisements make clear that the jobs are offered only to "EU passport holders", while others list a Hungarian passport, among other possible documents, as enabling jobs to be taken up (such as Polish or Czech visas). In this town, Hungary, next to the Czech Republic, appears as a destination country. In Solotvyno, job advertisements are rare and almost exclusively in Ukrainian, which contrasts with the low level of the use of the spoken language (the town may be too small to create its own "advert culture", as in Beregovo), and the contacts provided are usually in Uzhhorod and Ivano-Frankivsk. The number of job and visa adverts as well as cars with foreign license plates has clearly increased since 2011. The changes observed relate not only to the scale, but also and even more importantly to the patterns and strategies which people apply in their border-related activities.

The Luzhanka–Beregsurany checkpoint near Beregovo is always full of cars, pedestrians, and cyclists. Most of the regular commuters travel and return every day, others stay in Hungary for a few days. Many of those who cross the border on foot or by bicycle reach the farms and orchards on the Hungarian side of the border, where their relatively cheap labor is needed by the local landowners. Some others, after crossing the border, wait to be given a ride by cars going to the nearby town of Vasarosnameny (10 kilometers away) or—somewhat more distant—Nyiregyhaza (70 kilometers away).[4] Dozens of cars are also parked on both sides of the border, as many travelers prefer to reach it by car and cross on foot. The traffic in Solotvyno

4 There is also one bus a day from Beregovo to Nyiregyhaza and back, and one to Budapest twice a week.

is not as intensive as in Luzhanka, but cross-border commuting (on foot, by bicycle, and by car) to shop, work, or to trade at the open-air market in Sighet also takes place there. What can also serve as an illustration of the local (or translocal) familiarity with state borders is the fact that some local drivers travel to Hungary via the Solotvyno-Sighet bridge and Romania due to the better quality of the roads in the neighboring country. The alternative, which some people take, is to travel on Ukrainian territory to the nearest Ukrainian–Hungarian checkpoint in Vylok (98 kilometers away). The Uzhhorod–Vysne Nemecke checkpoint is open only to cars, trucks, buses (with regular connections to Presov, Košice, Prague, and Plzen), and motorbikes. The scale of traffic is much greater than in the locations previously mentioned. With no cyclists and pedestrians or hitchhikers, and no shops, markets, or large car parks nearby, the area around it seems far less lively than in Solotvyno and Luzhanka. Still, when the weather is good and the queues are long, drivers and passengers leave their vehicles, gather around, chat to each other or keep places in the line for others. With Uzhhorod being a relatively big city with a high number of cars registered abroad, the checkpoint is full of "passers" (Ukr. *peresichniky*)—drivers whose cars need to leave Ukraine every week, often without even entering the neighboring country. Many of these drivers, though, prefer to use the Chop (UA)–Zahony (HU) border crossing 30 kilometers away, which is much bigger but also known to be more traveler-friendly.

In Uzhhorod, Beregovo, and Solotvyno, some people travel to the neighboring country every day, whilst others do not do so at all. Slovakia, Hungary, and Romania also serve as transit countries for longer journeys: Debrecen (Hungary) and Košice (Slovakia) international airports, as well as bus stops and car parks in Sighet, Satu-Mare (Romania), Nyiregyhaza or Mataszelka (Hungary), where international buses stop. Thus, even traveling to more distant destinations involves local cross-border networks and strategies, as getting to any of these places requires using the regular bus connections (mostly from Uzhhorod, but also from Beregovo and the town of Mukachevo halfway between them), the services of local "taxi drivers", as people who provide international transport like to be called. There is a huge group of them in Beregovo. They know each other and often meet and talk in the lines at the border. They also use the same parking spots near the train station in Nyiregyhaza and they usually deliver to and pick up their passengers from the same trains to or from Budapest. Such is the case in Solotvyno, where the drivers also operate, driving cars registered in the EU. Like most of the inhabitants of the town, they drive EU-registered cars and take passengers to locations in Romania, Hungary, and Slovakia. Unlike those from Beregovo, they also serve connections within

Ukraine: mostly Hungarian consulates in Beregovo and Uzhgorod, or hospitals in the latter. As public transport in Solotvyno is inefficient and the choice of taxis not very wide, they are also likely to take the very local routes. They maintain contact with each other so that they can pass the clients (passengers) among themselves, or recommend each other when they cannot make the route requested. The size of the town and the state of its infrastructure enforces a certain flexibility on them. As their number of clients and the distances they have to go are uncertain, their earnings are far from stable. Using second-hand cars (sometimes up to 25 years old) also poses the risk of breakdowns, which subsequently requires some time out of action to fix it. The demand on transport services is much lower than in Beregovo, while in Uzhhorod it is sufficiently well developed to enable a choice between buses from that town or the trains from the nearby Chop station which, combined with huge traffic at the Uzhhorod–Vysne Nemecke checkpoint, does not leave much space for the cross-border taxi services.

Regardless of the checkpoints, out of the three neighboring countries it is Hungary that generates the most diverse plethora of attitudes, activities, and intimacies. After obtaining citizenship, numerous Transcarpathians work, study, and settle there. Others have their properties and registrations in both countries and share their lives between Ukraine and Hungary. Apart from the labor market (not as attractive as those in the Czech Republic, Poland, or Germany), Hungary offers a relatively well-developed health-care system and pensions which can be even 10 times higher than the Ukrainian ones. The demand for passports (often referred to as "European" ones) has boosted the property markets in the villages in eastern Hungary.

4. *Experiencing the border and studying it: an ethnographic revisit in uncertain times*

In terms of the changes that the region and its inhabitants have been experiencing in the face of political shifts and economic downturns, A, a teacher from Beregovo, personifies both the national and the regional turmoil. For 10 years (2004–2014), or "from Maidan to Maidan" as she describes it, referring to the two waves of opposition protests in Ukraine, with their epicenter at Kiev's Independence Square (*Maidan Nezalezhnosti*), she used to work as a school teacher in her hometown. Disappointed with the lack of positive changes regarding corruption, salaries, and mafia-like structures in public institutions (including schools) after the post-2014 breakthrough, she quit her job and was considering quitting her profession. However, through informal networks she got to know about a job offer at a school in one of the villages in Hungary, within a few kilometers of the Ukrainian border. This was where her Hungarian citizenship, acquired 2 years before, became useful. Like many other teachers from Beregovo and the neighboring villages, she commutes to work daily, either by bike, car, or school bus, which picks her up on the Hungarian side. Depending on the queue at the checkpoint, getting there takes between 2 and 3 hours. At first, she found it difficult to get accustomed to the new realities and different culture of work in the neighboring country, as well as to its language (her mother tongue being Ukrainian).

Daily commuting is not an easy task to cope with, and some teachers from Ukraine who also work in the same or nearby schools have settled in Hungary, some of them with their entire families. But A never seriously considered such a solution, as she enjoys returning to her home and family (husband and children) and sleeping in her own bed. She declares that she feels that she belongs *here* (Beregovo, Ukraine) and identifies herself as a Ukrainian patriot. When asked about her Hungarian citizenship, she did not consider it any kind of "treason" to her motherland. For her, it is just a way of finding a better-paid job—truly better, as her salary has increased at least five-fold. She has no insurance in Ukraine, but is insured and is entitled to health-care in Hungary.

Increased mobility across the border in turn creates demand for means of transport, and due to underdeveloped international public transportation in this section of the border (unlike the much bigger and busier Chop–Zahony checkpoint), paid hitchhiking from the border to the nearby towns is common, which increased together with the level of local mobility. In the face of the fall of the Ukrainian *hryvna* (in 2014), which was also the time when people started to travel more extensively, B gave up his job as an office worker in Beregovo in order to become a full-time driver in his family business. Driving a minivan with Hungarian license plates, he collects passengers to and from Nyiregyhaza and Debrecen (cities in Hungary 80 and 120 kilometers away, respectively), traveling to addresses as well as arranging pick-ups or drop-offs at the railway station in the former and the airport in the latter. The route and the timing are set according to the passengers and their needs, and if there are any seats left (sometimes he goes empty one way just to pick up some passengers in Hungary), he tries to find passengers at the border. Apart from buying lottery tickets in Hungary and occasional visits to the second-hand electronics shop, he is not interested in bringing any larger amount of goods home. Presenting his Hungarian passport, which he obtained in 2012, to the border guards of both countries, in 2016 he claimed it to be less confusing (both for him and for the officers) than swapping the passports in between the checkpoints, as many others (including his passengers) did. As he explained, the document was also supposed to serve as a kind of "insurance" that might enable his family's escape from Ukraine once "they start to shoot here". The year after, it was his associate who was driving in Hungary, while B picked the passengers up from or dropped them off at the checkpoint before or after they had crossed the border on foot. The initially less-confusing strategy of using only the Hungarian passport at the checkpoint became inefficient when the Ukrainian border guards started to count the days that foreign passport holders spent in that country. To secure their reentry into Ukraine, the country they actually live and originate from, frequent commuters had to change their strategy to presenting each country's officers with the passport of that country. With his Ukrainian passport being outdated, he could not, as he put it, "go abroad" for a while. In spite of identifying as a Hungarian and having Hungarian citizenship and making frequent visits to that country, he felt at home in Beregovo and he never wished to move elsewhere, not even to Hungary, where he had nothing but formal registration.

Back in 2006, C worked as a receptionist in Beregovo. With his salary hardly enough to make a living, at that time he was full of bitter words towards the country he lived in (Ukraine): the state of the economy and industry, corrupt political elites, unemployment, poverty, and the general lack of propriety. He did not spare his criticism of what he considered his actual motherland (Hungary) either. It was the country where he was treated like a foreigner, especially by the border guards, custom officers, and police. Back then, Hungary did not offer its co-ethnics from abroad the right to citizenship, which was rejected in the 2004 referendum[5]. He willingly and nostalgically (though not without bitterness) recalled his visits to the open-air market in the nearby city of Nyiregyhaza and his work at construction sites in Budapest, Sopron, and Komarom in the 1990s. Prior to that, he had traveled around the Soviet Union as a truck driver. After 2006, he changed his workplace a few times, but every time we met between 2006 and 2009, his material situation was far from stable. Prior to our meeting in 2016, I was wondering to what extent his life had changed after

5 In December 2004, the voters in Hungary were asked whether they were in favor of ethnic Hungarians (non-citizens and non-residents of Hungary) being granted the right to Hungarian citizenship. Although the majority of voted in favor, it was rejected due to the low turnout.

him acquiring a Hungarian passport, as I was convinced he had obtained it. I also had some doubts about whether I would still find him at his home in Beregovo, as I thought it quite possible that he had moved to Hungary or elsewhere. It turned out that he was still living his previous life, only it was a Ukrainian pension of 1000 Ukrainian *hryvna* (around 35 euros), not the precarious jobs he used to do before, which was supposed to secure his life. In fact, it was thanks to his small garden, where he grew fruit and vegetables, occasional support from his neighbors, meals provided by some Hungarian humanitarian organizations, and to him occasionally carrying cigarettes (into Hungary) and other goods (into Ukraine) across the border that he could make a living at all.

He had applied for Hungarian citizenship in 2011 (just after it became possible) and received it in 2012, but it did not change his situation much. For him, the retirement age in Hungary, which differs according to year of birth, was 64, while in Ukraine it was 60. Turning 62 in the summer of 2017, he was stuck between the two systems. Reaching retirement age was also rather unlikely to improve his situation. As he explained, in order to receive a Hungarian pension, one needs to register there and for that, he or she needs money to buy or rent a property, which C simply did not have. Selling the place he lived in was not a possibility, due to some ownership disputes. Bearing a Hungarian passport, he started to carry cigarettes across the border—an activity he, as a Ukrainian citizen, had given up more than 10 years before, after being fined and issued an entry ban.

One would be mistaken to think of dealing in contraband as a profitable activity. It does not appear to be so for people like him, who use what is left of their physical strength and health to work for the entrepreneurs paying 50 Ukrainian *hryvna* (less than 2 euros) for one trip across the checkpoint. The procedure is that goods that are cheaper in Hungary or the EU in general are brought to the border and then carried into Ukraine and shared between large numbers of people, so that the limits are not exceeded. This kind of work involves either physical carrying or sitting in a car loaded with cargo and pretending that part of it belongs to him and to other "passengers" like him. He also attempted to benefit from his Hungarian passport in summer 2016, when he went to work on a construction site in Budapest. He had hoped to spend 4 months there, earn 1,000,000 Hungarian *forints* and buy a small house in the village of Beregsurany on the Hungarian side of the Ukrainian–Hungarian checkpoint, 5 kilometers from Beregovo, which would secure his Hungarian pension. However, on his first day at work, he fainted, was taken to hospital, and had to go back home without even selling the Ukrainian cigarettes he had brought.

5. Conclusion

The impact of state borders on the life of the borderlanders is affected by the economic situation in the countries on either side, as well as by bilateral and international regulations regarding passports, visas, and work permits, or citizenship rules. The latter also influence the intensity of various forms of cross-border contacts and international mobility. However, the border is not experienced by everyone in the same way. As described by Alan and Josephine Smart, state borders structure the world according to one's citizenship and wealth, acting as full stops (which deny entry), semicolons (which require the travelers to obtain visas and work permits), or commas "slightly slowing movement at various checkpoints" (Smart/Smart 2008, p. 175). In my previous study, based on my 2009–2011 fieldwork in Solotvyno, I wrote that:

> Applying the metaphor to the bridge linking Solotvyno and Sighet [which could actually apply to any EU border crossing] would mean that it serves either as a 'full stop' or a 'semi-colon', and as a means of exercising control over the third-country nationals (needed but also 'dangerous') in the European Union. (Jóźwiak 2014, p. 36)

After six years and related changes, the scale of this "time-space punctuation" (Smart/Smart 2008) and the groups of people it affects are different, but the mechanisms of inclusion and exclusion persist. Despite an increasing pressure to leave the country and use the border in various ways possible, some of the local inhabitants cross the border on a regular basis (even every day), whilst others have never been to the other side. Nevertheless, the scale of cross-border activities and the strategies of familiarization with the state border have changed.

According to Hastings Donnan and Thomas Wilson, cross-border activities, on both official and grassroots levels, puncture the borders and subvert "the state's own design" for them (Donnan/Wilson 2010, pp. 6–7). Added to the popularity of Hungarian and Romanian TV and radio, strategies for securing a livelihood, which involve obtaining another state's citizenship or registering cars on the other side of the border, contribute to the transformation and increased role of the transnational spaces, in both social and geographical terms, in which people operate. Referring back to the question about the significance of political developments on national and international levels, we should acknowledge that cross-border links in Transcarpathia date back to the early 1990s, while the everyday presence of the neighboring countries in the form of the mass media has been the case for decades. What we observe in the second decade of the 21st century cannot be described as the "formation" of these spaces. These spaces, together with phenomena observed at and near the borders, can be interpreted as "gaps in Fortress Europe" and "blurred boundaries of the nation state". The abovementioned phenomena are at stake regardless of the political and economic conditions, it is the process of becoming blurred that changes.

These border-related grassroots responses to the (inter)national political conditions also reflect individual and collective agency and the limits to agency, entrepreneurship as well as "the precarious economy of the border" (cf. Arnold/Pickles 2011) in a time of instability and uncertainty. Carrying passports that are more powerful (Hungarian or Romanian passports) or less powerful (Ukrainian passports with visas or local border traffic documents) when leaving Ukraine makes one privileged in the context of selectivity performed at the borders of the EU. However, safeguarding the rights to cross the border, to reside abroad and to vote in a neighboring country (or its consulates at one's place of residence—a crucial aspect in the case of Hungary and Transcarpathia) does not eliminate social inequalities. Exclusionary mechanisms embedded in the functioning of the border are indirectly preserved. In order to fully enjoy the opportunities of the "golden tickets" to the EU, one needs certain resources which are not equally available. Carrying passengers on international routes requires capital to be invested in buying cars, registering them, and maintaining them. Working abroad requires networks (in order to find a job) or good health, in the case of physical labor. Receiving a Hungarian pension requires registration and actually settling in the country, for which, again, one needs funds.

When I was leaving B's car after he had taken me to the place I was staying in Beregovo, he encouraged me to call either him or his boss (who already had my number stored in his phonebook as the "Polish Sociologist") whenever I needed their service. When I last met A it was at her home with her friends and family members. Due to the summer holiday season, she did not have to worry about the queues at the border and the amount of time needed to get to and from work. Thanks to the holiday, she had more time not only to spend at home but also to look after a small business she ran with her husband in Beregovo. However, even without daily commuting, Hungary was still there. She gave me a lift in her car registered in that country, and the conversations around the table revolved around the Hungarian health-care system, pension fund, and the labor market. As was agreed among the company, it was all far from excellent, but still beyond comparison to what one can expect in Ukraine.

When in the summer of 2016 I called C on his cell phone, he was unable to meet as he was cycling to the border, "8 kilometers there and back in order to earn 40 *hryvnias*" [less than 1.5 euros]. When we met the next year, he recalled this and numerous similar situations when he had had to wait for a phone call and leave home when needed, never sure how much time he would have to spend at the checkpoint and how much he would earn there. "I am not in charge of myself," he said during our last meeting. On top of that, he still could not sell his house in order to possibly arrange a Hungarian pension.

References

Arnold, Denis/Pickles, John (2011): Global Work, Surplus Labor, and the Precarious Economies of the Border. In: Antipode 43, no. 5, p. 1598–1624, DOI: https://doi.org/10.1111/j.1467-8330.2011.00899.x.

Balibar, Étienne (2004): We, the people of Europe?: Reflections on Transnational Citizenship. Princeton/Oxford: Princeton University Press.

Brubaker, Rogers (1996): Nationalism reframed: Nationhood and the National Question in the New Europe. Cambridge University Press.

Burawoy, Michael (2003): Revisits: An Outline of a Theory of Reflexive Ethnography. In: American Sociological Review 68, no. 5, p. 645–679, DOI: 10.2307/1519757.

Donnan, Hastings/Wilson, Thomas M. (1999): Borders: Frontiers of Identity, Nation and State. Oxford: Berg.

Donnan, Hastings/Wilson, Thomas M. (2010): Ethnography, Security and the 'Frontier Effect' in Borderlands. In Donnan, H./Wilson, T. M. (eds.): Borderlands. Ethnographic Approaches to Security, Power and Identity. Lanham – Boulder – New York – Toronto – Plymouth. University Press of America, p. 1–21.

Erőss, Ágnes/Kovaly, Katalin/Tatrai, Patrik (2016): Effects of the Ukrainian Crisis in Transcarpathia: the Hungarian Perspective. CMR Working Papers 93. Warsaw: Centre of Migration Research, URL: http://www.migracje.uw.edu.pl/publikacje/effects-of-the-ukrainian-crisis-in-transcarpathia-the-hungarian-perspective-2/ (accessed: 23/10/2018).

Feldman, Gregory (2012): The Migration Apparatus: Security, Labor, and Policymaking in the European Union. Redwood City, CA: Stanford University Press.

Follis, Karolina S. (2012): Building Fortress Europe: The Polish-Ukrainian Frontier. Philadelphia: University of Pennsylvania Press.

Green, Sarah (2010): Performing Border in the Aegean: On Relocating Political, Economic and Social Relations. In: Journal of Cultural Economy 3, no. 2, p. 261–278, DOI: https://doi.org/10.1080/17530350.2010.494376.

Green, Sarah (2012): A Sense of Border. In: Donnan, H./Wilson, T. M. (eds.): A Companion to Border Studies. Malden – Oxford: Wiley-Blackwell, p. 573–592.

Iwański, Tadeusz (2015): A Ship Run Aground. Deepening Problems in the Ukrainian Economy. Warsaw: Centre for Eastern Studies, URL: https://www.osw.waw.pl/en/publikacje/osw-commentary/2015-06-16/a-ship-run-aground-deepening-problems-ukrainian-economy (accessed: 23/10/2018).

Jóźwiak, Ignacy (2014): Ethnicity, Labour and Mobility in the Contemporary Borderland. A Case Study of a Transcarpathian Township. In: Central and Eastern European Migration Review 3, no. 1, p. 27–39.

Marcus, George E. (1995): Ethnography in/of the World System: The Emergence of Multi-sited Ethnography. In: Annual Review of Anthropology 24, p. 95–117, DOI: https://doi.org/10.1146/annurev.an.24.100195.000523.

Simonyi, André/Pisano, Jessica (2011): The Social Lives of Borders: Political Economy at the Edge of the European Union. In: DeBardeleben, J./Hurrelmann, A. (eds.): Transnational Europe: Promise, Paradox, Limits. Hampshire/New York: Springer, p. 222–238.

Smart, Alan/Smart, Josephine (2008): Time-space Punctuation: Hong Kong's Border Regime and Limits on Mobility. In: Pacific Affair, 81, no. 2, p. 175–193, DOI: https://doi.org/10.5509/2008812175.

Tavory, Ido/Timmermans, Stefan (2009): Two Cases of Ethnography. Grounded Theory and the Extended Case Method. In: Ethnography 10, no. 3, p. 243–263, DOI: http://dx.doi.org/10.1177/1466138109339042.

Torpey, John C. (2000): The Invention of the Passport: Surveillance, Citizenship and the State. Cambridge University Press.

Yurchenko, Yuliya (2018): Ukraine and the Empire of Capital. From Marketisation to Armed Conflict. London: Pluto Press.

Zaiotti, Ruben (2007a): Of Friends and Fences: Europe's Neighbourhood Policy and the "Gated Community Syndrome". In: European Integration 29, no. 2, p. 143–162, DOI: https://doi.org/10.1080/07036330701252581.

Zaiotti, Ruben (2007b): Revisiting Schengen: Europe and the Emergence of a New Culture of Border Control. In: Perspectives on European Politics and Society 8, no. 1, p. 31–54, DOI: https://doi.org/10.1080/15705850701204087.

About the author

Ignacy Jóźwiak | University of Warsaw | Centre of Migration Research | ul. Patseura 7 02-093 Warsaw | Poland | T +48 22 55 46 779 | i.jozwiak@uw.edu.pl

Jóźwiak, Ignacy, holds a BA and MA in ethnology and a Ph.D. in sociology, which makes him consider himself a social anthropologist. He is a researcher at the Centre of Migration Research, University of Warsaw. Areas of research interest: labor migration to the EU countries, state borders, borderlands, and transnational spaces.

Passports and mobility at Spain's border with France, 1966–1978

Ariela House

Abstract

In 1966, Spain became the last of France's neighbors to admit French tourists with just a national identity card. However, travel to France with a Spanish identity card did not become possible until 1978. Focusing on the twelve-year period when French nationals were able to visit Spain with just an identity card, while Spanish nationals continued to need passports to travel to France, this paper considers the abolition of the passport requirement for tourists as an aspect of European integration and of the dictatorship and subsequent transition process in Spain.

Keywords

Passports, freedom of movement, tourism, Franco regime, European integration

1. Introduction

A series of bilateral agreements created a *de facto* passport-free tourism zone in Western Europe in the decades after the Second World War. The economic imperative to attract foreign tourists eventually led Franco's Spain to partially join this trend. In February 1966, Spain became the last of France's European neighbors to admit French tourists with just an identity card. Yet the ostensibly bilateral agreement was immediately applicable only to French nationals. When Spanish travelers would be able to visit France without passports was left up to the Spanish government. The partial integration of Spain into the *de facto* passport-free tourism zone while Spain remained a dictatorship reflected the country's position in Western Europe. A Cold War ally of neighboring democratic states and an increasingly popular vacation destination for their citizens, Franco's Spain faced minimal international pressure to end restrictive laws and practices that applied primarily to its own nationals. Authorities made use of their broad powers to deny, confiscate, and invalidate passports. Permitting travel abroad with the identity document that all Spaniards were required to have would have greatly limited possibilities for control. The differing political regimes in France and Spain meant that the border was experienced differently depending on the traveler's nationality. Differing documentation requirements were a concrete manifestation of the greater freedoms available to French nationals in comparison with those living under the dictatorship in Spain. However, the ability to enter Spain with just a French national identity card was also dependent upon the will of the Franco regime, which at one point temporarily reinstated the passport requirement for French nationals. Focusing on the twelve-year period when French nationals were able to visit Spain with just a national identity card, while the passport requirement remained in place for Spanish nationals, this paper argues that the expanding sphere of passport-free tourism was an important facet of European integration. It occurred outside the realm of European Community policy, thus permitting the participation of Spain, which did not become a member state until 1986.

The case of Spain under the Franco regime is particularly illustrative of the difference between passports and identity cards as documents for cross-border travel. Spanish passport legislation, archival documents produced by border control authorities, newspaper accounts, and a 1974 book by legal scholar José Manuel Castells Arteche that unfavorably compared the Spanish passport system to those of other countries will be used to demonstrate the extent to which passports were not accessible to everyone. Meanwhile, passport-free tourism had become the norm in much of Western Europe. Beginning in September 1974, Spain unilaterally suspended the 1966 agreement for several months, requiring that French tourists show valid passports at the border. The surprise expressed by French nationals who were affected by this measure shows that many in France had come to take the ability to travel to neighboring countries with just a national identity card for granted. Slightly more than three years later, Spanish nationals finally gained access to part of the Western European passport-free travel zone. Consideration of Spanish passport law and practice with regard to both Spanish and French nationals adds a new dimension to discussions on the expansion of freedom of movement in Europe and the nature of the Franco regime and the post-Franco transition process in Spain.

2. *Passports and Identity Cards as Travel Documents*

The *de facto* passport-free tourism zone in Western Europe emerged in the years after the Second World War through a series of agreements between governments. The trend toward passport-free travel led the Council of Europe to approve a "European Agreement governing the Movement of Persons between Member States" in December 1957. The convention followed the model of existing bilateral accords, stipulating that nationals of signatory countries could enter and exit the territories of other signatories for stays not exceeding three months with one of the documents listed in the appendix. These included identity cards for nationals of those states that issued them. France was, along with Belgium and Italy, one of the first Council of Europe members to adhere to the agreement (Turack 1972, p. 74). While this convention has subsequently been ratified by other states, expanding opportunities for passport-free travel between Council of Europe member states, French nationals first gained access to most of Western Europe with just their identity cards through bilateral agreements. These agreements predated the country of destination's adherence to the convention, as seen in Table 1.

	Entry with a French identity card (bilateral agreement)	**1957 Council of Europe convention entry into force**
Belgium	May 1949	January 1958
Luxembourg	June 1949	May 1961
Switzerland	May 1950	January 1967
Liechtenstein	May 1950	October 1998
F.R. Germany	December 1956	June 1958
Italy	March 1957	January 1958
Netherlands	May 1957	March 1961
Austria	June 1957	June 1958
United Kingdom	March 1961	–
Spain	February 1966	June 1982

Table 1: The expansion of passport-free travel for French nationals, 1949–1966

Sources: UNTS 1949a; UNTS 1949b; FDFA 1950; Traités et accords de la France 1956; UNTS 1958a; UNTS 1958b; Traités et accords de la France 1957; Treaty Series 1961; UNTS 1979a; Council of Europe 2018.

Discussion of passport-free tourism agreements can be found in legal scholarship from the period. In a 1972 book, Daniel C. Turack mentioned bilateral agreements between Western European states and considered the work of the Council of Europe and the OEEC (Organisation for European Economic Co-Operation) and its successor, the OECD (Organisation for Economic Cooperation and Development), to encourage the expansion of passport-free tourism. With regard to Spain, he cited a 1962 report by the

OECD's Tourism Committee, according to which the Spanish government was willing to admit French tourists without passports, but the French government was not yet willing to permit travel to Spain with just an identity card. Spain concluded such agreements with the Federal Republic of Germany in 1964 and with France and Switzerland in 1966 (Turack 1972, p. 58–59). Turack did not mention the clauses that, if activated, would have made these agreements apply reciprocally to Spanish nationals. José Manuel Castells Arteche, writing during the final years of the dictatorship in Spain, noted that agreements to allow tourism with just an identity card had become "widespread in continental Europe." Citing the agreements to allow tourists from West Germany, France, Switzerland, and Liechtenstein (included in the Swiss agreement) to enter Spain without passports, he accused the Spanish government of discrimination against Spanish nationals. Furthermore, these agreements had not been published in the official state journal (*Boletín Oficial del Estado*), where a wider audience inside Spain might have been made aware of their existence (Castells 1974a, p. 236–237). Most recently, in 1972, Spain had concluded an exchange of notes with the Benelux countries that was published in the official state journal. However, despite a change to passport legislation in 1971 that seemingly opened the door to applying such agreements reciprocally to Spanish nationals, the agreement included a provision that "suspended" travel to Belgium, Luxembourg, and the Netherlands with a Spanish identity card until subsequent notification by the Spanish government (Castells 1974a, p. 251–252).

The postwar trend towards passport-free tourism in Western Europe has received minimal attention in more recent studies. This may be attributed both to a tendency to focus on advances in freedom of movement that occurred within the framework of the primary institutions of European integration and to a belief that the move from passports to identity cards did not fundamentally change the nature of border crossing and police checks. Mark B. Salter notes that, unlike the Nordic Council, the Council of Europe failed in its early postwar aim of creating a passport union. Salter is correct to point out that, under the 1957 Council of Europe convention, travelers were still required to present some form of government-issued identification at the border: "Thus, the freedom was not to cross German–French borders without examination; rather, it was that the passport ceased to be the crucial and necessary document" (2003, p. 106–107). Tellingly, this quote fails to mention that it was not the 1957 Council of Europe convention that made travel between France and the Federal Republic of Germany possible with just an identity card, but rather a 1956 exchange of notes between the two governments (Traités et accords de la

France 1956). The bilateral agreements that first made tourist travel with just an identity card a reality in much of Western Europe have largely been forgotten. Sasha D. Pack's study on the role of European tourism in transforming Spain during the Franco regime provides valuable insight into the evolution of entry requirements for foreign visitors, particularly those traveling by car. However, with the exception of the Gibraltar border, he traces developments in this area only through 1961, thus omitting the passport-free tourism agreements that Spain entered into starting in 1964 (2006, p. 53–56, 91–96).

As John Torpey has argued, passports and other identity documents are tools that states use to monopolize the legitimate means of human movement, particularly across international borders. His study on the history of passports and their use in regulating movement makes brief mention of postwar passport-free tourism agreements in Western Europe (2000, p. 144–145). Yet, in the "typology of papers" that concludes his book, Torpey (2000, p. 159) distinguishes between internal passports designed to limit movement within a state's borders, international passports that are used as proof of nationality and provide access to consular services, and identity cards, which "are not normally, or not primarily, used to regulate movement, but simply to establish the identity of the bearer for purposes of state administration and of gaining access to benefits distributed by the state." The move from travel with a government-issued passport to travel with a government-issued identity card did not diminish the role of the sovereign state in controlling legitimate movement. However, given that national identity cards are primarily intended for use within state borders, the move to grant access to territories beyond these borders merits further discussion as a significant development in freedom of movement.

Identity cards and passports are different categories of government-issued documentation. Identity cards are normally issued to all nationals without exception and possessing one may be compulsory. In contrast, passports are not considered a necessary item because not everyone has reason to travel abroad and states may not make them as accessible as identity cards. The example of Spain under Franco starkly illustrates the difference between these two types of documentation. Possessing a national identity card was obligatory for all Spaniards aged 16 and over (BOE 1955). This meant that everyone except children had an identity card. Passports, however, were deliberately not made accessible to all Spanish nationals, as will be discussed in detail. Even in states considered full democracies, passports may be less readily available due to significantly higher issuance fees and longer processing times.

The elimination of the passport requirement for tourists made travel to a particular set of nearby countries more accessible, with obvious practical benefits for travelers and implications for the construction of a European identity. Bonn, Rome, and Madrid were closer to home for French nationals in 1970 than in 1950, not geographically speaking, but because they could now travel to these foreign capitals with the same identity document they used for everyday transactions in their home country. Though Spanish nationals benefited from the reciprocal abolition of entry visas in 1959, the elimination of exit visas in 1963 (Fernández 1991, p. 836) was as far as Franco's government was willing to go in relaxing the requirements for travel abroad, for reasons that become clear upon examination of passport law and practice under the dictatorship.

3. *Passports in late Francoist Spain*

The 1958 decree (*decreto*) regulating ordinary passports came at a time of increased political stability for the Franco regime. Nearly twenty years after the end of the Civil War in 1939, the regime had solidified its position at home and abroad. Spain was admitted to the United Nations in 1955 and joined the International Monetary Fund, the Export-Import Bank, and the OEEC in 1958. Membership in these international economic organizations demonstrated the Franco regime's newfound openness to the global market and its abandonment of the disastrous autarky policy of the postwar period. This significant policy shift laid the foundations for the economic boom of the 1960s, in which tourism would play a key role. The remittances of Spanish nationals working abroad and the inflow of foreign currency from tourism combined to correct Spain's balance of payments (Huguet 2003, p. 507). The economic importance of foreign tourism was undoubtedly the primary reason that Spain began to enter into agreements to allow nationals of certain countries to visit with just an identity card.

The new era of political stability was reflected in the decision to draw up a new passport law, but not in its content. José Manuel Castells Arteche categorized it as "postwar" legislation because "its principals remain immersed in the exceptionality of the preceding period." (1974a, p. 92). The new decree, dated June 20, 1958, was the first comprehensive passport legislation of the Franco era. It modified, but did not repeal, a 1935 decree that had remained in effect after the Civil War, albeit with the addition of further requirements for passport applicants. Castells argued that, while the 1958 decree could be considered a prolongation of its 1935 predecessor, it significantly increased the discretionary powers granted to authorities. Under the 1935 decree, the only grounds for depriving someone of the right to a passport were convictions for tax fraud or smuggling. In Castells' view, the 1958 decree gave authorities a *carte blanche* to deny passports, as stated in article 11: "Authorities may at any time deny any person the right to be issued a passport, or rescind one that has already been issued, on account of a crime or other reasons that could affect public order or national security" (1974a, p. 106). Furthermore, those who already held passports could be prevented from leaving Spanish territory under article 22:

> The Minister of Governance[1] is authorized to stop nationals from leaving national territory for the time considered opportune, even if they are in possession of their respective passports, if such a measure is advisable under the present circumstances or serious disturbances of public order are feared. (BOE 1958).

This article was nearly identical to that found in the 1935 decree (Castells 1974a, p. 107). The already restrictive nature of the decree enacted during the Second Republic likely explains why the Franco regime left it on the books.

Article 16 of the 1958 decree lists the documents that passport applicants were required to provide: two photographs, a national identity card plus a second document to prove their identity (birth certificate, family book, or previous passport), and a police record certificate. The need to first obtain a police certificate could significantly lengthen the application process. This requirement had been introduced in 1937, during the Civil War, in those parts of Spain that were already under Franco's control (Castells 1974a, p. 93). Other requirements varied according to the applicant's gender. Young men were required to present proof that they were meeting their military service obligations, first by completing an active service period and then by having their reservists' booklets (*cartilla militar*) stamped each year. As for women, requirements differed according to age and marital status, thus reflecting the regime's gender ideology, according to which a woman's proper place was in the home as an attentive and obedient wife and mother. Married women had to present a family book to prove their marital status when applying for a passport. Although it seems to be common knowledge in Spain that a married woman needed her husband's permission to obtain a passport during the dictatorship, this re-

1 Spain's Ministry of the Interior was known as the *Ministerio de la Gobernación* until 1977.

quirement is not actually specified in the passport legislation of the period. Women between the ages of 17 and 35 who were unmarried or widowed with no children had to present a certificate proving they had completed the "Social Service," a program administered by the Women's Section of the Franco regime's sole legal political party.

A 1971 passport decree replaced the one enacted in 1958 (BOE 1972). Its preamble claimed that the new regulations were conceived in accordance with "international agreements and circumstances, which have allowed greater flexibility in the issuance of passports and increased periods of passport validity." It is true that it extended the validity of Spanish passports from two years to five years—the international norm—while maintaining the administration's ability to limit validity to a shorter period, and that the application process was somewhat simplified by requiring fewer documents. However, requirements still included a criminal record certificate and, for young unmarried women, completion of the "Social Service." Powers to reject applications, cancel passports already issued, and limit the right of passport holders to leave Spanish territory were retained. The new decree altered the stipulation that passports were required for all travel abroad, found in its 1935 and 1958 predecessors, in a way that seemingly opened the door to allowing travel abroad with an identity card: "Those Spaniards who wish to travel abroad must first obtain a passport that proves their identity [*personalidad*], except for travel to a country or countries that do not have this requirement due to an existing exemption agreement" (BOE 1972; Castells 1974a, p. 241–242). However, during the last years of the Franco regime, the passport requirement remained in place for Spanish nationals wishing to leave the country, and authorities continued to make use of their powers to restrict access to passports.

The legal provisions for denying and confiscating passports were regularly used against political dissidents. Castells analyzes in considerable detail the Spanish Supreme Court's 1971 decision in the case of Alfonso Comín Ros, who had appealed a Ministry of Governance resolution denying him a passport. Comín applied for a passport on September 29, 1965 at Barcelona's central police headquarters (*Jefatura Superior de Policía*). He received no response. On March 1, 1966, he applied again, this time through the General Directorate of Security (*Dirección General de Seguridad*). Finally, on July 29, 1966, he sent a new passport application to the Ministry of Governance. Five months later, on December 20, 1966, he received notification of a General Directorate of Security decision, dated October 22, 1965, to deny his initial application. He appealed before the Ministry of Governance. In a resolution dated February 11, 1967, the Ministry asserted that the administration enjoyed complete "discretionary authority" (*facul-*

tad discrecional) to grant or deny passports. On October 25, 1971, Spain's Supreme Court upheld the Ministry's 1967 resolution (Castells 1974a, p. 161–162). The court found that, under existing law, passports could be denied for reasons that "might" affect public order, and police reports had implicated Comín in incidents "that are undoubtedly related to public order." These included "notes and petitions, talks, participation in events and meetings, [and] trips or contact with national and foreign persons" (Castells 1974a, p. 272–273). Comín was a known critic of the Franco regime. A left-wing Catholic intellectual, he had a long history as an activist, having participated in several clandestine students' and workers' organizations in Catalonia. In the years between his first passport application and the Supreme Court's decision on his appeal, he was sentenced to 16 months in prison for an opinion article deemed "illegal propaganda" and jailed for four months during the "state of emergency" declared in early 1969 to quell a wave of protests (Pérez 2006, p. 96–97).

Participants in protests against the regime saw their passports rescinded, even without being formally charged with or convicted of a crime. In a February 1978 column celebrating the elimination of the passport requirement for travel to France, the Catalan journalist Lluís Permanyer described how members of the Barcelona elite who were involved in protests during the late Franco period had attempted to regain their lost freedom to travel abroad. He referred specifically to the events of the "Caputxinada," a March 1966 meeting held at a Capuchin monastery in Barcelona to draw up the founding statutes of the Democratic Students' Union (*Sindicat Democràtic d'Estudiants*) that was raided by the police, and the December 1970 sit-in held by Catalan artists and intellectuals at the Benedictine abbey of Montserrat to protest against the "Burgos trial"[2] (1978, p. 70):

> Then came a period in which, in intellectual and political circles, it was common to come across many people whose magical green books [passports] had been taken away: for participation in the "Caputxinada" or the sit-in at Montserrat, or because they were on the list of those who had signed one of those manifestos that were constantly circulating. Thus began the exhausting and humiliating pilgrimage to implore the benevolent issuance of another passport and, if this failed, the search for an important figure who could intercede.

---

2 In December 1970, 16 members of ETA were tried in a military court in Burgos. Nine were sentenced to death, which elicited widespread protests. Under diplomatic pressure from governments that included France, Franco commuted the death sentences on December 30 (Morán 1997, p. 76–77).

It goes without saying that not everyone who had a passport denied or taken away was sufficiently well-connected to gain an audience with someone in a position to reconsider this decision.

The General Directorate of Security periodically drew up lists of opponents of the regime who were not to be issued passports. On December 31, 1972, a young man from Galicia arrived at the border post in the Basque town of Irun bearing a safe conduct from the Spanish consulate in Toulouse that authorized him to return to Spain. He stated that he had departed for France with a valid passport, issued in Santiago de Compostela in 1969 and renewed in 1971 at Spain's Consulate General in Paris. The Irun border police, following their standard procedure in cases of Spanish nationals who claimed to have lost their passports while abroad, searched the files they had on hand and telephoned the police in Santiago de Compostela and the young man's hometown. They discovered that he had been issued a passport, as he claimed, but that he had subsequently been placed on the General Directorate of Security's annual list of student activists who were not to be granted passports. Nonetheless, the higher authorities whom the border police consulted authorized the student to re-enter Spain and continue his journey home. He had been listed as an activist too late for the General Directorate of Security to prevent his departure to France. However, he would undoubtedly have been refused a new passport had he tried to apply for one after returning to Spain. His police file in Galicia indicated that he was a "member of the communist party" (GAHP, GC, 242/3).

Discriminatory practices in access to passports were not limited to measures intended to prevent political dissidents from leaving the country. There is evidence of discrimination based on socioeconomic status in deciding whether to approve passport applications. When border police in the Catalan town of Puigcerdà reported a man to provincial authorities for having entered France without an exit visa in 1961, they remarked that he claimed to be a chemist, whereas in his passport he was listed as a laborer. The police found this "very odd, given that, in the absence of other circumstances, it is easier to obtain a passport as a doctor [*facultativo*] than as a laborer" (AHG, GC, 774/1). This suggests that class discrimination in the issuance of passports was commonplace. The Spanish Emigration Institute (*Instituto Español de Emigración*) aimed to control emigration by Spanish workers. In a March 8, 1962 memo, the General Directorate of Security ordered passport-issuing authorities to thoroughly investigate the travel plans of applicants suspected of intending to seek work abroad. If these suspicions were confirmed, the application for an ordinary passport would be denied and the applicant would be directed to apply to emigrate through official channels (AHL, GC, 3576). Thus, an applicant who was poor, but able to pay the issuance fee of 150 pesetas, might be denied a passport based on the suspicion that he or she intended to emigrate. Under a 1963 decree, illiterate individuals who did not participate in a literacy program could not obtain passports (Castells 1974a, p. 233). This requirement may be compared to the "Social Service" obligation for young unmarried women in that it was a coercive measure that limited opportunities for those who failed to enroll in programs intended to mold them into proper Spaniards.

The most far-reaching use of the "discretionary authority" to deny, confiscate, or invalidate passports occurred in early 1974 and affected passport holders in Spain's four Basque provinces. On December 20, 1973, the head of Franco's government, Luis Carrero Blanco, was killed when a bomb exploded under his car in Madrid. The Basque armed organization ETA quickly claimed responsibility for the assassination in a press conference held in southwestern France (Morán 1997, p. 79). The General Directorate of Security soon implemented restrictive measures that applied to all holders of passports issued in the provinces of Araba, Bizkaia, Gipuzkoa, and Navarre. As of January 20, 1974, passports from these provinces were no longer valid for travel abroad without a special inspection stamp. It was widely reported in the press that this measure aimed to prevent the use of falsified passports. However, as José Manuel Castells Arteche pointed out in a March 1974 article, it was well-known that "activists" normally used documentation that allowed them to pass themselves off as hailing from outside the Basque Country. Castells noted that Basque travelers were also being asked to provide "justification" to border police as to their reasons for traveling, a requirement that had not been officially communicated to the public (1974b, p. 138–139). In Gipuzkoa, which includes the major border-crossing point of Irun, the requirement that all passports be presented for inspection was first announced in a note signed by the provincial chief of police and published in local newspapers on January 9 (El comisario jefe provincial 1974a, p. 8):

> As ordered by the General Directorate of Security, all Spaniards holding passports issued by this Provincial Police Station or the Local Police Stations in Irún, Eibar, Zumárraga and Fuenterrabía who need to use them to travel abroad via any border, port, or airport within national territory must, as of the 20th of this month, present them in the respective departments previously mentioned, during normal opening hours, in order that they be submitted for inspection.

Holders of passports issued in Donostia had to hand in their passports in a strict alphabetical order, presumably due to the high volume of passports requiring inspection in this provincial capital, located just 20 kilometers from the French border. The police did not accept passports belonging to those whose surnames began with the last letter of the alphabet until April 17 (El comisario jefe provincial 1974b, p. 8). Thus, a passport holder called Zabala would have been unable to leave Spanish territory for more than three months.

In Castells' view, this blanket measure was legally dubious, as the provisions for invalidating passports under the 1971 decree clearly applied to cases in which authorities had cause to deny specific individuals the right to travel abroad. Castells suggested that Spanish law did provide a legal option for such a measure, in the form of a *decreto-ley* specifically suspending the right of inhabitants of the affected provinces to travel (1974b, p. 138–139). However, authorities under the Franco regime were unconcerned with such legal technicalities when exercising the broad discretionary powers they enjoyed—certainly in practice, if not always according to the letter of the law—to restrict the right to travel abroad even of people who had been issued passports. Possessing a national identity card was compulsory, which meant that student activists, communists, Catalans who participated in protests, and residents of the four Basque provinces had identity cards that could not be taken away. Retaining the passport requirement meant that these people could easily be prevented from traveling abroad at the regime's discretion, unless they were willing to cross the border illegally outside the authorized crossing points where the police conducted regular passport checks.

4. *Passport-free travel for French nationals and Spain's suspension of the 1966 agreement*

By the end of the 1950s, a French national identity card had become sufficient documentation for entering all of the European countries that border France, with the sole exception of Spain. Spain's partial incorporation into the passport-free tourism zone in Western Europe began with the conclusion of an exchange of notes with the Federal Republic of Germany on July 22, 1964. West Germans were to benefit from the agreement almost immediately, beginning on August 1, but "the date of its entry into force in respect of Spanish nationals" was to be "communicated by the Spanish government through the diplomatic channel" (UNTS 1979b). The next such agreement came approximately a year and a half later, on January 13,

1966, when the Spanish foreign minister and the French ambassador to Spain concluded a similar exchange of notes. Again, the text left the decision as to when the agreement was to apply reciprocally to Spanish nationals visiting France up to the Spanish government: "This new provision will apply to French nationals beginning on 15 February 1966 and to Spanish nationals beginning sixty days after the date that your [Spain's] government will specify through diplomatic channels" (UNTS 1979a). This agreement was the final piece in making a passport unnecessary for French nationals traveling to neighboring countries, approximately nine years after West Germany and Italy began to admit French tourists with an identity card. The fact that France's more democratic neighbors allowed their own nationals to leave the country with just an identity card, while Spain did not, was of little significance to the French tourists who now benefited from passport-free travel to Spain. The 1966 agreement did not need to be reciprocal in order to help cement the idea in France that an identity card was all that was needed for travel to neighboring countries.

Thus, even though Spain's political regime differed considerably from those of other neighboring countries, the Spanish government's sudden decision in 1974 to unilaterally suspend the 1966 agreement came as a shock to many in France. At the beginning of the year, Spanish authorities' reaction to the assassination of Carrero Blanco by ETA had included the blanket invalidation of passports issued in the Basque provinces, as has been described. Also in early 1974, Spain requested the extradition of ten people accused of involvement in the assassination. However, the French government rejected the request, citing an 1877 treaty that forbade extradition for political crimes (Morán 1997, p. 81). Then, on September 13, 1974, a bomb exploded at a café in Madrid located opposite the headquarters of the General Directorate of Security, in an attack for which ETA never claimed responsibility. The bombing killed and injured people with no relation to Spain's security apparatus. One week later, on September 20, Spain's Council of Ministers issued a statement denouncing the "apparent status as political refugees" that ETA "terrorists" enjoyed in France, which had allowed them to "make the French Basque region the base for the subversive operations they carry out in Spain." The Spanish government resolved to "ask the French government to adopt the appropriate measures in order to put an end to this situation, which is incompatible with the friendly relations that exist between the two countries." Furthermore, surveillance and control at the French border would be stepped up (Consejo de Ministros 1974, p. 3).

That afternoon, Spanish border police in the Basque town of Irun began to require that French tourists show a valid passport. The following day, the new policy was in place at all checkpoints on the border with France. The Perpinyà[3]-based daily *L'Indépendant* wrote of a "disagreeable surprise"; border police in the Catalan town of La Jonquera, Spain's most-transited point of entry, had waived the new requirement only for a troupe of majorettes set to perform at Barcelona's annual city festival and for truck drivers, who were given a two-day window to apply for passports. Most French travelers who arrived at the border that Saturday morning were forced to turn around (No author 1974, p. 1). The new entry requirement for French nationals was likewise front-page news in *Le Monde*, which noted that Spain had violated the terms of the 1966 agreement: "In Paris, it has first of all been observed that Madrid is not respecting the 1966 accord, which can only be abandoned two months before its annual renewal, which occurs each February by tacit agreement" (Novais 1974, p. 1).

In French Catalonia, the prefecture of the Pyrénées-Orientales department issued 33,000 passports, a remarkably high number, in the six months that followed the suspension of the 1966 agreement. However, many French nationals who did not live near the border were unaware that their identity cards no longer sufficed for travel to Spain, even months after the passport requirement was reinstated. "It is staggering how numerous they are," wrote the Perpinyà edition of *La Dépêche du Midi* on March 17, 1975, citing the recent examples of a couple from Limoges headed to a wedding and a man from Lille traveling to a family funeral. Refused entry at the Spanish border, they were able to plead their cases at the prefecture in Perpinyà and were issued passports that same day (J.K. 1975, "Régionale" section, p. 1).

A few French nationals who did manage to enter Spain without passports paid a harsh price for their ignorance regarding the new entry requirement. In November 1974, two teenagers from Val-d'Oise hitchhiked across the border at La Jonquera in a car with Spanish license plates. The driver dropped them off in Figueres, slightly more than 20 kilometers from the border, where they were stopped by a pair of Civil Guard officers and arrested when they failed to produce valid passports. Under questioning, they declared that they were certain that only an identity card was needed to enter Spain and that nothing had been said to them at the border. The two teenagers were jailed in the Girona provincial prison before being deported to France on November 26, one week after their arrest

---

3 "Perpignan" in French and officially. This paper uses Catalan and Basque place names for towns and cities on both sides of the border, except when quoting primary sources.

(AHG, GC, 841/19). This was the standard procedure when a French national was arrested for illegal border crossing, but two months earlier the boys' trip to Spain would have been perfectly legal under an agreement that, by its own terms, remained in effect.

Two months later, a 19-year-old French student took advantage of a short school vacation to travel to Spain with a West German friend who had a car. The two entered Spain at La Jonquera on February 28, 1975. The French student later declared that their papers had not been inspected at the border. Had border police examined the driver's papers, they would have detected no irregularities, because Spanish authorities had not suspended the 1964 agreement with the Federal Republic of Germany. The two friends did not make the return trip together. On March 4, the French student boarded a train from Barcelona to Cervera de la Marenda, the first town on the French side of the border on the Catalan coast. Upon arrival, already on French soil but subject to an exit examination by Spanish police under an agreement that had created "juxtaposed controls" at border train stations (BOE 1969), he showed his identity card and was arrested for illegal border crossing. The student explained under questioning that he believed that his trip was perfectly legal and that he had not encountered any difficulties during his brief stay in Spain:

> He also says that he did not know that a passport was necessary to enter Spain, because this is the first time he has come to our country, and that in addition he knew that at least in the past it was possible to enter Spain with the aforementioned document, being unaware of the passport requirement for French subjects.

The young man spent a few days in the Figueres prison before being transferred to Portbou for deportation. On March 12, he was deported across the border to Cervera de la Marenda, the same town where he had been arrested eight days earlier while attempting to return home (AHG, GC, 842/31).

The sovereign state's role in controlling human movement includes determining who may enter its territory and under what conditions. There is nothing to stop it from suddenly changing requirements, other than concern about potential diplomatic and economic consequences. Spain's decision to suspend the 1966 agreement may be seen a sign that the Franco regime was less concerned with maintaining diplomatic protocol than more democratic European governments, but all states can unilaterally determine both entry requirements for foreigners and exit requirements for nationals. Though French officials protested that Spain was not respecting the terms of the 1966 exchange of notes, reopening the Spanish border for tourists who lacked passports does not appear to have been a diplomatic priority. France continued to honor the agreement that allowed Spanish border police to conduct exit checks at the train station in Cervera de la Marenda, which is how the 19-year-old student came to be arrested on French soil. The eventual reinstatement of the 1966 agreement appears to have been economically motivated.

The attempt to pressure the French government into taking action against alleged ETA members proved entirely unsuccessful and had serious economic repercussions for businesses that relied on customers from across the border. Though a significant number of people, particularly residents of the border zone who made frequent trips to the other side, applied for a passport after many years without one, there were also many in France who decided not to visit Spain. On January 21, 1975, the Girona section of *La Vanguardia Española* reported that the hotel industry in Alt Empordà, which includes the northernmost portion of the Costa Brava, had seen its French clientele fall by approximately forty percent (Vila 1975, p. 33). A February 5 article in the same Barcelona-based newspaper, titled "Anti-tourism Passports," accused authorities of making a politically-motivated decision that had little to do with any real concern about the security of the border: "From the beginning, it was thought that this decision had been made for reasons that were more political than practical for police control, and four months later it has been confirmed that this situation is causing serious harm to commerce and tourism" (No author 1975, p. 5).

On Friday, March 21, 1975, just nine days after the 19-year-old student was deported, Spanish authorities stopped requiring French nationals to show passports at the border (Lecuona 1975, p. 1). Palm Sunday was two days away. Given that Holy Week marked the beginning of the tourist season, the timing of Spain's reinstatement of the 1966 agreement indicates that it came as a direct response to the demands of the tourism industry. The Spanish government had failed to force the French government to change its extradition policy. That the decision to end passport requirements came just before Palm Sunday suggests that *La Vanguardia Española* was right to conclude in February 1975 that the suspension of the agreement had been politically motivated and was not necessary to protect Spain's internal security. By March 1975, Spanish authorities had decided that it no longer made sense to continue a policy that had failed to advance Spain's position in the extradition quarrel with France and now threatened to derail the upcoming tourist season. The consequences of Spain's suspension of the 1966 agreement show that opportunities for passport-free travel were beginning to shape the identity of Western Europeans. The two French boys arrested in November 1974 were not yet seventeen years old, making them just eight in 1966, when Spain became the last state among France's European neighbors to accept entry with just a French identity card. The student arrested in March 1975 was not much older. None of them was from the border region, where news of the passport requirement had undoubtedly spread quickly as many locals saw their weekend trips to Spain suddenly interrupted. The teenagers' statements that they had no idea that a passport was now required are perfectly believable and suggest that French youth in the 1970s did not know a world in which a passport was necessary for travel to neighboring countries.

5. The "transition" to passport-free travel for Spanish nationals in 1978

Requirements for Spanish nationals wishing to travel abroad were finally brought in line with Western European norms beginning in late 1977, two years into the transitional period that followed Franco's death in November 1975. Franco had named Juan Carlos de Borbón, the grandson of the king who went into exile after the proclamation of the Second Republic in 1931, his successor as head of state. Carlos Arias Navarro, appointed by Franco following the assassination of Carrero Blanco, continued in office until July 1976, when the new king appointed Adolfo Suárez. Suárez, the minister in charge of the Franco regime's political party at the time of his appointment, initiated a process of dismantling the regime's political institutions from within to transition to a parliamentary system with democratic elections. The victory of his Union of the Democratic Centre (*Unión del Centro Democrático*) coalition in the June 1977 election made him Spain's first democratically elected prime minister since the Second Republic. It was the government that emerged from this election that acted to reform passport law and make bilateral agreements for passport-free travel apply reciprocally to Spanish nationals.

First, the 1971 decree regulating the issuance of passports was replaced with a new royal decree (*real decreto*) dated September 23, 1977 (BOE 1977). Its preamble cited Spain's "political evolution," the expansion of its diplomatic relations, and its recent ratification of the International Covenant on Civil and Political Rights to explain the pressing need for a new passport law. In keeping with article 12 of the international covenant, which deals with the right of citizens to enter and leave their country, article 1 of the decree made it clear that political dissidents who had not been charged with or convicted of a crime could no longer be denied passports, as had been common practice under the Franco regime:

> All Spanish citizens have the freedom, excepting obligations under the law, to enter and exit national territory and, to this end, have the right to obtain a passport or equivalent document. This right cannot be limited for political or ideological reasons.

The "Social Service" requirement for young, unmarried women was eliminated, but a police record certificate continued to be required.

Then, on December 1, 1977, the Council of Ministers voted to activate the reciprocity clauses in all existing exchanges of notes to eliminate passport requirements for tourists. Activation procedures differed according to the terms of the agreements. The first country that Spanish nationals were able to visit with just their identity cards was the Federal Republic of Germany, beginning on December 20, because the 1964 exchange of notes did not specify a waiting period following notification by the Spanish government. The 1966 exchange of notes with France was finally published in the official state journal on January 30, 1978 (BOE 1978a). It appeared alongside a letter from Spain's foreign minister formally notifying France's highest diplomatic representative in Madrid of the Spanish government's decision that the agreement was to apply to Spanish as well as French nationals. The letter was dated December 6, 1977 and the passport requirement for Spanish tourists entering France was abolished 60 days later, in accordance with the waiting period stipulated in the original agreement, on February 4, 1978. More than twelve years after French nationals gained the freedom to cross the Pyrenean border with their identity cards, Spanish nationals could finally travel on equal terms.

In the years that followed the decision to make the exchanges of notes with the Federal Republic of Germany, France, Switzerland, and the Benelux states applicable on a fully reciprocal basis, Spain entered into further agreements to allow travel in Western Europe with a Spanish national identity card. The Spanish and Austrian foreign ministers concluded the first of these new accords on February 1, 1978. It went into effect 60 days later. In sharp contrast to the practices of the Franco regime, the new Spanish government was quick to publish the agreement with Austria in the official state journal and register it with the United Nations for inclusion in the *Treaty Series* (BOE 1978b; UNTS 1978). The political situation in Spain had changed since the 1972 exchange of notes with the Benelux countries and all subsequent agreements of this type were to apply to nationals of both contracting states from the start. Further agreements to abolish passport requirements were concluded with Portugal in April 1979 (BOE 1979) and with Italy in November 1980 (BOE 1981). Spain joined the Council of Europe in 1977 but did not ratify the 1957 convention on the movement of persons until 1982 (Council of Europe 2018). Bilateral agreements were responsible for Spanish nationals gaining the ability to enter the territories of several Western European states, including the six founding members of the European Economic Community, without passports by 1981.

6. *Conclusion*

In his February 1978 newspaper column, Lluís Permanyer reflected on the significance of no longer needing a passport to travel to France after the experience of the last years of the Franco regime: "I believe that being able to cross the Pyrenees without the need to show a passport will make us feel a little more equal to the much-envied citizens of democratic Europe" (1978, p. 70). The new Spanish government's decision to permit travel abroad with a Spanish identity card broke with the repressive policies of the dictatorship and allowed Spanish nationals to directly benefit from European integration in the realm of freedom of movement. The Franco regime, making use of the sovereign state's monopoly over the legitimate means of movement, had maintained the passport requirement in order to more easily control who was able to travel abroad, even as it began to enter into agreements to permit nationals of certain Western European states to enter Spain with just an identity card.

The surprise expressed by the French teenagers arrested for illegal border crossing and their compatriots who were turned away at the border while the 1966 agreement was suspended between September 1974 and March 1975 suggests that many French nationals had come to take the ability to travel to all neighboring countries without the need to show a passport for granted. The agreements that created a *de facto* passport-free tourism zone in Western Europe were significant because they created a dichotomy between nearby European countries that could be visited with just a national identity card and the rest of the world, which was accessible only with a passport. The elimination of the passport requirement for travel to France was a sign that Spain was moving closer to joining the ranks of "democratic Europe," eight years before it became a European Community member state.

The border experience was altered by the elimination of the need for passports, a type of documentation primarily issued for the purpose of travel. Passports were substituted by identity cards, which are primarily used for identification within one's own country. This change created a fundamental difference between the experience of crossing borders within

Europe as a citizen of one of the states that participated in the passport-free travel zone and crossing other borders at which a passport was still required. The importance of agreements to allow passport-free travel must be considered in light of the fact that documentation requirements for French and Spanish tourists crossing the border between the two countries remain today as they were in 1978. While free movement of workers has always been a central tenet of European Community policy, much travel between member states continues to fall under the category of tourism: trips of fewer than three months that involve neither employment nor establishing residency. Furthermore, the Schengen agreement has not eliminated the need for travelers to be prepared to show a valid travel document if requested by border control authorities, whether during sporadic checks or when generalized border checks are temporarily reinstated due to security concerns. For nationals of those European Union member states that issue national identity cards, this document is sufficient. This has been the case for tourist travel at many Western European borders for over sixty years, and for Spanish nationals traveling to France for four decades.

References

BOE (Boletín Oficial del Estado) (1955): Orden de 24 de diciembre de 1955 por la cual se señalan los plazos máximos para solicitar el Documento Nacional de Identidad, así como la obligatoriedad de su presentación por todos los españoles mayores de dieciséis años cualquiera que sea su sexo y edad. 12/29/1955, p. 7956.

BOE (1958): Decreto por el que se regula la expedición de pasaportes españoles ordinarios. 7/14/1958, p. 1257–1258.

BOE (1969): Canje de Notas entre los Gobiernos de la República francesa y el de España aprobando el Acuerdo relativo a la creación en la estación de Cerbere, en territorio español [*sic*], de una Oficina de Controles nacionales yuxtapuestos, elaborado por la Comisión mixta hispano-francesa el 20 de mayo de 1969. 10/16/1969, p. 16161–16162.

BOE (1972): Decreto 3276/1971, de 23 de diciembre, por el que se regula la expedición de pasaportes ordinarios a los españoles. 1/17/1972, p. 824–826.

BOE (1977): Real Decreto 3129/1977, de 23 de septiembre, por el que se regula la expedición de pasaportes ordinarios a los españoles. 12/10/1977, p. 27024–27026.

BOE (1978a): Canje de notas relativo a la supresión de la obligatoriedad del pasaporte para facilitar el turismo entre España y Francia de 13 de enero de 1966 y comunicación de España por la que se da plena vigencia al mismo. 1/30/1978, p. 2217–2218.

BOE (1978b): Convenio entre el Gobierno Español y el Gobierno Federal Austriaco sobre circulación de personas, firmado en Viena el 1 de febrero de 1978. 3/29/1978, p. 7127.

BOE (1979): Acuerdo entre el Gobierno de España y el Gobierno de la República de Portugal, sobre suspensión de pasaportes. 7/24/1979, p. 17344–17345.

BOE (1981): Canje de notas constitutivo de Acuerdo de 14 de noviembre de 1980 entre España e Italia para la supresión del pasaporte. 2/5/1981, p. 9332.

Castells Arteche, José Manuel (1974a): El derecho al libre desplazamiento y el pasaporte en España. Madrid: Seminarios y Ediciones.

Castells Arteche, José Manuel (1974b): La revisión de unos pasaportes. In: Cuadernos para el diálogo, March 1974, p. 138–139.

Council of Europe (2018): Chart of signatures and ratifications of Treaty 025. www.coe.int/en/web/conventions/full-list/-/conventions/treaty/025/signatures?p_auth=6jdApVfq, 5/31/2018.

Consejo de Ministros (1974): El Gobierno pide a Francia que resuelva el problema planteado por los refugiados de la E.T.A. In: La Vanguardia Española, 9/21/1974, p. 3.

El comisario jefe provincial (1974a): Necesidad de presentar los pasaportes en Comisaría. In: El Diario Vasco, 1/9/1974, p. 8.

El comisario jefe provincial (1974b): Revisión de pasaportes. In: El Diario Vasco, 3/31/1974, p. 8.

El gobernador civil (1974): Se suspende, por el momento, la recogida de pasaportes. In: El Diario Vasco, 1/24/1974, p. 8.

FDFA (Swiss Federal Department of Foreign Affairs) (1950): Accord par échange de notes relatif à la circulation des personnes entre la France et la Suisse, 4/24/1950. Documents provided to the author via e-mail.

Fernández Fuster, Luis (1991): Historia general del turismo de masas. Madrid: Alianza Editorial.

Huguet, Montserrat (2003): La política exterior del franquismo (1939-1975). In: Pereira, Juan Carlos (ed.): La política exterior de España (1800-2003): historia, condicionantes y escenarios. Barcelona: Ariel, p. 495–516.

J.K. (1975): Le passeport attend sa condamnation. In: La Dépêche du Midi, 3/17/1975, p. Régionale 1.

Lecuona, Juan Antonio (1975): Frontera: Los franceses no necesitan pasaporte. In: La Voz de España, 3/22/1975, p. 1.

Morán Blanco, Sagrario (1997): ETA entre España y Francia. Madrid: Editorial Complutense.

No author (1974): In: L'Indépendant, 9/22/1974, p. 1.

No author (1975): Pasaportes antiturísticos. In: La Vanguardia Española, 2/5/1975, p. 5.

Novais, José Antonio (1974): Madrid demande à Paris plus de rigueur à l'égard des révolutionnaires basques. In: Le Monde, 9/22–23/1974, p. 1.

Pack, Sasha D. (2006): Tourism and Dictatorship: Europe's Peaceful Invasion of Franco's Spain. New York: Palgrave Macmillan.

Permanyer, Lluís (1978): Aquél pasaporte. In: La Vanguardia Española, 2/7/1978, p. 70.

Pérez i Granadós, José L. (2006): Comín i Ros, Alfons Carles. In: Catalunya durant el franquisme: diccionari biogràfic. Vic: Eumo Editorial, p. 96–97.

Salter, Mark B. (2003): Rights of Passage: The Passport in International Relations. Boulder: Lynne Rienner Publishers.

Torpey, John (2000): The Invention of the Passport: Surveillance, Citizenship and the State. Cambridge: Cambridge University Press.

Traités et accords de la France (1956): Accord sous forme d'échange de lettres entre la France et l'Allemagne sur le régime de la circulation des personnes sous le couvert de la carte d'identité. basedoc.diplomatie.gouv.fr/exl-php/recherche/mae_internet___traites (no. 19560021), 10/15/2018.

Traités et accords de la France (1957): Accord par échange de lettres franco-autrichien sur la suppression de l'exigence du passeport entre les deux pays. basedoc.diplomatie.gouv.fr/exl-php/recherche/mae_internet___traites (no. 19570037), 10/15/2018.

Treaty Series (1961): Exchange of Notes between the Government of the United Kingdom of Great Britain and Northern Ireland and the Government of the French Republic concerning Arrangements to Facilitate Travel between the United Kingdom and France. treaties.fco.gov.uk/docs/pdf/1961/TS0032.pdf, 5/31/2018.

Turack, Daniel C. (1972): The Passport in International Law. Lexington (Mass.): Lexington Books.

UNTS (United Nations Treaty Series) (1949a): Exchange of notes constituting an agreement between Belgium and France designed to facilitate the movement of persons between the metropolitan territories of Belgium and France. No. 447, vol. 30, p. 45–51.

UNTS (1949b): Exchange of notes constituting an agreement supplementary to the above-mentioned agreement extending its application to the Belgian–Luxembourg and French–Luxembourg frontiers. Extension of no. 447, vol. 31, p. 489–490.

UNTS (1958a): Agreement between Italy and France on the movement of persons. Signed at Paris, on 28 February 1957. No. 4253, vol. 291, p. 191–195.

UNTS (1958b): Exchange of notes constituting an agreement between the Netherlands and France for the purpose of facilitating the movement of persons between the two countries. No. 4305, vol. 299, p. 43–49.

UNTS (1978) Agreement concerning the movement of persons. Signed at Vienna on 1 February 1978. No. 16553, vol. 1082, p. 27–35.

UNTS (1979a): Exchange of notes constituting an agreement between Spain and France relating to the abolition of the passport requirement with a view to facilitating tourism. No. 18106, vol. 1150, p. 421–426.

UNTS (1979b): Exchange of notes constituting an agreement relating to the abolition of the passport requirement with a view to facilitating tourism (with annex). Bonn, 22 July 1964. No. 18111, vol. 1151, p. 25–34.

Vila, J. (1975): La exigencia de pasaporte a los turistas franceses repercute en la hostelería del Alto Ampurdán. In: La Vanguardia Española, 1/21/1975, p. 33.

Archives

AHG: Arxiu Històric de Girona (Girona Historical Archives)
GC: "Govern Civil" collection

AHL: Arxiu Històric de Lleida (Lleida Historical Archives)
GC: "Govern Civil" collection

GAHP: Gipuzkoako Artxibo Historiko Probintziala (Gipuzkoa Provincial Historical Archives)
GC: "Gobierno Civil" collection

About the author

Ariela House | University of Barcelona | Department of History and Archaeology | Montalegre, 6 | 08001 Barcelona | Spain | T +34 628 73 58 21 | ariela.house@gmail.com

Ariela House recently completed a Ph.D. in history at the University of Barcelona. Her research focuses on border control between France and Spain from 1958 to 1978, including changing visa and passport requirements, short-term passes available primarily to borderland residents, and the detection and punishment of illegal border crossing. She holds a bachelor's degree, *summa cum laude*, in government, with a minor in history, from Smith College in Massachusetts, and a master's degree from the University of Barcelona.

The economic impact of cross-border work on the municipalities of residence: an example at the French–Luxembourgish border

Isabelle Pigeron-Piroth and Rachid Belkacem

Abstract

This chapter seeks to investigate whether the proximity of a border can be seen as an engine of regional development, or a disruptive element. The impacts of cross-border activity on demographic evolution but also on unemployment or economic activity at the French–Luxembourgish border will be identified. Quantitative data from the municipal level (French census for 2014) will be used, with a special focus on the French border municipality of Longwy (formerly one of the main steel-producing areas in France).

Keywords

Cross-border work, Greater Region Saar-Lor-Lux, economic impact, Lorraine

1. Introduction

In European border areas, especially around Luxembourg and Switzerland, cross-border mobility of workers (between two different countries) is extensive and increasing. The Greater Region Saar-Lor-Lux, a cross-border space constituted by regional entities from four different countries (Lorraine in France, Saarland and Rhineland Palatinate in Germany, Wallonia in Belgium and Luxembourg), counted 232,000 cross-border commuters in 2017. Cross-border work is anchored in local economies and has many impacts. The cross-border commuters experience the border in their everyday life, through their specific status, their home–work mobility, and the differences (economic, legal, etc.) between the place where they live and the place where they work. In this chapter, we address the issue of the economic impacts of cross-border work on the French municipalities of residence in the vicinity of Luxembourg (the north of Lorraine, because of the considerable flow of cross-border commuters and the historical context of economic activity). Can borders (through the importance of cross-border work) be seen as an engine of growth and regional development, or as a brake on economic development for these municipalities? Our aim here is to enrich the common knowledge and understanding of border experiences in relation to work by identifying some economic impacts related to the proximity of a border and the number of cross-border commuters in the places of residence. The impacts on population growth, local unemployment, and economic activities will be analyzed on a small territorial scale (municipal if possible, or employment area).

From a theoretical perspective, economic science provides instruments and concepts to enable better understanding of mobility. The first way of considering mobility is to analyze it as one of the fundamental conditions of the ideal functioning of the labor market. In the benchmark model of economics, in particular the model of the market first formalized by L. Walras in 1874, mobility of economic agents has a central status. All the theoretical analysis consists in showing that mobility of workers is useful for firms as well as for workers themselves, and in different situations (in employment or in unemployment). On the one hand, there is a scarcity of resources in comparison with the unlimited needs of individuals. Individuals, such as cross-border workers, thus offer their availability and work to companies (which may be located across the borders). They have to make choices, taking constraints into account (distances, travel time, etc.). On the other hand, the rationality of economic agents' behavior is the second postulate of this theory. Workers (including cross-border workers) always make the best choices. They are rational because they seek to maximize their satisfaction by minimizing their effort. Employers are also rational because they seek to maximize their profit by minimizing the costs associated with the use of workers and capital. In this theory, work, whatever its nature or its institutional form (temporary work, border work, fixed-term contract, etc.) is summed up by the rationality of labor supply and demand. Following on from this benchmark model, several studies have legitimized the central role of mobility in the labor market in the context of unemployment. For some authors, professional mobility between various companies allows a search for information on potential future jobs (theories of job search from Stigler 1962; Jovanovic 1979a, 1979b). According to the human capital theory, mobility also enables the realization of investment in the human resources of workers (Becker 1964). In this frame of theoretical research, by being mobile, cross-border workers would accumulate various forms of work experience, increasing their employability and thus their future income. By contrast, immobility is considered a loss of experience. Is cross-border mobility of workers only a factor in the fit between labor supply and demand? Can it be analyzed differently? This empirical study also enriches the theoretical analysis of cross-border mobility. As a conclusion, we will provide some reflections on this topic.

In order to examine an economic impact, our aim is to analyze the data on a geographical scale that is not too large. We decided to use the municipal level (where available) as a way of revealing the link with cross-border work, providing some elements of explanation that will have to be studied (and confirmed) in future analyses. On its website, the French Statistical Institute (INSEE) publishes municipal data from the national censuses that record population and working (or non-working) population. They provide some insights into the recent evolution of the proportion of cross-border commuters in the municipalities, and into population characteristics.

It is indeed difficult to answer this question about economic impacts. Firstly, there is a lack of comparable and harmonized data. Different countries are involved, and methods of measuring (employment or unemployment, for example) differ from one country to another. Secondly, the geographical scale is a real issue: choosing the appropriate one is not easy. One may pitch it too large or too small, and data are not available for all the levels in a harmonized and comparable way. Lastly, different elements are interconnected, so that the causal effects are not easy to identify.

To address the economic impacts of cross-border commuters, we begin this chapter by outlining the spatial and temporal framework of this study (point 2). We identify some impacts of mobility on demographic dynamics (point 3), on local unemployment (point 4), and on economic activities (point 5) in the vicinity of the French–Luxembourgish border.

2. *Cross-border mobility of workers in the Greater Region*

Within the Greater Region Saar-Lor-Lux, 232,000 people were living and working in two different countries in 2017 (OIE).

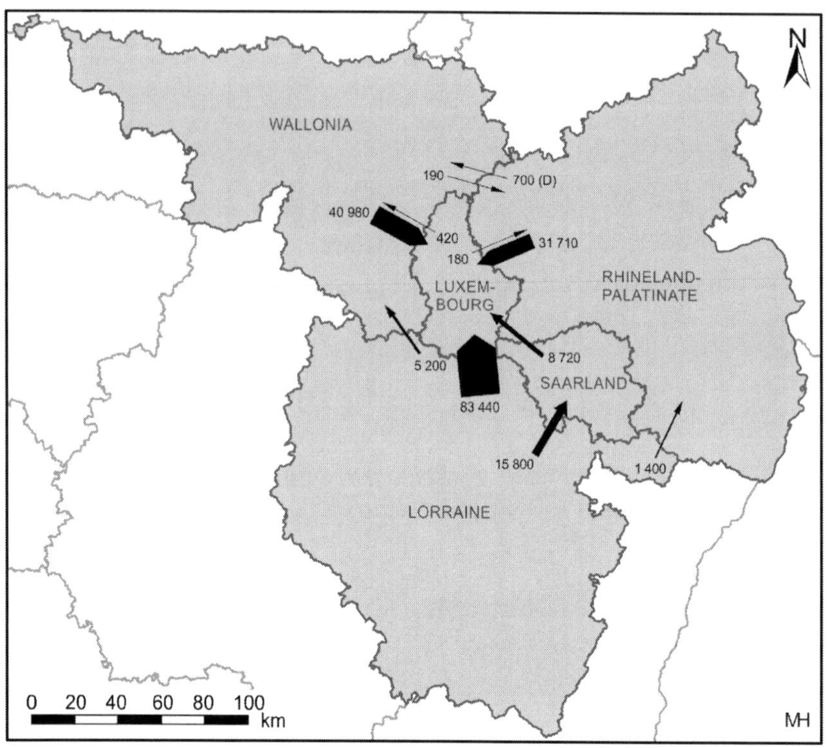

Figure 1: Cross-border commuters in the Greater Region Saar-Lor-Lux (2016)
Source: Data: IBA/OIE, Map: Malte Helfer

While most cross-border commuters work in Luxembourg, the French region of Lorraine is the main region of residence (around 105,000 in 2016). The large majority of the cross-border commuters living in France commute to Luxembourg. Moreover, there is a decreasing but still important flow of cross-border commuters from Lorraine to Germany (Saarland).

2.1 The durability of the phenomenon

Cross-border work is a lasting phenomenon that is anchored in local economies. In Lorraine, almost 10% of the working population works abroad (50% in the *Zone d'emploi de Longwy* (employment area) located near Belgium and Luxembourg). In small municipalities in the immediate vicinity of the border, more than 75% of the working population works abroad (Figure 2).

Cross-border work is important for local economies not only on the French side of the border but also on the Luxembourgish one. Indeed, 187,700 cross-border commuters worked in Luxembourg in 2018. Over the last 25 years, the numbers of cross-border commuters coming from France, Germany, and Belgium have multiplied by a factor of 4.5 in this country. They now constitute 44.4% of the salaried population working in Luxembourg. Twenty-five years ago, only 23% of the salaried population in Luxembourg came from abroad (France, Germany, and Belgium). The French cross-border commuters working in Luxembourg are the most numerous: they constitute half of the group.

The economic growth of Luxembourg is partly due to this workforce coming from abroad (Belkacem/Pigeron-Piroth 2015a). Indeed, in sectors such as industry, trade, construction, finance, or science, more than the half of their workers are cross-border commuters.

2.2 *A growing proportion of cross-border commuters in the French municipalities near Luxembourg*

The closer to the border the municipalities are, the more they are affected by cross-border work (Figure 2). Fewer than 5 kilometers from the Luxembourgish border, more than 75% of the working population of some French municipalities is employed in Luxembourg. These are mainly small municipalities offering little employment. Their geographical location is closer to the jobs offered on the Luxembourgish side of the border. Moreover, the attractiveness of employment poles located on the other side of the border is reinforced by the differentials (higher wages, for example) and metropolization of the city of Luxembourg. During the last ten years, most of the French municipalities have seen a rise in the proportion of cross-border commuters.

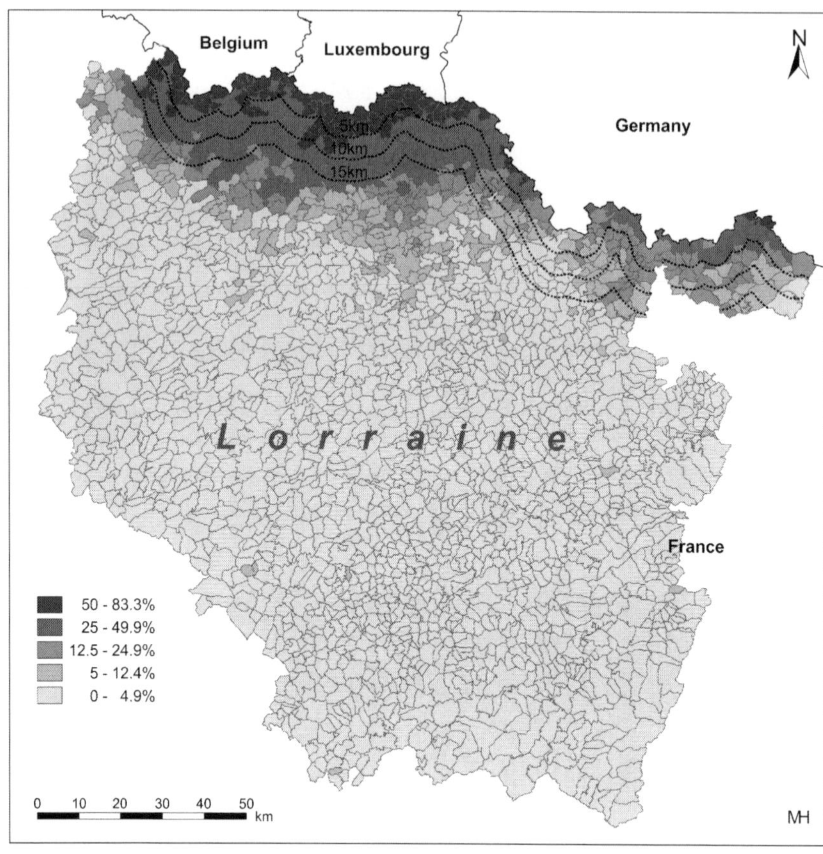

Figure 2: Percentage of cross-border commuters in the working population of French municipalities (2014)

Source: data: INSEE (Census 2014), calculation and map: University of Luxembourg

Furthermore, these French municipalities are attractive for the cross-border commuters who want to settle close to the border and reduce the home–work commute. Most of these municipalities have experienced strong demographic growth, mainly due to cross-border commuters and also the lower real estate prices in comparison to Luxembourg.

3. Population growth near the Luxembourgish border

To address the economic impacts of cross-border work in the French municipalities of residence, we first examined the growth of the population. The data are available at the municipal level. Taking into account the group of municipalities situated fewer than 15 kilometers from the borders (i.e. most of the municipalities with more than 25% of the salaried population working abroad according to Figure 2), their population fell continuously before 1990. From 1990 onwards, the population of this group increased again from one census to the next. On average, the annual rise was 0.32% per year over the last 25 years (+0.06% for Lorraine as a whole over the same period).

3.1 Taking the context into account

The explanations for this can be diverse and, of course, contextual elements have to be taken into account to understand these trends better. For example, the neighborhood of Longwy (a town of 14,200 inhabitants in the north of Lorraine, bordering Belgium and Luxembourg) is a really interesting case study. In the past, it was an important industrial center with numerous furnaces and around 30,000 workers (in 1960). Longwy and its region suffered greatly when this activity stopped, and lost many inhabitants. During this process of deindustrialization, working abroad became a solution for many workers from the steel industry, who found jobs in the Luxembourgish steel industry (or other activity sectors). Indeed, the development of cross-border commuting from the area of Longwy began earlier in comparison to other French towns and cities (like Thionville or Metz, for example, which are both further from the border). In a recent study, an attempt was made to measure the individual and territorial determinants of cross-border commutes in comparison with other commutes taking place inside France (Pigeron-Piroth et al. 2018). One of the main results is that of course the distance, but also a low density of jobs around the municipality of residence in France (low number of jobs per km^2 around the municipality of residence), greatly increased the tendency to undertake cross-border commuting. That means that a lack of employment around the municipality of residence constitutes an explanation for cross-border commuting.

The social and demographic context varies from one municipality to another. According to data from the three last censuses, the area of Longwy (the *zone d'emploi* includes 100 municipalities, with a population of

111,885 people in 2014) has recently experienced a growth in population after a long period of decline. This increase is mostly due to migration (the new incomers). The proximity of Luxembourg and its job opportunities is a reason to move to Longwy. Moreover, the recent changes in the area (development of leisure activities, highlighting of the historical heritage of the town, etc.) have contributed to the diversification of the local economy and the image of the area, in contrast to its industrial history.

The profile of the cross-border commuters has changed very little in the area of Longwy. The social transformation of the population is indeed very slow and most cross-border commuters are still (low-skilled) workers. Finally, Luxembourgish metropolization has had less impact on the profiles of cross-border commuters in the area of Longwy (Chen et al. 2018, p. 16) compared with other French cities and towns like Metz or Thionville, where the numbers of highly qualified cross-border commuters have increased greatly.

3.2 *Small municipalities near the border*

For other small municipalities directly near the Luxembourgish border, the demographic growth is strong. For example, the border village of Zoufftgen had about 1,100 inhabitants in 2014. Since 2009, the annual average growth of the population here has been 6.2%. The settlement of new inhabitants in this municipality (mainly cross-border commuters) also has an impact on the sociodemographic characteristics of the population. Indeed, in 2014, the inhabitants with a higher education degree were strongly over-represented here (constituting 45% of the population compared with 27.5% for France as a whole). The numbers of these people continue to rise, while the numbers of people without a degree are decreasing and now correspond to fewer than one inhabitant in five (31.6% at the national level). This example underlines the attractiveness of the municipalities located near the border for the cross-border commuters who want to reduce the length of their commute.

Demographic growth of a municipality is a factor of dynamism, and a positive element, especially when this population has higher wages (wages are higher in Luxembourg, as are the social benefits). This greater buying power of cross-border commuters is indeed injected into the local economy via their local spending (on goods or services). They also pay local French taxes. However, the issues for the municipalities facing such a rise in population are numerous: cohesion with the established population, increase in real-estate prices, increase in the demand for services or schools, mobility issues, etc. This growth of population is not neutral and has to be managed in order to be affordable and positive for the municipalities concerned.

4. Evolution of the unemployment rate near the border

Another way of analyzing the impact of cross-border commuting would be to gauge the impact on the rate of unemployment, arguing that cross-border commuting lowers this unemployment rate in places of residence. French territories are suffering a high unemployment rate in comparison to the other territories of the Greater Region. The smaller the geographical scale, the greater the impact that can be identified. However, calculating the rate of unemployment at the municipal level can be problematic because of the size of the municipalities (which can be really small in France) or the structural effect hidden by this rate (age of the resident population, for example). That is why we decided to analyze the unemployment rate at a higher (and logical) level: the *zone d'emploi* (employment area). Created by INSEE from the commutes, this level is a way of taking into account the area where most of the people live AND work.

4.1 Restrained evolution of the unemployment rate

Within the region of Grand Est as a whole, the unemployment rate is 8.9% (1st trimester of 2018, INSEE). The Grand Est region includes Lorraine, Alsace, and Champagne Ardennes, and is situated in the north-east of France. This is the new regional scale used in France since 2016. This region is the only French region that shares its boundaries with four countries (Belgium, Luxembourg, Germany, and Switzerland). Consequently, it is affected the most by cross-border work.

According to the *zone d'emploi* (employment area), there is a huge diversity of unemployment rates within Grand Est (from 5.2% to 12.3%) (Figure 3). Longwy and Thionville, the two towns most affected by cross-border commuting in the direction of Luxembourg, have employment rates close to the regional rate (and slightly lower for Thionville).

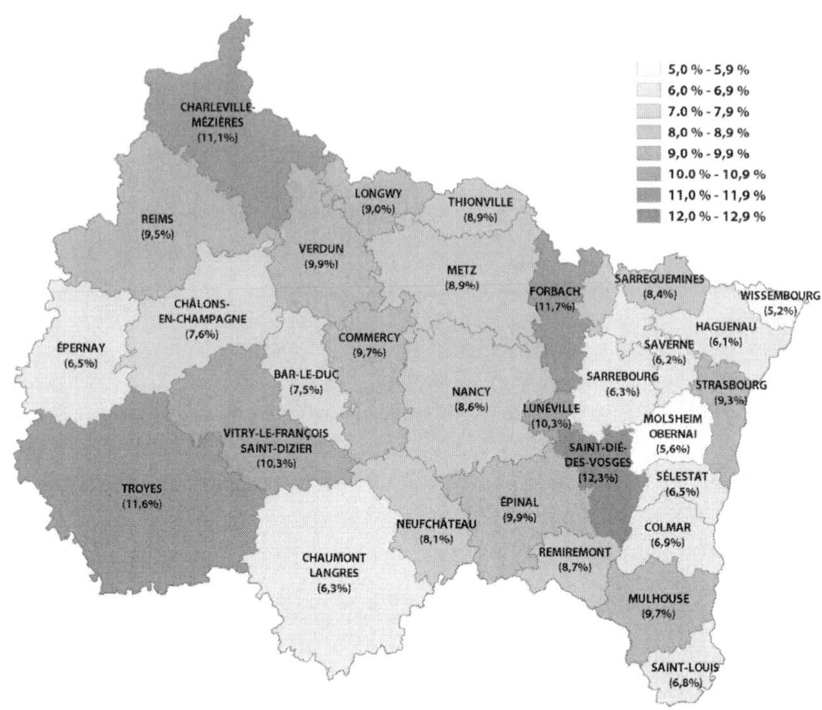

Figure 3: Unemployment rates for the French "zones d'emploi" in the Grand Est region (1st trimester of 2018)

Source: INSEE

The vicinity of Luxembourg and the opportunities for finding jobs in this country restricted the unemployment rates near the border. As explained previously, in the neighborhood of Longwy, the industrial crisis destroyed many jobs in this area a few decades ago. The possibility of finding a job just on the other side of the border (in the industrial sector) was an opportunity and reduced the unemployment rate. Today, the type of jobs held by cross-border commuters from Longwy is more diverse, but industry remains an important sector for the inhabitants of this region. Looking for a job on the other side of the border became common for most jobseekers. Moreover, the status of cross-border commuters has been regularized by bilateral tax conventions (to determine in which country the cross-border commuters have to pay taxes) and by European regulation (Regulation (EC) No. 883/2004 on social security). This status of cross-border commuters has greatly facilitated the rise in this activity, despite some problematic aspects of this status (for example, the differences in retirement age in the different countries). Moreover, some obstacles still remain and have slowed the development of the cross-border labor market (traffic jams, difficulties in having qualifications recognized in the other countries, etc.) (Belkacem/Pigeron-Piroth 2015b).

4.2 A matter of matching

The proximity of Luxembourg is of course not the only factor that affects the unemployment rate. Unemployment is indeed really complex to explain: the factors which affect it are numerous and there are different ways of measuring it. This is not only a matter of quantitative matching (between jobseekers and jobs), but also one of qualitative matching. Characteristics of supply and demand do matter. The Luxembourg labor market does in fact need an increasingly specialized and qualified workforce. Moreover, language skills are important and vary in Luxembourg from one job sector to another (Pigeron-Piroth/Fehlen 2015). The development of financial sector and science jobs in Luxembourg, for example, demands highly qualified people. There can be a mismatch between the needs of the Luxembourgish economy and the profiles of some jobseekers, with the result that some unemployment rates remain high. The other aspect to take into consideration when analyzing the unemployment rate is the supply side (employment opportunities) in the place of residence. How does job creation around the commune of residence look?

5. Economic activity in the French area

Despite the growth in the number of jobs offered in Luxembourg (2% per year on average between 2008 and 2013), the neighboring French territories faced a decrease in jobs over the same period (-1.7% per year in *Zone d'emploi* (employment area) *de Longwy*) (INSEE 2016). There is no real dissemination of employment growth across the borders. The border acts as a barrier in this case, and places territorial limits on job creation.

From a qualitative point of view, identifying the impact of Luxembourgish growth on the evolution and/or the transformation of local employment in the French territories is of real interest. Does the proximity to the border (and to neighboring labor markets) have an impact on economic activities that succeed and that develop in the French area? The French statistical institute showed that local employment was less developed in the immediate vicinity of the border. Moreover, employment related more to the "in-place economy", that is to say jobs (production of goods and services) created locally to meet the needs of the population living in this area, or tourists (François/Moreau 2010). This could include, for example, leisure activities, but also trade, services, etc.

Indeed, in the area of Longwy the majority of the new enterprises created in 2015 belonged to the sectors of trade, transportation, or accommodation and food service activities. Several shopping and leisure centers have been built recently, creating more than a thousand jobs.

Nevertheless, some negative impacts of the proximity of borders can also be identified. The attractiveness of Luxembourg as an international employment pole can be problematic for the economic development of the French regions. The quantity and also the variety of jobs, and especially the high level of wages, can create competition between Luxembourg and the French region, which is economically less attractive. This area has to find territorial specialization complementary to the development of Luxembourg; the in-place economy as mentioned above constitutes an initial idea.

6. *Conclusion*

The everyday life of cross-border commuters is shared between a place of residence in one country and a place of work in another. The French–Luxembourgish border has a high level of cross-border flow, and some French municipalities have a high percentage of cross-border commuters in their resident population. The impacts of this huge cross-border phenomenon are numerous. Cross-border commuters, as they cross the border every day, experience the differences in laws, rules, prices, wages, labor markets, and so on. Throughout this chapter, we have tried to identify some impacts of these many types of mobility on the places of residence, in such a way as to answer this question: is the proximity of the border a positive or a negative point for demography, unemployment, or economic activity?

This chapter has provided insights into some economic impacts of cross-border commuting in French municipalities. Firstly, there is demographic growth near borders, in rural areas and in some industrial regions (Longwy) where the population was previously decreasing. The proximity of Luxembourg has a clear attractive effect and creates a dynamism in the area near the border. Secondly, taking into account the crisis this industrial area faced, unemployment has been somewhat limited. Without the job opportunities in Luxembourg, the unemployment rate could have been much higher. Moreover, the local economy is being diversified with the development of the in-place economy in this region. Jobs in Luxembourg offer a higher level of wages, which contributes to the local economy through consumption of goods and services, for example. However, on the other hand, cross-border mobility of workers can hinder the development of these regions because of the "competition" with Luxembourg, through the brain drain, by increasing the expenses borne by the small municipalities facing a strong growth in population, or also by increasing social and territorial inequalities.

Cross-border work plays a significant role in European functional integration between border territories (Commissariat Général à l'Egalité des Territoires 2017). For territories in northern Lorraine, cross-border commuting brought about by the proximity of the border can be seen as a shared human resource for border areas. Indeed, rather than being simply a matter of supply and demand (as in economics research literature), cross-border mobility can be considered a constructed territorial resource for individuals and for territories. Social and institutional approaches in terms of regulation indeed constitute another way of analyzing mobility. In this approach, actors' practices, institutions, rules, traditions, and conventions are central functions to understanding the evolution of employment. This theoretical perspective finds its origins on the one hand in the institutional economics that emerged in the United States at the beginning of the twentieth century with Veblen (1901) and Commons (1924), and on the other hand in the French regulation school with Robert Boyer and Michel Aglietta. The objective aimed at by these different authors is to understand economic and social transformations (Aglietta 1982, p. 14). The notion of regulation thus means "any dynamic process of adaptation of production and social demand, the conjunction of economic adjustments associated with a configuration yielded by social relationships, institutional and structural forms ..." (authors' own translation) (Boyer 1980, p. 492). In this theoretical perspective, cross-border work is a social construction. Indeed, the mobility of cross-border workers is codified by various regulations. The Treaty of Rome in 1957 established the free movement of workers within the European area. European regulations apply to social security. Bilateral conventions between countries supplement these arrangements in order to regulate tax status. The practices of the individual and collective actors (workers, companies, employment agencies, etc.), who have a history, an identity, and a culture, provide a reality to these flows. The mobility of workers necessitates regulation of the workforce in terms of the quantitative needs of companies (number of workers) and the qualitative needs (skills of the workers). Cross-border workers can thus be defined as shared human resources for cross-border areas (Belkacem/Pigeron-Piroth 2015a). Hence, we suggest considering geographical mobility a territorially constructed resource for both the individuals and the territories.

References

Aglietta, Michel (1976): Régulation et crise du capitalisme. L'expérience des Etats-Unis. Paris: Calmann-Lévy 1st edition.

Becker, Gary (1964): Human Capital, A Theoretical and Empirical Analysis with special reference to education. National Bureau of Economic Research.

Belkacem, Rachid/Pigeron-Piroth, Isabelle (eds.) (2012): Le travail frontalier au sein de la Grande Région Saar-Lor-Lux. Pratiques, enjeux et perspectives. Nancy: PUN-Presses Universitaires de Lorraine.

Belkacem, Rachid/Pigeron-Piroth, Isabelle (2015a): Cross-border labour in the Greater Region Saar-Lor-Lux: evolutions and effects on the status of the workers and on regional economic and social development. In: Forum Socjologiczne, no. 4, p. 240–254.

Belkacem, Rachid/Pigeron-Piroth, Isabelle (2015b): Un marché de l'emploi intégré ? L'emploi frontalier et ses dimensions socioéconomiques. In: Wille, C. (ed.): Lebenswirklichkeiten und politische Konstruktionen in Grenzregionen. Das Beispiel der Grossregion SaarLorLux: Wirtschaft-Politik-Alltag-Kultur. Bielefeld: Transcript, p. 39–57.

Boyer, Robert (1980): Rapport Salarial et analyses en terme de Régulation: une mise en rapport avec les théories de la segmentation du marché du travail. In: Economie Appliquée, no. 2, p. 491–508.

Chen, Jianyu/Gerber, Philippe/Ramadier, Thierry (2018): Dynamiques socio-spatiales des actifs lorrains au regard de la métropolisation transfrontalière luxembourgeoise. In: Espace populations sociétés 2017, no. 3, p. 0–24.

Commissariat général à l'égalité des territoires (2017): Dynamiques de l'emploi transfrontalier en Europe et en France.

Commons, John R. (1924): Legal foundations of capitalism. New York: Macmillan.

Doeringer Peter B./Piore, Michael J. (1971): Internal labor market and manpower analysis. Heath Lexington Book, Mass.

François, Jean-Paul/Moreau, Gérard (2010): Impacts du travail frontalier en Lorraine: entraînement de l'emploi et développement du présentiel, avec effet d'ombre à la frontière. In: Economie Lorraine, no. 234.

INSEE (2016): Les dynamiques socio-économiques du Grand Est dans son environnement régional et transfrontalier 4. INSEE Dossier.

Jovanovic, Boyan (1979a): Job Matching and the Theory of Turnover. In: Journal of Political Economy 87, no. 5, p. 972–900.

Jovanovic, Boyan (1979b): Firm-Specific Capital and Turnover. In: Journal of Political Economy 87, no. 6, p. 1246–1260.

OIE (2016): Situation du marché de l'emploi dans la Grande Région. Dixième rapport de l'Observatoire Interrégional du marché de l'emploi pour le Quinzième Sommet des Exécutifs de la Grande Région.

Pigeron-Piroth, Isabelle/Le Texier, Marion/Belkacem, Rachid/Caruso, Geoffrey (2018): Déterminants individuels et territoriaux des navettes internes ou transfrontalières des actifs résidant en France. In: Espace, Populations; Sociétés, no. 3, p. 0–30.

Pigeron-Piroth, Isabelle/Fehlen, Fernand (2015): Les langues dans les offres d'emploi au Luxembourg (1984–2014). University of Luxembourg.

Piore, Michael J. (1969): On-the-job training in the Dual Labor Market; public and private responsibilities in on-the-job training of disavantaged workers. In: Werber, A.-R. (ed.): Public-private manpower policies. Madison (Wisc.), p. 101–131.

Piotet, Françoise (2014): L'ampleur de la mobilité géographique en France, quelques données chiffrées. In: Les mondes du travail, no. 14, p. 27–37.

Stigler, George (1962): Information in the Labor Market. In: Journal of Political Economy 70, no. 5, p. 94–105.

Veblen, Thorstein (1901): Gustav Schmoller's Economics. In: Quarterly Journal of Economics, vol. XVI, p. 69–93.

About the authors

Isabelle Pigeron-Piroth | University of Luxembourg | Campus Belval, Maison des Sciences Humaines | Institute of Geography and Spatial Planning | 11, Porte des Sciences | 4366 Esch-Sur-Alzette | Luxembourg | T +352 46 66 44 6402 | isabelle.piroth@uni.lu

Pigeron-Piroth, Isabelle, MA in economics, research associate at University of Luxembourg; employment and mobility in cross-border contexts, cross-border labor markets.

Rachid Belkacem | University of Lorraine | Campus Lettres et Sciences Humaines | Laboratoire Lorrain des Sciences Sociales | 23, boulevard Albert 1er – BP 13397 | 54015 Nancy cedex | T +33 3 82 39 62 43 | rachid.belkacem@univ-lorraine.fr

Belkacem, Rachid, Ph.D. in economics, lecturer in Economics and Management at University of Lorraine; labor markets from comparative international and cross-border perspectives, economic and social development in cross-border contexts.

Cross-border everyday lives on the Luxembourg border? An empirical approach: the example of cross-border commuters and residential migrants[1]

Christian Wille and Ursula Roos

Abstract

Luxembourg is characterized by phenomena of mobility that include cross-border commuters and residential migrants. While both groups have been mainly examined from a socioeconomic perspective, this paper adopts a sociocultural approach. We will focus on the question of the extent to which cross-border mobility in everyday life promotes cross-border lifeworlds. This will involve examining people's social contacts at their place of work and/or place of residence as well as the spatial organization of practices of the everyday life of both groups. The paper gives insights into everyday lives at the EU's internal borders, whose organization into nation states is subordinate and at the same time constitutive.

Keywords

Border studies, residential migration, cross-border commuting, integration, Luxembourg

1. Introduction

With foreign nationals constituting 45.3% of the country's resident population (cf. Statec 2014, p. 9), Luxembourg is shaped in a singular way by phenomena of immigration. Other characteristic features of the Grand Duchy are local phenomena of cross-border mobility that are especially conspicuous in border regions. Of particular relevance here is the phe-

---

1 Originally published as Wille, Christian/Roos, Ursula (2018): Grenzüberschreitende Lebenswelten an der luxemburgischen Grenze? Eine empirische Annäherung am Beispiel von Grenzpendlern und Wohnmigranten. In: Pallagst, Karina/Hartz, Andrea/Caesar, Beate (eds.): Border Futures – Zukunft Grenze – Avenir Frontière. Zukunftsfähigkeit Grenzüberschreitender Zusammenarbeit. Hannover: Akademie für Raumforschung und Landesplanung, p. 168–189.

nomenon, which has been on the increase since the 1980s, of cross-border commuters, i.e. workers from the neighboring regions with employment in the Grand Duchy, as well as the more recent phenomenon of residential migrants, i.e. people moving from Luxembourg to neighboring Germany, France, or Belgium. Both groups are—even if partly with opposite tendencies—regularly mobile in border-crossing activities, be it to get to their place of work or residence, or be it to engage in everyday practices in the neighboring country.

Phenomena of cross-border commuters and residential migrants on the Luxembourgish border have so far received little attention in sociocultural research. Current studies about cross-border commuters (e.g. Belkacem/ Pigeron-Piroth 2012 and 2015) and residential migrants (e.g. Carpentier 2010; Wille 2011) in the Greater Region have focused, with only a few exceptions, (Wille 2012, Franziskus/de Bres 2012; Boesen/Schnuer 2015; Wille 2016) mainly on the socioeconomic implications of these forms of mobility. This contribution, then, centers on the sociocultural aspects, aiming to shed light on cross-border or rather on spatially fragmented everyday lives along the Luxembourgish border. At the same time, these reflections also point to the more general question of how significant the EU's internal borders actually are in border regions—particularly 30 years after the signing of the Schengen agreement. This study will investigate the development of social contacts at people's places of employment and/or of residence as well as the spatial organization of the everyday practices that can be observed among cross-border commuters and residential migrants along Luxembourg's border. For both partial aspects of the realities of cross-border life, quantitatively and qualitatively gathered results are amalgamated from various studies (Table 1) per group under review.

We will begin by first sketching a statistical portrait of the cross-border commuters and residential migrants that takes into account key developments—in particular since 2000. Building on this, we will then look at the abovementioned partial aspects of cross-border life realities on the basis of empirical findings, and finally we will compare the groups of cross-border commuters and residential migrants with each other. Reconnecting the observations to the question of this contribution shows that one can indeed speak of cross-border everyday lives along Luxembourg's borders.

Studies	Wille 2012	Wille et al. 2016	Roos 2016
Context of the study	Ph.D. project (University of Luxembourg und University of the Saarland)	Project "IDENT2 – Regionalisierungen als Identitätskonstruktionen in Grenzräumen" (University of Luxembourg)	Ph.D. project (University of the Saarland)
Period when study was conducted	2006/2007	2012/2013	2012/2013
Sample of the study	cross-border commuters with employment in Luxembourg (N=233) of these living in: Saarland (n=28) Lorraine (n=85) Rhineland-Palatinate (n=106) Wallonia (n=14) Interviewed cross-border commuters with place of work in Luxembourg (N=25) of these living in: Saarland (n=3) Lorraine (n=5) Rhineland-Palatinate (n=15) Wallonia (n=2)	cross-border commuters [2] (N=287) of these living in: Saarland (n=13) Lorraine (n=157) Rhineland-Palatinate (n=25) Wallonia (n=92) residential migrants from Luxembourg (N=56) of these living in: Saarland (n=6) Lorraine (n=16) Rhineland-Palatinate (n=12) Wallonia (n=22)	resident population of the district town of Merzig (N=856) of these: Persons without migrant background: n=487 Persons with migrant background: n=366, of these 40 residential migrants with Luxembourgish nationality Interviewed residential population with migrant background in the district town of Merzig (n=12), of these one residential migrant with Luxembourgish nationality
Methodology	Quantitative survey Qualitative interviews	Quantitative survey Qualitative interviews	Quantitative survey Qualitative interviews

Table 1: Data drawn on in this article

2. Cross-border commuters

In the following, we will first discuss the group of cross-border commuters who have shaped the Luxembourg labor market for over 30 years and represent 44% of the labor force employed in Luxembourg today. Statistically, their emergence can be traced back to the 1960s, but it is only since the 1980s that the employment of cross-border commuters has developed a

2 It is assumed that these cross-border commuters primarily work in Luxembourg.

striking dynamic. This will be outlined below (cf. Wille 2012, p. 143–200), followed by a discussion of the extent to which cross-border commuters have social contacts in their countries of residence and employment, and in which everyday practices they engage there.

The increasing employment of cross-border commuters that began in the 1980s has continued almost unabated to the present day, with a majority of workers coming from France, their numbers having multiplied tenfold between 1980 and 2000. Until 1985, the annual growth rate of this commuter flow in Luxembourg, the most significant since 1987, did not exceed the 8% mark; from 1986 onwards, though, it increased significantly, and by 1992 it ranged between 13 and 22%. This increase was due to the difficult labor market situation as a result of the steel crisis, which was particularly palpable in the border regions of Lorraine. Between 1985 and 1994, commuters from France benefited in particular in the area of market services (386.2%) and the construction industry (361.1%); in the manufacturing industry their growth rates were lower (cf. Statec 1995, p. 260).

The development of the commuter flow from Belgium, which increased more than fourfold between 1980 and 2000, follows the general development of cross-border worker employment. Until 1983, the annual growth rates of the previously most significant commuter flow did not exceed the 3.5% mark; from 1984 onwards, they increased significantly, with an annual increase of a little less than 10%. In 1987, the Belgians were supplanted by the French as the largest cross-border commuter group, which was due to the development of employment in the services sector in Luxembourg, with a concomitant clear decline in employment in the former strongholds of the iron and steel industry in France. Nevertheless, the flow from Belgium increased between 1987 and 1991, with annual growth rates between 10 and 13%. Despite the economic recession in the early 1990s, in the subsequent years an increasing number of workers commuted from Belgium, with the momentum initially slowing down, but picking up speed towards the end of the decade, with annual growth rates between 7 and 10%. Between 1985 and 1994, the cross-border commuters from Belgium benefited in particular from the development of market services (254.8%) and the construction industry (232.7%); in the manufacturing industry, the growth rate (6.6%) was significantly lower compared to that of commuters from France and Germany (cf. Statec 1995, p. 260).

The development of the flow from Germany, which increased elevenfold between 1980 and 2000, also follows the general trend of cross-border commuter employment in Luxembourg. Even though the numbers of cross-border commuters from Germany compared to those from France or

Belgium remained on a relatively low level until the turn of the century, the annual growth rates can compare with those of the other commuter flows. Until 1983, they were below 10%, but from 1984 onwards they suddenly accelerated, and by 1991 they ranged between 17 and 22%. After the economic slowdown in the 1990s, the annual rates of change grew again to above 10%. Between 1985 and 1994, cross-border commuters from Germany benefited from job growth in particular in the market services industry and in the construction industry (cf. Statec 1995, p. 260).

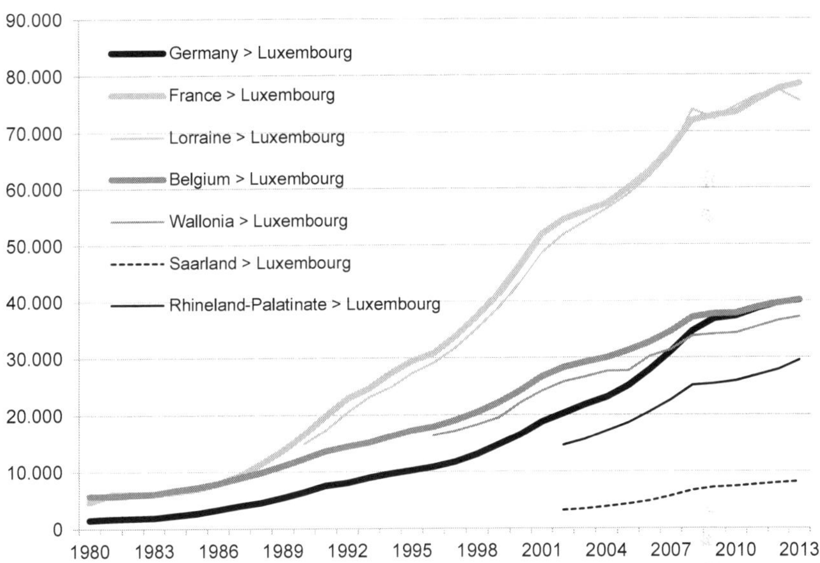

Figure 1: Development of cross-border commuter employment by country of origin, 1980–2013

Sources: Bundesagentur für Arbeit (Germany), Inspection Générale de la Sécurité Sociale (Luxembourg), Institut national de la statistique et des études économiques (France), Institut national d'Assurance Maladie-Invalidité (Belgium)

The remarkable development of cross-border commuter employment since the 1980s not only justifies looking into the question of the cross-border or spatially fragmented everyday lives along the Luxembourg border, but has also led to an atypical situation in Luxembourg: between 1998 and 2008, employment in Luxembourg grew by 51%, in particular in the corporate services sector. Here the shift, already registered in the 1990s, of the labor force with Luxembourgish nationality from the manufacturing industry to the (semi-)public sector continued. This segmentation of the labor market increased Luxembourg's reliance on foreign labor, since the development in the private economic sector was sustained mainly by cross-border commuters and resident foreign nationals.

In the following, we will take a closer look at the development of the volume of commuting since the turn of the millennium. In 2013, Luxembourg counted 158,758 cross-border commuters (including 2.7% atypical commuters), half of whom came from neighboring France (78,454) and a quarter each from Germany (40,105) and Belgium (40,199). Their number has grown 1.5-fold since 2003, with the flow from Germany showing particular momentum—so that in 2012 there were more commuters coming to Luxembourg from Germany than from Belgium for the first time. The development since the turn of the millennium did not, however, proceed evenly: in the course of the economic crisis in the early 2000s, growth initially slowed down, picking up speed again from 2004 onwards. The economic and financial crisis of 2008 had a much deeper impact. While it did not lead to a reduction in cross-border commuters employed in Luxembourg, it did slash the high development rates of previous years—especially in the manufacturing industry and in the finance industry. The flows from France and Belgium were particularly affected, even though—like the commuters from Germany—they were able to achieve minor increases in employment in 2009. While the slowed-down momentum of development was able to recover slightly by 2011, it is still far removed from the pre-crisis level (cf. IBA 2014, p. 18).

With regard to everyday lives along the Luxembourg border, one needs to additionally take into account the places and regions of residence of cross-border commuters, which show that the attraction of the Luxembourg labor market extends beyond the directly bordering regions (cf. Wille 2012, p. 143–200). In France, for instance, in 2008 more than half (57.3%) or a fifth (20.1%) of cross-border commuters lived in Thionville or Longwy; however, the catchment area expanded increasingly towards the south and the east of Lorraine. Thus the regions around the Bassin Houiller or Sarreguemines, mainly in the ambit of the German labor market, showed relatively high growth rates in cross-border commuting between 2000 and 2008; the areas around Metz and Nancy in the south also showed a palpable increase in Luxembourg cross-border commuters domiciled there. The cross-border commuters from Wallonia, by contrast, in the period of investigation, lived for the most part in direct proximity to Luxembourg: 17.8% in the province of Liège and 77.5% in Belgian Luxembourg (2008). The ratio of cross-border commuters resident in the province of Luxembourg declined between 2000 and 2008; by contrast, the province of Liège increased in importance, which shows an expansion of the range of influence of the Luxembourg labor market. In the two German federal states too, the Luxembourg cross-border commuters lived predominantly near the border: in 2008 slightly less than two thirds (64.0%) of cross-border commuters from the Saarland were resident in the rural district of Merzig-Wadern, close to the Luxembourg border, and a further 17.7% lived in the neighboring district of Saarlouis. In Rhineland-Palatinate, the catchment area was concentrated around the region of Trier; in addition, 42.5% of commuters from Rhineland-Palatinate lived in the district of Trier-Saarburg and 25.9% in the rural district of Bitburg-Prüm.

2.1 Social contacts at the place of residence/work

To investigate the question of the extent to which cross-border commuters employed in Luxembourg have social contacts at their place of residence and work, we will first draw on the findings of Wille et al. (2016) regarding the practices of commuters in relation to visiting family and friends (Table 2). Due to data constraints, the observations focus on commuters living in Lorraine and Wallonia, which are compared with the border-region residents of the respective resident regions as a comparison group.

We can observe that cross-border commuters primarily visit friends and family in their country of residence. As regards friendships in Luxembourg, they report making only half as many visits to friends than in their country of residence—but still significantly more frequently than other border-region residents—which points to friendly relations in the country of work. But compared to friends, cross-border commuters make distinctly less frequent visits to relatives in the Grand Duchy, but more frequently than the border-region residents as a whole. That friends are visited more often than relatives in a neighboring region corresponds to the general trend (cf. Wille 2015, p. 149) and is connected to the (non-)existence of cross-border family relations.

Region of residence	**Lorraine**		**Wallonia**	
	cross-border commuters (n=157)	border region residents (n=867)	cross-border commuters (n=92)	border region residents (n=517)
Visiting friends in …				
France	88	75		
Luxembourg	44	17	54	17
Belgium			85	76
Visiting relatives in …				
France	88	76		
Luxembourg	13	7	21	6
Belgium			80	76

Table 2: Visiting practices of cross-border commuters and border-region residents with place of residence in Lorraine or Wallonia, in percent (multiple entries)

Source: Wille et al. 2016

The findings show that cross-border commuters have contact to friends and family in Luxembourg—albeit to a lesser extent than in their country of residence—but that these are significantly more pronounced than cross-border social contacts of border-region residents as a whole. We can say that everyday cross-border mobility common among cross-border commuters encourages the development of social relations, in particular friendships, in Luxembourg.

For the further discussion of friendly relations in the country of work, we draw on findings by Wille (2012, p. 296). In that study, two-thirds (67.9%) of cross-border commuters employed in Luxembourg state that they regard people living in their country of work as belonging to their circle of friends. This applies more to commuters from Rhineland-Palatinate (75.5%) and to a lesser degree to those from Lorraine (56.5%). A closer look at the friendly relations of all the cross-border commuters interviewed shows, however, that the majority of these are (former) colleagues (87.3%), a fact that some cross-border commuters confirm in interviews (cf. Wille 2012, p. 298):

> Of course, I also know Luxembourgers, but only among my colleagues —current and former colleagues. I still have contact to a few of them

> from the firm where I did an internship once and we meet occasionally during the lunch break or some such. (Saarland-Luxembourg)
>
> Yes, I do know some Luxembourgers. But these acquaintances, as I'd call them, all develop via my work. Going out and getting to meet people, that's not the case. (Rhineland-Palatinate–Luxembourg)
>
> It does occasionally happen that after work I go out with colleagues or former colleagues to have a beer in a pub in Luxembourg. But that doesn't happen that often, because of all the driving. I have a demanding job and when I finish work at eight in the evening I want to go home, then I want to do something private. (Rhineland-Palatinate–Luxembourg)

We can say that friendly relations outside of the work context seem to develop only rarely. The reasons given by cross-border commuters are long journeys to the workplace or family obligations, and point to insufficient time to make new contacts with residents of the Grand Duchy. This leads to the question to be discussed in the following of how far cross-border commuters spend time in Luxembourg outside of their work.

2.2 *Everyday cross-border practices*

To explore the question of which everyday practices the cross-border commuters from Lorraine and Wallonia who were interviewed engage in in their countries of residence and work, we draw on findings by Wille et al. (2016) (Table 3).

		Lorraine (region of residence)		**Wallonia (region of residence)**	
Everyday practices	performed in...	cross-border commuters (n=157)	border region residents (n=867)	cross-border commuters (n=92)	border region residents (n=517)
Shopping	France	77	63		
	Luxembourg	78	48	91	49
	Belgium			71	55
Grocery shopping	France	83	71		
	Luxembourg	53	23	76	27
	Belgium			78	69
Recreation in the countryside/Tourism	France	76	64		

		Lorraine (region of residence)		Wallonia (region of residence)	
Everyday practices	performed in...	cross-border commuters (n=157)	border region residents (n=867)	cross-border commuters (n=92)	border region residents (n=517)
	Luxembourg	53	33	48	34
	Belgium			68	62
Attending cultural events	France	73	61		
	Luxembourg	45	18	46	12
	Belgium			69	59
Going out	France	63	53		
	Luxembourg	59	23	56	15
	Belgium			65	50
Seeing the doctor	France	87	77		
	Luxembourg	38	9	45	7
	Belgium			83	78

Table 3: Spatial distribution of everyday practices of cross-border commuters and border-region residents with place of residence in Lorraine and Wallonia, in percent (multiple entries)

Source: Wille et al. 2016

What becomes clear here is that, compared to border-region residents, cross-border commuters, on the whole, engage more frequently in everyday practices in Luxembourg and make more use of facilities in the Grand Duchy. Nevertheless, the cross-border commuters conduct their everyday practices primarily in their country of residence, although their country of work also plays an important role—such as for grocery shopping and leisure. Cross-border commuters primarily carry out consumer activities in Luxembourg and go out there. The more or less equal importance of country of residence and country of employment is here partly due to the necessary lunchtime restaurant visits and buying articles of daily use. It is worth mentioning in this context that for cross-border commuters the opportunities for doing the grocery shopping, which is necessary in any case, often lie 'on the way', and that the shops in their place of residence are already closed by the time they arrive home (cf. Wille 2012, p. 301). This is also confirmed by a commuter in an interview (cf. Wille 2012):

> Well, I do occasionally get my groceries on the way home because the bigger shops are open longer than the local ones here [in Rhineland-Palatinate]. They are located exactly so that you pass them on the way

> home—although I don't shop that often in Luxembourg because the price difference for food products is relatively high. (Rhineland-Palatinate–Luxembourg)

The second most frequent everyday practices performed in Luxembourg are leisure activities and visits to cultural events, which slightly less than half of the cross-border commuters carry out in their country of work (Table 3). What is particularly appreciated are the multilingual cultural opportunities in Luxembourg City, which in terms of cultural policy is intended to compete with other large European cities:

> I also spend time in Luxembourg outside of my work. In the first two years that was different, but then, gradually... you also get a wider range of cultural activities there than here where I live—here it's just countryside. (Rhineland-Palatinate–Luxembourg)

> Occasionally, I also spend some time in Luxembourg. I go to restaurants, the theatre, and cultural events. (Lorraine–Luxembourg)

> In the summer, I sometimes drive over with the family, perhaps to Echternach—then the border doesn't really exist; we also go for walks with the kids, or cycling. (Rhineland-Palatinate–Luxembourg)

Finally, we can observe among the cross-border commuters a clear preference for the country of residence when going to see the doctor, which is why visits to the doctor – which cross-border commuters can also carry out abroad – are the least frequent everyday practice in Luxembourg (Table 3). Conversations with cross-border commuters have indicated that one advantage of seeing the doctor in the Grand Duchy is that waiting times for consultation appointments with specialists in Luxembourg are distinctly shorter than in France, for instance.

The findings show that cross-border commuters perform everyday activities in the country of employment, and they do this more often than the rest of border-region residents. This finding should however not obscure the fact that despite everyday cross-border mobility, many cross-border commuters prefer the country of residence for carrying out everyday practices. Cross-border commuters explained this, such as in Wille (2012), with financially more favorable leisure activities in the country of residence, long travelling hours, lack of social contacts in Luxembourg or with a habitus centered on the private sphere:

> I rarely spend time in Luxembourg outside the job – very rarely. I occasionally go to a fair or a movie, but otherwise I don't go to Luxembourg any more – because then I'm glad not to have to take the car

> again. And I don't stay there directly after work either. (Rhineland-Palatinate–Luxembourg)

> No, I live in Metz, and that's a long way away. I don't spend much time in Luxembourg outside my work. I have lunch in Luxembourg, but I don't eat there in the evenings, because I don't know of many places to go in Luxembourg. My partner also lives in Metz and my friends are mostly here. I've never thought of going out in Luxembourg because that doesn't interest me. (Lorraine–Luxembourg)

> Even for lunch, I often eat at the canteen in the bank, and I arrive by train at eight thirty and take the train back at six. So it's rare that I stay in Luxembourg after work. (Lorraine–Luxembourg)

3. *Residential migrants*

After having taken a closer look at the cross-border commuters, this section now turns to cross-border residential migration, which was detectable in the Greater Region up until the 1990s, in particular at the border between the Saarland and Lorraine (cf. Wille 2011). On the Luxembourg border, residential migrants are still a recent phenomenon, which has, however, gained considerable significance since the turn of the millennium and is increasingly shaping life in the districts in Germany, France, and Belgium that are close to the border. The residential migrants include not only Luxembourgers, but also French people, Germans, and Belgians as well as other foreign nationals who move primarily due to the price differences for real estate and building lots that exist between Luxembourg and the bordering countries. In the following, we will first outline the development of residential migration since the turn of the millennium, and then investigate the questions of what effects moving house has on social contacts at the former and the new place of residence, and how everyday practices are distributed spatially after relocating.

Statements about the volume and the features of cross-border residential migrants can only be made with great caution, since there is as yet insufficient detailed information on the migration movements that are of interest to us. The present data have been made available by regional statistical offices in the Saarland, in Rhineland-Palatinate, in Lorraine, and in Wallonia, and differ greatly in their significance.[3] We therefore have to draw primarily on information regarding the subgroup of atypical cross-border commuters, who are better covered by the Luxembourg office of statistics. These are people who, after moving out of Luxembourg into a neighboring region, continue to work in the Grand Duchy, thus differentiating themselves—in an atypical way—from the group of cross-border commuters who do not work in their country of origin.

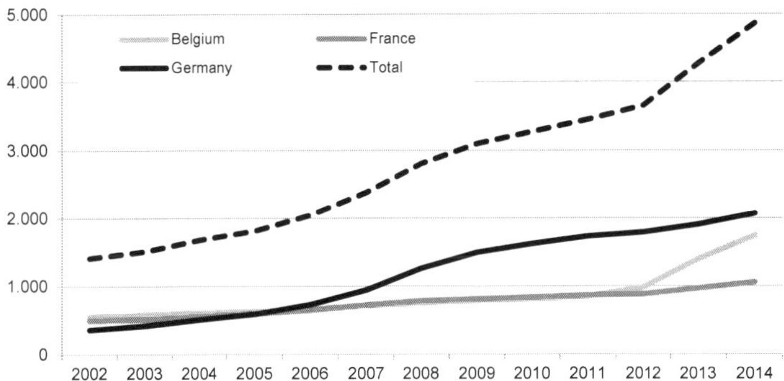

Figure 2: Development of cross-border commuters with Luxembourgish nationality and Luxembourg as country of work by countries of residence 2002–2014

Source: Inspection Générale de la Sécurité Sociale (Luxembourg)

In 2014, the number of atypical cross-border commuters with Luxembourgish nationality totaled only 4,865 people, but since 2002 it has increased 3.5-fold—particularly in the border regions (Figure 3). The majority commutes to Luxembourg from Germany (42.5%), followed by Belgium (35.8%) and France (21.7%). This distribution is the result of a shift that has occurred in the last decade: while until the early 2000s, more than two-thirds of the atypical cross-border commuters still lived in the Belgian and French regions, it is Rhineland-Palatinate and Saarland that have gained importance in recent years. Since 2006, they have constituted the largest group of atypical commuters with Luxembourgish nationality (Figure 2). The most recent developments show that atypical cross-border commuters increasingly come from Belgium to Luxembourg to work (Figure 2), which, however, can be interpreted as a real increase in the phenomenon

3 The office of statistics in Lorraine (INSEE) provides figures for the number of people of Luxembourgish nationality living in Lorraine in the years 1999 and 2010; the office of statistics in Wallonia (IWEPS) provides no figures.

to only a limited extent. This is connected to the fact that since 2010 it has become easier to acquire Luxembourgish citizenship—provided one can prove Luxembourgish ancestry—and that this has been acquired by many Belgians in recent years. Some of the cross-border commuters employed in Luxembourg anyway have since then been listed in the official statistics as atypical cross-border commuters.

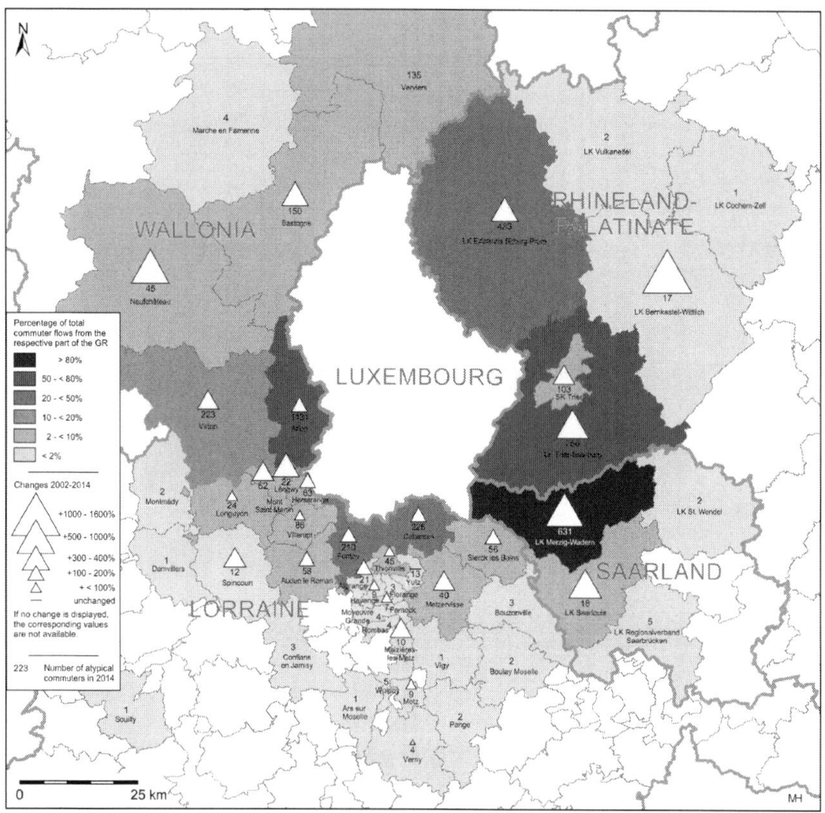

Figure 3: Cross-border commuters with Luxembourgish nationality and Luxembourg as country of work by residential districts 2014, and changes in percent 2002–2014

Source: Inspection Générale de la Sécurité Sociale (Luxembourg), cartography: Malte Helfer

In their study of atypical cross-border commuters, Brosius/Carpentier (2010) additionally incorporate people of non-Luxembourg nationality and observe for the years 2001 to 2007 that the Luxembourgers constitute only a quarter of this group. By contrast, people of German, French, and Belgian nationality constitute a remarkably high percentage (57%), followed by Portuguese (10%) and people of other nationalities (8%). The atypical cross-border commuters of French, Belgian, and German nationality have, in the course of cross-border residential migration, almost without exception chosen their new place of residence in their land of origin.

In the following, we will take a closer look at the volume and the key developments of residential migration in the different regions of the Greater Region. On the basis of the available official statistics, we will take into account here not only atypical cross-border commuters, but also people of Luxembourgish nationality as well as people who have moved from Luxembourg.

In 2011, 2,725 Luxembourgish nationals lived in the Saarland. Since 2001, their number has increased more than threefold. Particularly strong changes compared to the previous year can be observed in the years 2006 and 2007, in which the number of Luxembourgers increased annually by up to a third (33.2% in 2008/2007). But with the economic and financial crisis, the momentum collapsed abruptly, so that growth slowed down markedly in the following years—albeit with a continuous positive tendency. The number of annual moves from Luxembourg to the Saarland has also increased more than threefold in the last decade: whereas in 2000, 161 moves from Luxembourg were registered, in 2011 it was already 576. Here we can observe that after 2008, an annually increasing number of non-Luxembourgers moved out of the Grand Duchy.

In Rhineland-Palatinate, the number of Luxembourgers has increased by more than four times since 1995: while 1,422 Luxembourgish nationals lived in the federal state that year, in 2012 it was already 5,637. Within this period, we can distinguish between three phases: in the years 2000–2004—with rates of annual change still below 10%—we can observe an initial increase in moves by Luxembourgers; between 2004 and 2008, the annual rates of change increased by up to 20%; and finally the momentum slowed down markedly after 2008. The majority of Luxembourgers (90%) lived in close proximity to the border: 43% in the rural district of Trier-Saarburg, 36.2% in the Eifel district of Bitburg-Prüm and 10.2% in the urban district of Trier. As regards the moves to Rhineland-Palatinate, in 2012 1,242 people from the Grand Duchy were counted, comprising 726 Luxembourgers and 516 non-Luxembourgers. The percentage of annual moves accounted for by non-Luxembourgers has remained at around 40% since the mid-2000s.

Analogously to the increase in moves from Luxembourg, the number of atypical cross-border commuters who reside in Germany has also increased, as mentioned above. Almost all of the 2,067 Luxembourg commuters (2014) with Luxembourg nationality coming from Germany lived in the neighboring Rhineland-Palatinate and in the Saarland. The majority lived in Rhineland-Palatinate (1,366), and here particularly in the districts Trier-Saarburg and Bitburg-Prüm. Approximately a third lived in the Saarland (657), where they lived primarily in the border district of Merzig-Wadern. The most significant residential communities of the atypical cross-border commuters living in Germany are the municipalities of Perl, Trier, Mettlach, Nittel, Palzem, Freudenburg, Wincheringen, and Konz. Since the mid-2000s, areas further away from the Luxembourg border have also been affected by the phenomenon of residential migration.

In 1999, 2,550 Luxembourgers lived in Lorraine, and 2,399 in 2010. This corresponds to a drop of 6% within eleven years. The available statistics, however, only provide information on people of Luxembourgish nationality, while those of other nationalities who moved from Luxembourg (e.g. French or Portuguese) are not included here. But we can assume that their proportion of the Lorraine resident population is not insignificant, since 84% or 59% of the gainfully employed French and Portuguese who have moved their place of residence into the neighboring country moved to Lorraine (cf. Brosius/Carpentier 2010, p. 32). The atypical cross-border commuters with Luxembourgish nationality have more than doubled (112%) in the last decade (2002–2014); in 2014, their numbers amounted to 1,055. Two-thirds of them lived in the Moselle department, in particular in the cantons of Cattenom and Fontoy. Around one third was registered in Meurthe-et-Moselle department, particularly in the cantons Villerupt, Audun-le-Romain, Herserange, and Mont-Saint-Michel.

There are no statistical data available regarding resident Luxembourgers or the annual number of moves from Luxembourg into Wallonia. But the information on the 1,743 (2014) Luxembourgers living in Belgium who work in the Grand Duchy provides some pointers. 89% of them lived in the Wallonian province of Luxembourg; their numbers there increased threefold between 2002 and 2014, and in 2014 amounted to 1,553 people. They lived primarily in the Arrondissement d'Arlon (72%), followed by the Arrondissement de Virton (14.4%). The most significant areas of residence of atypical cross-border commuters living in Belgium include Arlon, Aubange, Messancy, Bastogne, und Attert (cf. Gengler 2010, p. 270). Recently we have also been able to observe an increase in the atypical cross-border commuters in the Arrondissement Verviers, which belongs to the German-speaking community of Belgium.

For the past decade, we can, in summary, observe a continuous increase in cross-border residential migrants from Luxembourg and, coupled with that, an increase in atypical cross-border commuting. Here, neighboring Germany is particularly popular as a country of residence compared to neighboring France and Belgium. It needs to be pointed out that the situation outlined above only very approximately reflects the actual development and the extent of residential migration, because the number of those who move while keeping their place of residence in Luxembourg, for all kinds of reasons—and are thus not included in the statistics on population movements—is presumably significant. We can therefore assume that the phenomenon of cross-border residential migration is far more marked than it has been possible to describe here.

3.1 Social contacts at the place of residence/work

In the following, we will look at the development of social contacts also with regard to the group of residential migrants. Drawing on Wille et al. (2016), we will examine the question of how far individuals' social relations with various groups of people in the former and the new place of residence have changed since moving into a neighboring region.

With regard to Luxembourg, one can first observe a reduction in social contacts there, since the interviewees state that since moving, they see friends (41%) and family (14%) in the Grand Duchy less frequently. This is also confirmed by the findings provided by Roos (2016, p. 352): even though residential migrants maintain contact with friends/acquaintances and relatives in Luxembourg—since their circle of friends there is often larger than in their new place of residence—despite their good intentions, their visits become less frequent the longer they live in the neighboring country:

> In the beginning I always said to my friends: 'Once a week I'll always be down there.' Now not any more at all. There is nothing that makes me want to go there. If it wasn't for my grandchild, I'd go there even less often. (Residential migrant in Germany)

This development in their visiting habits is often explained by the greater geographic distance and subsequently longer travelling times. Carpentier/Gerber (2010, p. 89f.) observe here a doubling of driving times among atypical cross-border commuters after moving. To avoid additional journeys, Roos' (2016) interview partner combines work-related and personal appointments, or invites friends and family to their new place of residence:

> When there is something on in Luxembourg and I have to work anyway, when I'm doing a late shift for instance and they have something organized and then the next day I have a late shift or an early shift again, then I stay down there. Then I stay there. [...] But when there's something on, I say to my mother: 'Come on up.' As long as my father still drives—he's 76 [...]—and likes to drive, he can come here. My mother also likes to come here. It's something totally different for her. (Residential migrant in Germany)

The quantitative and qualitative findings show that moving primarily reduces social contact to friends in the Grand Duchy, while family relations remain stable. But on the other hand new friendships develop in the course of these migrants changing their place of residence, as more than half of the interviewees had made friends at their new place of residence, although new social contacts with locals (69%) seem to be more common than with fellow residential migrants (55%). These findings provided by Wille et al. (2016) can be explained by the residential migrants' stated intentions to integrate locally—as, for instance, described by Boesen/Schnuer (2015)—as well as by the desire of some to distance themselves from their own group of fellow residential migrants. Such efforts at local integration are also reflected in the results presented by Roos (2016, p. 351, 353), according to which there is a great variety of neighborly contact with locals, which develops in everyday life, but also at parties or in situations of mutual support:

> We reach out to people. It's not that we stand in a corner and don't talk to anyone, for example, when something happens. (Residential migrant in Germany)

> If you're pruning roses and someone stops, then sure, you have a chat. Happened to me a couple of times. Someone came along and said: 'Oh, but you have to do some more pruning here.' OK, I've no idea. This is my first garden. I prune where I think it's right. 'No, but you have to do some more here.' (Residential migrant in Germany)

> Also, when there's work to do, you help each other. One of our neighbors is coming over now to borrow our trailer. Also, when there's something that needs to get done: 'Can you give me a hand for an afternoon?' they immediately say yes. We do too because we're used to it from back home. There we also did that, that everybody lends a hand. (Residential migrant in Germany)

In terms of social contacts beyond the immediate living environment of one's home, a residential migrant living in the district town of Merzig mentions membership of associations that promote contact with locals:

> Joining clubs and associations. That's something you can do immediately. It's easy to make friends there. Then there's always someone who knows someone else and so on. (Residential migrant in Germany) (Roos 2016, p. 354).

Among the residential migrants interviewed, the desire for social inclusion at their new place of residence is directed primarily at the local population. Contact to other Luxembourgers, by contrast, is less explicitly sought; in the interview we can even observe tendencies to dissociate oneself. For instance, for the interviewee, the municipality of Perl was out of the question as a place of residence, because too many residential migrants from Luxembourg live there:

> But Perl didn't appeal to me at all. Not that I'm a racist, but there are just too many Luxembourgers. That's too many for me. (Residential migrant in Germany)

Despite this kind of rejection, social contacts also develop between residential migrants and other non-locals. Such informal networks common in the context of migration serve for the exchange of information, experience and the collective use of material goods. For networks between non-locals to form, places of sociability relevant to everyday life such as the neighborhood (34%), place of work (29%), or associations (13%) seem to play an important role, since the residential migrants also state that these are places where they have got to know other people who moved from the Grand Duchy (cf. Wille et al. 2016).

We can observe that, for practical reasons, contact to existing friends and family at a migrant's former place of residence is limited in the course of them changing their place of residence, in particular contact to friends in Luxembourg. At the same time, however, friendships develop at their new place of residence through encounters in the neighborhood, associations, and at their place of work, primarily with the local population and to a lesser extent with other residential migrants.

3.2 Everyday cross-border practices

In a further step, we will inquire how residential migrants from Luxembourg organize their everyday practices in spatial terms. Wille et al. (2016)

have investigated which (selected) everyday practices residential migrants perform in which of the countries in question. Here we can generally observe that after moving, residential migrants visit Luxembourg particularly frequently for everyday practices (Table 4), which suggests a "certain attachment to the country of origin" (Carpentier/Gerber 2010, p. 97).

	Shopping	Grocery shopping	Recreation/ Tourism	Cultural events	Going out	Seeing the doctor	Club and association activities
France	38	30	51	28	21	18	16
Luxembourg	86	65	56	65	65	86	22
Belgium	33	23	34	32	23	23	9
Germany	41	34	39	33	23	20	6

Table 4: Spatial distribution of everyday practices by countries for residential migrants from Luxembourg in the Greater Region, in percent (multiple entries, N=56)

Source: Wille et al. 2016

This is evident in particular in shopping activities and doctor's visits, which show a strong discrepancy between which ones are performed in the country of residence and which in Luxembourg (Table 4). With regard to doctor's visits, the interviewees differentiated between GPs and specialists. While a number of the interviewees in Wille et al. (2016) and Roos (2016) had already looked for a new GP at their place of residence—which is probably due to the geographic proximity and a greater regularity of visits compared to specialists—primarily the latter continue to be consulted in Luxembourg. This is explained by the fact that specialists will have been familiar with the interviewees' medical history for many years and that this has created a relationship of trust:

> I still go to see several doctors in Luxembourg. Those are my doctors that I've been going to for years. But otherwise, my daughter goes to the ophthalmologist here, and she also wants to look for a dentist here. But for the rest … And we just have this one GP here. For that, we don't go to Luxembourg anymore, only to the specialists. (Residential migrant in Germany)

> Well, I also still have some doctors in Luxembourg who have treated me for four years and who know my medical history. So it's easier for me to go there than to explain my medical history all over again. (Residential migrant in France)

Next, we will turn to shopping and attending cultural events, which occur approximately twice as often in the Grand Duchy than in the migrants' country of residence (Tab. 4). Restaurants, bars, cinemas, theatres, etc. in Luxembourg hold a particular attraction, since here there is a wider discrepancy between the opportunities for such activities in the country of residence and in the Grand Duchy (Table 4).

Shopping behavior was determined, for some of the interviewees (cf. Wille et al. 2016; Roos 2016, p. 353), primarily by the differences in price and range of products between the different countries (cf. Wille 2015, p. 136) and maximization of personal benefit. Thus, certain products—such as food and clothes—are mostly bought in the country of residence, where they are as a rule cheaper, while alcohol, petrol, and tobacco continue to be bought in the Grand Duchy:

> We cherry-pick. What we like better in Luxembourg we do there. [...] Shopping we do here. We don't do any shopping in Luxembourg anymore. [...] We fill up our cars with gas in Luxembourg. (Residential migrant in Germany)

Other interviewees in Wille et al. (2016), however, emphasize that for them it is not the price but the quality of the products that is important, which is why they shop in Luxembourg despite the higher prices. But this is financially only possible because their place of residence is in the neighboring country and money can be saved this way and invested elsewhere:

> Well, I come from the country, meaning I like to know where the things I buy come from... when I buy meat then I like to buy Luxembourgish meat. When I buy vegetables then I also go to the market. That's just the cook in me, who always pops up; it's not that I don't trust their stuff, but it's just a different quality. And with the prices that we save in Belgium with housing I can still afford the quality from Luxembourg. If I were living here [in Luxembourg], I probably wouldn't go shopping here; that's the irony of it. (Residential migrant in Belgium)

We can see a relatively balanced distribution of everyday practices between country of residence and Luxembourg in the migrants' touristic practices and recreation in green surroundings. Even though interviewees visit the

Grand Duchy most frequently for these activities, leisure opportunities in neighboring France seem to be equally attractive (Table 4). In addition, interviewees in Wille et al. (2016) mention leisure activities in Belgium and Germany, for instance motorbike trips or visits to concerts, restaurants, open-air swimming pools, or Christmas markets:

> In the Saarland for instance, when it's nice weather and warm outside, there are swimming pools that we don't have in the region. They have big open-air pools and big lawns. When we can't go on a vacation, the children like that. Yes, and Rhineland-Palatinate, we have some friends there too. Once in a while we go there for the weekend. We also like to go to the Christmas market in Trier, because we used to live in Grevenmacher. (Residential migrant in France)

Also for the generally poorly developed practice of attending association events, Luxembourg continues to be important, even though residential migrants in France participate relatively frequently in local associations (Table 4). And after moving, a residential migrant in Germany did decide to join an association at his new place of residence because he expected social integration would be easier this way.

The quantitative and qualitative results show that Luxembourg continues to be an important reference for residential migrants after moving. Besides the reasons already mentioned, this is also due to the atypical cross-border commuters among the interviewees, whose employment brings them back to Luxembourg regularly. With regard to this subgroup, the findings presented by Carpentier/Gerber (2010, p. 91) permit more differentiated statements than is possible with the above data; they observe that the new place of residence of the atypical cross-border commuters indeed plays a role in the way they conduct everyday practices. One needs to take into account, however, that more than half of the interviewees included German, Belgian, and French nationals. Even before moving, they had already conducted numerous everyday practices in their country of origin. Luxembourgers and Portuguese, by contrast, performed their activities almost exclusively in the Grand Duchy. Among them, one can observe a continued strong attachment to their country of origin after moving, since around half of their everyday activities continue to take place in Luxembourg. With atypical cross-border commuters of German, French, and Belgian nationality, by contrast, one can observe a shift of everyday practices into their new country of residence.

Against this background, we can say that residential migrants continue to conduct particular everyday practices after moving (also) in Luxembourg, in the case of atypical cross-border commuters who benefited from their everyday cross-border mobility. Probably there are differences between residential migrants with Luxembourgish and Portuguese nationality who for the most part no longer reside in the Grand Duchy and have a stronger geographic anchoring, and residential migrants with nationalities of their new countries of residence, who probably concentrate their everyday activities more on their new place of residence.

4. Conclusion

This contribution has examined two mobile groups of people at the Luxembourgish border in order to gain insights into the everyday lives of cross-border workers. To this end, we discussed the development of their social contacts at their place of work and/or residence, as well as the spatial organization of everyday practices of cross-border commuters and residential migrants.

Our observations have shown that cross-border commuters do indeed maintain relationships with friends and family in Luxembourg, albeit distinctly less than in their country of residence. Compared to other border-region residents, their social contacts—in particular friendships—in the neighboring country or country of employment are more marked, which can be ascribed to the everyday cross-border mobility of cross-border commuters and the concomitant contacts at their place of work. We further observed that friendships outside of the context of work tend to be rare, a fact which cross-border commuters explain with long journeys, family obligations, and generally a lack of time. So while cross-border commuters maintain social contacts in both their country of residence and that of their work, their contact to friends and family in their country of residence predominates.

As regards residential migrants, we were able to establish that, after moving, they visit friends and relatives in the Grand Duchy less often than before. This applies in particular to friendships, which is explained by longer travelling times. On the other hand, residential migrants form new friendly contacts at their place of residence, in particular with members of the local population. Typical places of sociability such as the neighborhood, clubs and associations, or place of work are especially relevant. For the most part, their connections with relatives remain stable after moving, while those with friends are reduced, with new contacts developing at their place of residence.

As far as the spatial organization of everyday practices is concerned, it became clear that cross-border commuters conduct these more frequently in Luxembourg than the border-region inhabitants on the whole. These primarily involve consumption and going out, which are often connected with working in the Grand Duchy. Nevertheless, commuters prefer their country of residence for everyday activities, which is explained by more favorable leisure opportunities in their country of residence, long journeys, or a lack of social contacts in Luxembourg. Thus, while cross-border commuters also perform their everyday activities in Luxembourg, they do this very selectively and are guided by economic considerations.

For residential migrants—in particular those of Luxembourgish and Portuguese nationality—we can establish that they continue to conduct certain everyday practices in the Grand Duchy after moving, and also complementing others in their region of residence. A relevant factor here is not only the subgroup of atypical cross-border commuters who connect errands with their work in Luxembourg. Equally important are habits, (new) financial scope, trust (in doctors or in the quality of products), and economic considerations. Residential migrants continue to perform their everyday activities on both sides of the Luxembourgish border after moving, with the Grand Duchy remaining an important region of reference for many of them.

The comparison of cross-border commuters and residential migrants shows that one can indeed speak of cross-border everyday lives at the Luxembourgish border. Both groups maintain social contacts on both sides of the border; connections with relatives remain for the most part unchanged in the course of cross-border mobility. On the other hand, new mobility-related friendly contacts develop in their immediate work and residential environments. Everyday practices are also carried out by both groups on both sides of the Luxembourgish border, with the Grand Duchy being visited for different reasons: while cross-border commuters prefer their country of residence for everyday practices and make use of opportunities in Luxembourg for rational and practical reasons, for residential migrants it is often routines and emotional reasons that play a role in them conducting their everyday practices in Luxembourg.

Against this background, the aforementioned effectiveness of European interior borders can be qualified for the region under review, which however should not obscure the (latently) continuing spatial fragmentations, such as the preferences for their country of residence voiced by cross-border commuters or the characterization, made by some residential migrants, of their new place of residence as a “place to sleep”. In addition, the organization in nation states with their system-related differences (e.g. the level of taxes and prices or the real estate and labor market) has to be regarded as territorial fragmentation, which, however, encourages cross-border lifeworlds at the Luxembourgish border—motivated by maximization of personal benefit—and continues to be constitutive for the issues discussed here.

References

Belkacem, Rachid/Pigeron-Piroth, Isabelle (eds.) (2012): Le travail frontalier au sein de la Grande Région Saar-Lor-Lux. Pratiques, enjeux et perspectives. Nancy: Éditions Universitaires de Lorraine.

Belkacem, Rachid/Pigeron-Piroth, Isabelle (2015): Un marché de l'emploi intégré? L'emploi frontalier et ses dimensions socio-économiques. In: Wille, C. (ed.): Lebenswirklichkeiten und politische Konstruktionen in Grenzregionen. Das Beispiel der Großregion SaarLorLux. Wirtschaft – Politik – Alltag – Kultur. Bielefeld: Transcript, p. 39–57.

Boesen, Elisabeth/Schnuer, Gregor (2015): Wohnen jenseits der Grenze. Regionale Integration und ihre lokalen Verwirklichungen. In: Wille, C. (ed.): Lebenswirklichkeiten und politische Konstruktionen in Grenzregionen. Das Beispiel der Großregion SaarLorLux. Wirtschaft – Politik – Alltag – Kultur. Bielefeld: Transcript, p. 179–201.

Brosius, Jaques/Carpentier, Samuel (2010): Grenzüberschreitende Wohnmobilität von in Luxemburg ansässigen Erwerbstätigen: Quantifizierung und Charakterisierung des Phänomens. In: Carpentier, S. (ed.): Die grenzüberschreitende Wohnmobilität zwischen Luxemburg und seinen Nachbarregionen. Luxembourg: Saint Paul, p. 15–36.

Carpentier, Samuel (ed.) (2010): Die grenzüberschreitende Wohnmobilität zwischen Luxemburg und seinen Nachbarregionen. Luxembourg: Saint Paul.

Carpentier, Samuel/Gerber, Philippe (2010): Welche Konsequenzen hat die grenzüberschreitende Wohnmobilität auf die täglichen Fahrten und die Aktivitätsräume? In: Carpentier, S. (ed.): Die grenzüberschreitende Wohnmobilität zwischen Luxemburg und seinen Nachbarregionen. Luxembourg: Saint Paul, p. 87–113.

Franziskus, Anne/De Bres, Julia (2012): Le rôle de la langue luxembourgeoise dans les pratiques linguistiques des frontaliers au Luxembourg. In: Belkacem, R./ Pigeron-Piroth, I. (eds.): Le travail frontalier au sein de la Grande Région Saar-Lor-Lux. Pratiques, enjeux et perspectives. Nancy: Éditions Universitaires de Lorraine, p. 129–149.

Gengler, Claude (2010): Expatriation „à la luxembourgeoise“. In: Pauly, M. (ed.): ASTI 30+. 30 ans de migrations, 30 ans de recherches, 30 ans d'engagements. Luxembourg: Binsfeld, p. 262–275.

IBA – Interregionale Arbeitsmarktbeobachtungsstelle (2014): Die Arbeitsmarktsituation in der Großregion. Teilbericht Grenzgängermobilität. Saarbrücken.

Roos, Ursula (2016): Migration und Integration in ländlichen Räumen am Beispiel der saarländischen Kreisstadt Merzig. Eine empirische Untersuchung unter besonderer Berücksichtigung der Erfahrungen und Sichtweisen von Personen mit Migrationshintergrund. Universität des Saarlandes. (download: https://goo.gl/jD AHBU)

Statec (1995): La main d'œuvre frontalière au Luxembourg. Exploitation des fichiers de la sécurité sociale. Cahiers Economiques 84.

Statec (2014): Luxemburg in Zahlen, Luxembourg.

Wille, Christian (2011): Atypische Grenzgänger in der Großregion. In: GR-Atlas – Atlas der Großregion SaarLorLux, Paper Series 30.

Wille, Christian (2012): Grenzgänger und Räume der Grenze. Raumkonstruktionen in der Großregion SaarLorLux. Frankfurt/M: Peter Lang.

Wille, Christian (2015): Grenzüberschreitende Alltagspraktiken in der Großregion SaarLorLux: eine Bestandsaufnahme. In: Wille, C. (ed.): Lebenswirklichkeiten und politische Konstruktionen in Grenzregionen. Das Beispiel der Großregion SaarLorLux: Wirtschaft – Politik – Alltag – Kultur. Bielefeld: Transcript, p. 133–156.

Wille, Christian (2016): Mobilität und Raum. Vorder- und rückseitige Regionalisierungsprozesse in der Großregion SaarLorLux. In: Cicotti, C./Cuoghi, S. (eds.): La rencontre avec l'autre. Phénoménologie interculturelles dans l'Europe contemporaine. Brussels: Peter Lang, p. 75–103.

Wille, Christian/Reckinger, Rachel/Kmec, Sonja/Hesse, Markus (eds.) (2016): Spaces and Identities in Border Regions. Policies – Media – Subjects. Bielefeld: Transcript.

About the authors

Christian Wille | University of Luxembourg | Campus Belval | Maison des Sciences Humaines | UniGR-Center for Border Studies | 11, Porte des Sciences | L-4366 Esch-sur-Alzette | Luxembourg | christian.wille@uni.lu

Wille, Christian (Ph.D.) is a senior researcher at the University of Luxembourg and head of the network UniGR-Center for Border Studies. He has published the books "Spaces and Identities in Border Regions" (2016), "Living Realities and Political Constructions in Border Regions", (2015) and "Cross-border Commuters and Spaces of the Border" (2012). His research area includes cultural border studies, transnational everyday lives, and spatial, identity, praxeological theories.

Ursula Roos | Gymnasium Ottweiler | Seminarstraße 43 | 66564 Ottweiler | Germany | u.roos@gym-otw.de

Roos, Ursula (Ph.D.) teaches geography and chemistry at a secondary school in Ottweiler. Prior to her current position, she was a research associate at the Institute of Geography and Spatial Planning at the University of Luxembourg, and at the geography department at Saarland University. Her research interests are migration and integration studies, especially in rural areas, as well as border studies. She holds a degree in geography and chemistry from Saarland University (2011) and a Ph.D. in Geography (2015). Her Ph.D. thesis focuses on migration patterns as well as the individual integration processes of international migrants in rural areas.

Moving from nation into region. Experiences and memories of cross-border dwelling in the Greater Region SaarLorLux

Elisabeth Boesen

Abstract

Relocating one's home to the other side of a national border is a practice of border crossing that is currently gaining in importance in (European) borderlands. The Greater Region SaarLorLux represents an interesting case for study due to the complex composition of the group of residential migrants and the diversity of the border crossing movements. By analyzing individual 'moving stories', the contribution proposes a view on this form of migration that aims at an understanding of the 'multiplicity of place' and thus of an important dimension of border experiences and regional identification processes. The article also addresses general questions on the relationship between migration, memory, and homemaking.

Keywords

Residential migration, borderland, dwelling, memory, identity

1. *Introduction*

Cross-border residential mobility (CBRM), i.e. the fact that people relocate their home a short distance across a national border, is a relatively new form of cross-border movement that appeared in the wake of the formal opening of intra-European borders, and is mainly linked to national disparities in the real estate market in border regions. People move to the other side of a national border because housing and especially building land is less expensive there. We observe this kind of mobility at the Dutch–German, the Polish–German, the Italian–Slovenian, and the Slovak–Hungarian borders—to name but a few examples. These residential moves take place above all where an urban center adjoins a national border, with a predominantly rural area on the other side (Jagodic 2012); examples are Nijmegen, Bratislava, Trieste, Basel—and Luxembourg.

These moves could thus be subsumed under the general phenomenon of peri-urbanization, their distinguishing feature being the fact that the urban agglomerations in question expand beyond a national border. The ensuing developments and problems therefore concern research on spatial planning and politics, while classical issues of migration studies—cultural identity, social integration, community formation, etc.—are, apparently, of less importance. It is in fact a matter of debate whether the term 'migration' is appropriate here. Some scholars argue that insofar as these residential moves do not (strongly) affect the activity space of the movers, they cannot be considered as migration. Instead, they opt for the term 'residential mobility' (cf. Gerber/Carpentier 2013; Kaufmann 1999), while others propose newly coined expressions, like 'elastic migration' (van Houtum/Gielis 2006) or 'short-distance transnationalism' (Strüver 2005). This terminological indecision reflects the conceptual ambiguity of the phenomenon.

Research on these developments is relatively limited, which might in part be due to the fact that the numerical importance of these movements is small when compared to, for example, work-related commuting. Another reason for the relative neglect might be seen in a more general inclination to privilege conflict over harmony in border studies (cf. Minghi 1991), whereas cross-border residential movement typically takes place in highly integrated borderlands (cf. Martinez 1994). It is, however, surprising that CBRM is also largely ignored in more recent research that deals with the problem of why people—in contrast to goods, capital, and information—prove to be relatively immobile and borders continue to act as barriers in cases where, as in the EU, formal mobility restrictions have more or less disappeared (cf. van Houtum/van der Velde 2004; van der Velde 2012; Klatt 2014). Could this lack of academic interest in the phenomenon be related to the conceptual difficulties that it poses? CBRM calls major conceptual frames like mobility/immobility, national dichotomies, and residential move/migration into question and thus alludes to the complexity of bordering processes and border experiences and, generally, to the relationship between space and movement. While the study of this relationship has of late been very much dominated by 'nomad thought' (cf. Thrift 1994; Cresswell 2006), research on cross-border residential mobility obliges us, so to speak, to (re)consider the complementary aspect, i.e. the processes of dwelling, of being sedentary in variably extended spaces (cf. Bissel 2013; Schnuer 2014).

In recent years, there has been some academic work on dwelling inspired in part by classic texts, above all Heidegger (cf., e.g., Casey 1997; Ingold 2000). This renewed interest can be interpreted as a consequence of the general turn to mobility in the social sciences and humanities, the new mobilities paradigm implying, as it were, immobility as the correlate to movement. One can also argue that dwelling is especially important to those who travel, and that in an era of 'thinned-out places' home becomes more important (Harvey 1996; Casey 2001). At the same time, there is increasing attention on the forms of dwelling that characterize a mobile lifestyle, that is, on mobile dwelling in the literal sense (cf. Rolshoven 2006) and to poly-topical or multi-local residence (Stock 2015; Weichhart 2015). Recently there have been considerable efforts at defining and typifying multi-locality, one of its most important forms, perhaps the essential form, being multi-local dwelling, the practice of dwelling in alternating places.[1]

It is not rare that CBRM in the Greater Region SaarLorLux results in individuals being attached to two places of residence, one being their place of concrete everyday life and the other, which is located in Luxembourg, being their official place of residence where their letterbox is installed.[2] One can also come across people who alternate between two places, spending several days a week in Luxembourg and the rest in a neighboring borderland. Normally, however, CBRM means abandoning one's place of residence in one country—in the present case, Luxembourg—and taking up a new place of residence on the other side of the national border. I argue that this kind of move and the border experiences related to it can bring about a particular form of 'multiple dwelling' and that the analysis of the complex process of movement helps us understand societal developments and identification processes in border regions.

CBRM is not only, as argued above, conceptually vague, but also indeterminate as regards the experiences, aspirations, and self-conceptions of those who move. Many of them have become, as it were, migrants unintentionally. They have relocated their house across the border without intending to move there in a more encompassing sense, but find themselves afterwards as having moved or being involved in an ongoing process of

1 Cf., for example, the work done by the *Arbeitskreis Multilokale Lebensführung und räumliche Entwicklungen der Akademie für Raumforschung und Landesplanung* (ARL).

2 Unfortunately, we do not have exact data on the number of 'illegal', i.e. unregistered residential migrants from Luxembourg in the adjoining borderlands. Their number may be quite important, as is shown by the example of Wincheringen, a Moselle village with 2,200 officially registered residents, where the mayor estimates the number of non-registered residents to be 100 to 150, the great majority of whom have their official residence in Luxembourg (interview with E. Schömann, October 2, 2015).

moving, of leaving their former social world and recreating a new one that is mainly located in another country (Boesen 2015). CBRM is thus a highly complex matter, both with respect to the conditions and motivations involved in relocating one's home and with respect to the integration and identification processes that are brought about by it. These multilayered processes are revealing of general developments in European borderlands, in that they call into question the mobile/immobile dichotomy and common categorizations that are based on it, like for instance the differentiation between 'traditional' and 'transnational borderlanders' (cf. Strüver 2005; Klatt 2016; Martinez 1994). Moreover, a processual perspective that focuses on how the people themselves experience and conceptualize their residential move is complementary to the notion of the border as implying two fundamental but opposed attitudes or desires, namely that of retreating from the other and that of longing for it (cf. van Houtum/Eker 2015, p. 204). Apart from revealing the ambivalence of personal needs and experiences, individual migration memories also bring to light the complexity of the historico-cultural and social categories involved.

I would hold that the 'moving stories' we encountered in the SaarLorLux borderlands are nevertheless about migration, albeit a particular type of migration, namely migration from a national into a non-national realm —from nation into region. Furthermore, I argue that this form of migration engenders memory processes, which, although distinct, might be illuminating for general questions about the relationship between memories, mobility and belonging. I will try to develop my argument by presenting and analyzing two 'migration stories', two examples of residential migrants that stem from research in German villages located at the border with Luxembourg, which have been particularly affected by CBRM in the last ten to fifteen years. In the last part, I will turn to general questions on the relationship between migration, memory and homemaking. Before coming to the examples, I will make a few introductory remarks on CBRM in the Greater Region.

2. *The Greater Region SaarLorLux*

In the Greater Region SaarLorLux, CBRM means above all residential flows from Luxembourg to its neighboring borderlands (cf. Wille/Roos, in the present volume; Carpentier 2010; Wille/Schnuer/Boesen 2014; Boesen et al. 2015; Reichert-Schick 2017). The phenomenon is very pronounced here and, more importantly, also particularly complex, and therefore deserves special consideration. First, it is important to note that by virtue of its small size, Luxembourg has three nearby national borders (with Belgium, France, and Germany) and therefore offers a threefold option to people considering residential migration. While all three border regions experienced a massive influx of new residents from Luxembourg in the last fifteen to twenty years, one can observe considerable differences in the composition of the three groups of residential migrants, and thus in the development of the individual borderlands. The vast majority of those who move to France and Belgium are French and Belgian nationals respectively, whereas more than 50% of the migrants who opt for residence in Germany are of Luxembourgish nationality (Carpentier 2010).

A further particularity of CBRM in the Greater Region is related to the composition of Luxembourg's population, with almost 48% being of non-Luxembourgish nationality (STATEC 2018). The group of incomers from Luxembourg in the adjoining border regions—and especially in the German borderland—is highly differentiated with respect to national background, and also with respect to socioeconomic characteristics. Apart from national Luxembourgers, it embraces a high number of international migrants working in diverse sectors, including in the financial sector and in European institutions, amongst others.

This hints at another distinctive feature of the region, namely the degree of mobility and the complexity of mobility patterns that characterize Luxembourg society and the Greater Region as a whole. Suffice it to say that apart from the high number of immigrants, the Luxembourgish labor market also attracts more than 175,000 daily commuters from the surrounding border regions, who represent almost 45% of the country's work force (STATEC 2018). Hence, the mobile/immobile dichotomy is also called into question by a, so to speak, generalized mobility (Lannoy/Ramadier 2007). It is worth mentioning, for example, that an important part of the 'immobile' autochthonous population of the surrounding border regions —in certain villages more than 80% of the active population—are cross-border commuters (cf. Pigeron-Piroth/Belkacem in this volume). All this indicates the inadequacy of national dichotomies, the idea of a clearly demarcated here and there, which underlie much of the research on residential mobility and on European borderlands in general—including those approaches that adhere to a transnational perspective.

In the following, I will largely ignore the described variability and complexity, in that I will concentrate on the German borderland. Moreover, I will further narrow the view by selecting one specific group of newly arrived residents from Luxembourg, namely those with Luxembourgish nationality. I will thus focus on 'the Luxembourgers'. The restriction of our research to the German part of the Luxembourgish borderland was motivated by the fact, already mentioned, that the group of residential migrants is particularly diversified here. In contrast to the Belgian and French borders, where the majority of residential migrants are Belgian and French nationals respectively, the migrant group in German borderland villages embraces not only a large proportion of national Luxembourgers but also a high number of international migrants, who have turned small rural communities into cosmopolitan places with up to 40 nationalities. In the present context, I limit myself to the Luxembourg nationals among these migrants, because they are a most promising subject regarding the experiences and narratives related to cross-border residential moves. The Luxembourgers can be seen as representing prototypical migrants in as much as they have left their native country in order to settle in a new one, while for others setting up residence across the border meant either return migration—Germans moving back to Germany—or just a further stage in their intermittent movement across Europe or the world. As we will see, however, the Luxembourgers are at the same time very peculiar migrants because, in a sense, they did not leave 'home'.

3. *'Moving stories'*

My analysis is based on the results of a study that consisted of qualitative research in four rural localities that have witnessed a considerable influx from Luxembourg in the last ten to fifteen years but show significant differences with regard to size and infrastructure (cf. map). In these villages, we carried out participant observation and conducted narrative interviews with residents who had moved in from Luxembourg—Luxembourgish nationals as well as others—and with the local autochthonous population, including interviews with mayors and other experts.[3] We did 70 interviews altogether, among them 21 interviews with individuals and couples with Luxembourgish nationality.

Here, I will present two migration stories, originating from Mr. Da Silva and Mr. and Mrs. Weber respectively.[4] It goes without saying that the two examples are not meant to represent the totality of Luxembourgish residential migrants in the German borderland. Neither do they represent the

---

3 The project "Cross-border residence. Identity experience and integration processes in the Greater Region" was conducted by Gregor Schnuer and me and financially supported by the *Fonds National de la Recherche Luxembourg*.

4 The names have been changed.

totality of those who we interviewed. The two examples resemble each other in that they present 'success stories'. In both cases, the new place of residence in the German borderland turned out to be the right choice; neither Mr. Da Silva nor the Webers think about returning to Luxembourg. In this respect at least, they are actually representative not only of the totality of our interviewees with Luxemburgish nationality but also of the great majority of Luxembourgish residential migrants in general. In a quantitative analysis of cross-border residential mobility, 88% of the participants were satisfied or very satisfied with their decision to move (Carpentier 2010, p. 118; cf. also Wille/Roos, in this volume).

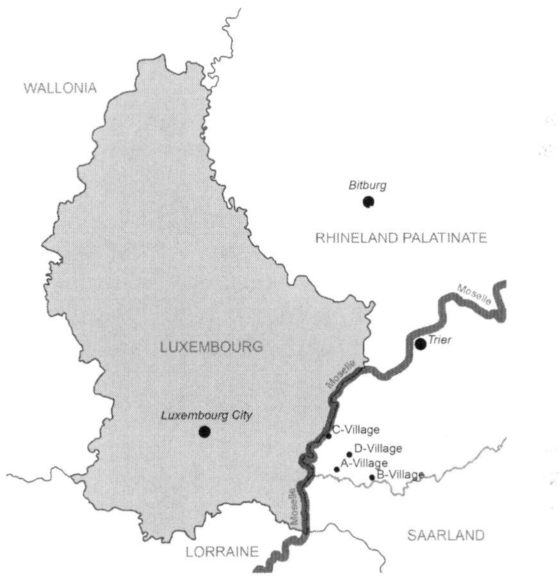

Map: Geographical situation of the case studies, cartography: Gregor Schnuer

The two examples are also close to each other in that they are located in the same village, namely A-Village (see map), which indicates that Mario Da Silva and the Webers might have similar ideas about desirable village size, infrastructure, proximity to the border, landscape preferences, etc. They have chosen a very small village at a distance of 6 kilometers from the border. In 2000, A-Village had only 170 inhabitants, with no non-Germans among them. Since then the village has witnessed a growth of more than 20%, and by now, about 20% of its inhabitants are of Luxembourgish nationality. On the other hand, we also find clear differences between the two cases, and thus gain an impression of the diversity of residential migrants' social and biographical situations, of their reasons for moving, and their reflections about identity and belonging.

3.1 Case I

Mario Da Silva moved to A-Village 19 years ago and can therefore be described as one of the pioneers among the Luxembourgish residential migrants in the German border region. He recounts at length how in the late 1990s he and his future wife—both of them of Portuguese ancestry and both born in Luxembourg—were searching for a building lot in their Luxembourgish home region, the Moselle. Back then, building land was very scarce because landowners simply refused to sell, wishing to preserve the land for their own offspring. However, he and his wife agreed that they were *Miseler*, 'Mosellians', and that they didn't want to move to another region. After having searched in vain on the Luxembourgish side of the river, Mr. Da Silva came across a plot of land in a German village where he was attending a colleague's birthday party. He fell in love with the place on the spot and bought the plot, which was located in a small residential area at the edge of the village, the next day.

Mr. Da Silva underscores the spontaneity of his decision, which was taken without him having previously considered moving to Germany and without him being aware of its pros and cons, e.g. the differences in taxes, municipal charges, etc. His spontaneous decision turned out to be a lucky one. He explains that looking back, he is more than happy that in Luxembourg people refused to sell their land to them because "I am definitely happier here […] my family is certainly happier here." According to him, A-Village is different from his home village in Luxembourg in that there is much more neighbourliness, helpfulness, and sociability.

Mr. Da Silva explains that he sees himself as a Luxembourger rather than as a Portuguese. At the same time, however, he feels at home in A-Village: "Sometimes I really feel as if I were born here, as if I were from here." He seems to have no problem reconciling these various relationships. After having explained that the village he lives in and the border region in general is, according to him, somehow part of Luxembourg, he concludes: "But I simply say: 'I am from here'".

3.2 Case II

Mr. and Mrs. Weber came to A-Village in 2008. When they decided to move across the border, they were in their mid-thirties and had already bought and elaborately renovated a house in the south of Luxembourg. Mr. Weber explains that they never once had the intention to leave the place where they lived, but then their shared hobby, namely horses, brought about their wish for a bit of land and a home where they could keep the animals themselves. Their search for something affordable brought them to Germany. In the middle of A-Village they found an old farmhouse that perfectly suited their needs, with stables, sheds, and sufficient pasture.

What the Webers described as a 'hobby' turned into much more than that once they arrived at their new home. By moving there, they opted for —or they found—a new way of life, with the animals being of central importance. "When you come home from work in the evening, it is like being on holiday," as Mrs. Weber puts it. Life in the village and their spare-time work with the animals especially has become an indispensable compensation for their stressful work in Luxembourg. As regards the future of their children, who are still small, their attitude resembles that of Mr. Da Silva. They will attend school in Germany, which is not self-evident, as many Luxembourgish parents living in the German borderland prefer to send their children to school in Luxembourg. For the Webers, this is not an option because, as Mrs. Weber explains: "Our future is in A-Village. We will not move back to Luxembourg."

At the same time, Mr. Weber points out that, historically speaking, there is no difference between Luxembourgers and the people of A-Village, that "they are all the same" anyway. "One can establish a border anywhere, but this doesn't mean that one changes the people." But he also admits that before moving to A-Village, they themselves were not aware of how similar they were to their new neighbors, for example as regards the linguistic closeness of the local variant of Moselle Franconian to Luxembourgish, which allows the Webers to speak Luxembourgish in A-Village. In a similar way to Mr. Da Silva, Mrs. Weber explains that they feel like they have been living in A-Village for thirty years already. "And this means that it is simply home"—a feeling they did not have to the same extent in their former place of residence in Luxembourg.

These brief presentations of two individual narratives show that moving to the other side of the national border is, in the first place, understood and legitimized by concrete practical reasons. The most elementary reason is given by Mr. Da Silva; he and his fiancée were in need of a place where they could take up residence independently of their parents. The Webers were, so to speak, looking for a place where they could take up residence with their horses. In other cases, the former home had become too small or too big, sometimes, e.g. after a divorce, also too expensive. However, our examples also show that these practical and rational motives are not the end of the story. To put it differently, they reveal that the move only just begins with taking up residence at the new place. Many interviewees clearly feel the need to legitimize the fact of living on the other side of the border in a more personal way, by explaining that they are now in the right place, whereas their former place of residence was, as it were, the wrong one. This relation is emphatically expressed by Mrs. Weber, who states that she feels more at home in the new place than she ever did in their former place in Luxembourg.

Mr. Da Silva and the Webers both describe themselves as having moved to a place where almost everything is different from their former residence in Luxembourg and from dwelling in Luxembourg in general, while they claim at the same time that they are still in a place that can be identified with Luxembourg. They describe this in clearly different ways. The Webers hint repeatedly at the common historico-cultural background between their former and their current place of residence and the ultimate irrelevance of the border—the people are the same, they speak a common language, and are of the one *Stamm* ('tribe'), as Mr. Weber expresses himself. Mr. Da Silva's notion is much more egocentric, being grounded in his own feelings of belonging—of belonging to a place that is part of Luxembourg although located on the other side of the national border.

To put it differently, the Webers and Mr. Da Silva have left Luxembourg without arriving in another country. This means, on the one hand, that the border has moved, so to speak, eastward. Luxembourg is virtually expanding—not as a state territory but as a region. A-Village and the whole German border region belong somehow to Luxembourg, as Mr. Da Silva claims, while Mr. Weber insists upon the historical and ethnic-cultural unity of the people by underlining that formerly, i.e. before the Congress of Vienna, the current border did not exist. In both cases, Luxembourg constitutes an essential part of the spatial and sociocultural entity that comes into being at the new place of residence. This new place makes it thus possible to stick to one's own Luxembourgish identity—in part even to revitalize it—as a regional identity. On the other hand, however, 'migration into the region' is often accompanied by a markedly critical attitude towards Luxembourg and the Luxembourgers. This critical view is already apparent in my brief presentation of the two cases. When Mr. Da Silva is enthusiastic about the openness and helpfulness of his neighbors and Mrs.

Weber talks about her intense feeling of home in A-Village, they tell us something about their former experiences—or, more precisely, about how they remember their former lives.

4. Memories of belonging and estrangement

As stated at the beginning, the growing significance of CBRS in European border regions is related to political changes and the ensuing structural economic developments. Building land is, roughly speaking, half as expensive on the German side of the Moselle as on the Luxembourgish side. Interviewees mention these price differences when talking about the decision to relocate across the national border but, in most cases, do not dwell on financial considerations. In their relocation stories, other reasons for moving and other circumstances are more prominent. Apart from detailed accounts of personal and familial incidents—divorce, illness, neighborhood conflicts—the interviews contain above all memories of the former place of residence and are thus rather 'place stories'[5]. These memories are, however, anything but nostalgic reminiscences of a lost home.

The migration story of the Webers is especially revealing in this respect. Their move across the border turned out to be a move into a new way of life, not only because of the rural surroundings and their spare-time work with their animals, but also because they quickly developed neighborly and social relations of an intensity that they found, in retrospect, deplorably absent in their native Luxembourg. The Webers describe this transformation also, and above all, by comparing their new house to the old one. While the renovation and styling of their first house was done with the utmost commitment and precision—in the 'Luxembourg mode', as they say—in A-Village they confined themselves to the necessities. Here they can, as they put it, live up to their own needs and are no longer under pressure to meet the expectations of others.

The story of the Webers is typical insofar as complaints about the excessive materialism reigning nowadays in Luxembourg were almost commonplace among our Luxembourgish interviewees—a materialism that is felt as a social compulsion to keep pace with or, better still, to outdo one's neighbors in competitive conspicuous consumption. Their story is, however, also typical in that their explicit dissociation from life in their former home goes along

5 On the importance of place stories in migration research and on the related concept of geographical identification or 'idiotopy' (cf. Pascual-de-Sans 2004).

with a strong desire to identify with a new home that stretches across the border and includes Luxembourg. The drastic descriptions of different lifestyles and forms of social intercourse go hand in hand with the claim that the people are the same on either side of the border and that, irrespective of the border, there is a fundamental unity. Like Mr. Weber, some of the interviewees underlined this assertion by hinting at the fact that most of the German border villages in question were part of the Duchy of Luxembourg until 1815. More importantly, however, the notion of unity was embedded in memories of arriving and settling down in the new village, that is, in recent experiences of unexpected familiarity and feelings of belonging, experiences which in certain cases were expressly associated with childhood memories and idyllic notions of life in the Luxembourg of former times.

What do stories such as this tell us about the importance of memories for place-making? In recent years, there has been quite some work on the relationship between memory and migration, and approaches which try to differentiate between various forms and functions of nostalgia. An example is Hage's work on Lebanese migrants in Australia, where he defines nostalgia as one part of the process of homebuilding in which intimations of lost homelands that—along with intimations of new homelands—trigger memories are "affective building blocks used by the migrants to make themselves feel at home where they actually are" (2010, p. 419). In our case, these intimation-triggered memories of the former home are almost universally negative. The Luxembourgish interviewees reminisce about the increasing materialism in their country, about social coldness, lack of openness, and the demise of neighborly relations. Another of these almost ubiquitous memories of life back home is that of being prevented from using one's native tongue, Luxembourgish, in everyday life by non-Luxembourgish waiters, shop employees, medical staff, etc., who rudely insist upon being spoken to in French. In the German borderland, the migrants are pleasantly surprised to find that they are welcome to speak Luxembourgish.

Our interviewees thus tell about the loss of home—loss not in the sense that home was left behind but in the sense that it has changed and is no longer familiar. Or, in Hage's words: because it no longer triggers memories that help the migrants feel at home in the present. This altered place has sharp contours when regarded from the other side of the border. In her study on migrants from former Yugoslavia, Spela Drnovšek Zorko describes what she calls 'methodologies of migrant memory', meaning by that "a space of possibility for seeing differently that is provoked by encounters between memories of homing" (2016, p. 92). This 'seeing differently', she further notes, can bring about memories of a past home that does not emerge as homely and easily inhabited, memories of a home that has become strange, or even brings about, as in the Luxemburgish example, clearly negative memories (Drnovšek Zorko 2016, p. 88ff.).

While Drnovšek Zorko proposes a sensory perspective on these memories, understanding home as embodied by sense-memory (Drnovšek Zorko 2016, p. 84ff.), our examples suggest a different, more elementary approach. Here, memories are clearly related to doings, i.e. to the practices of place-making. The case of the Webers is particularly revealing because they describe their encounter with memories of homemaking in the literal sense, i.e. of building or creating a physical home. But the same holds true for non-material domains of everyday life, such as, for example, neighborly contact and linguistic interactions. By recounting and more or less explicitly comparing these practices and habits, the migrants 'give shape' to their place of belonging.

5. Conclusion

As claimed at the beginning, cross-border residential moves are a particular kind of migration, particular not only as regards individual border experiences and issues of belonging, but also in view of more encompassing processes of identification and place-making. Strikingly, our Luxembourgish interviewees hardly ever mentioned Germany and the Germans, neither when looking back at their decision to move abroad nor when recounting their experiences at their new place of residence in Germany. Their move thus does not seem to lead from their home country into another country, but from a country into another entity. For convenience, I propose calling this entity 'region'.

'Region' designates a multiplicity of socio-spatial entities. It comes into being—or rather shows itself as a possibility—no less in the small village of A-Village than in the transborder region called 'Moselle' and in the Greater Region. The realization of this space resides in individual acts of identification and experiences of belonging that are 'nourished' by memories of home, by a nostalgia which enables to feel at home in the present and to look forward to the future.

While this feeling at home is no longer produced by the memories relating to the former dwelling place in Luxembourg, it is apparent in the memories of arriving in the new place: memories of being encouraged to speak Luxembourgish at the local bakery, of being welcomed by friendly neighbors, and being invited to assume customary social obligations. To put it briefly, by memories of being fully able and accepted to engage in all kinds of local relationships.

The stories of our interviewees contain different kinds of memories of home, different not only in the sense that they are positive or negative, but also in the sense that they exhibit different temporalities. Their accounts of their former home are about recent changes that foster feelings of estrangement and strong impulses to dissociate. Their memories of their current place of residence, on the other hand, refer to the retrieval of elements from an undefined past and to timeless familiarity. They are the 'antidote' to the estrangement that accompanies their memories of transformation, in that they enable the creation of a space of belonging that comprises Luxembourg —albeit a Luxembourg different from that which they have just left behind. This homely Luxembourg is not confined to the past, but as part of the region it lives on in the present and is projected into the future.

References

Bissel, David (2013): Pointless Mobilities: Rethinking Proximity through the Loops of Neighbourhood. In: Mobilities 8, no. 3, p. 349–367.

Boesen, Elisabeth (2015): Wohnen jenseits der Mosel. Zur 'Wohnmigration' zwischen Luxemburg und dem deutschen Grenzraum. In: Forum 356, p. 8–11.

Boesen, Elisabeth/Nienaber, Birte/Roos, Ursula/Schnuer, Gregor/Wille, Christian (2015): Phantomgrenzen im Kontext grenzüberschreitender Wohnmigration. Das Beispiel des deutsch-luxemburgischen Grenzraums. In: Europa Regional 22, no. 3–4, p. 114–128.

Carpentier, Samuel (2010): La mobilité résidentielle transfrontalier entre le Luxembourg et ses régions voisines. Luxemburg: Editions Saint Paul.

Cresswell, Tim (2006): On the Move. Mobility in the Modern Western World. Oxford: Routledge.

Casey, Edward S. (1997): The Fate of Place. A Philosophical History. Berkeley: University of California Press.

Casey, Edward S. (2001): Body, Self and Landscape: A Geophilosophical Inquiry into the Place-World. In: Adams, P. C./Hoelscher, S. D./Till, K. E. (eds.): Textures of Place: Exploring Humanist Geographies. Minneapolis: University of Minnesota Press, p. 403–425.

Drnovšek Zorko, Spela (2016): See(m)ing Strange: Methodologies of Memory and Home. Crossings. In: Journal of Migration & Culture 7, no. 1, p. 81–95.

Gerber, Philippe/Carpentier, Samuel (2013): Impacts de la mobilité résidentielle transfrontalière sur les espaces de la vie quotidienne d'individus actifs du Luxembourg. In: Economie et Statistique, INSEE, p. 77–96.

Ingold, Tim (2000): The Perception of the Environment. Essays on Livelihood, Dwelling and Skill. London: Routledge.

Hage, Ghassan (2010): Migration, Food, Memory and Home-Building. In: Radstone, S./Schwarz, B. (eds.): Memory, History, Theories, Debates. New York: Fordham University Press, p. 416–427.

Hardwick, Susan W./Mansfield, Ginger (2009): Discourse, Identity, and "Homeland as Other" at the Borderlands. In: Annals of the Association of American Geographers 99, no. 2, p. 383–405.

Harvey, D. (1996): Justice, Nature and the Geography of Difference. Massachusetts: Blackwell Publishers, p. 210–247.

Jagodic, Devan (2012): Living (beyond) the Border: European Integration Processes and Cross-border Residential Mobility in the Italian–Slovenian Border Area. In Jagetic Andersen, D./Klatt, M./Sandberg, M. (eds.): The Border Multiple. The Practicing of Borders between Public Policy and Everyday Life. Farnham: Ashgate, p. 201–218.

Kaufmann, Vincent (1999): Mobilité et vie quotidienne: synthèse et questions de recherche. In: 2001 Plus, no. 48, p. 1–64.

Klatt, Martin (2014): (Un)familiarity? Labor related Cross-Border Mobility in Sonderjylland/Schleswig since Denmark joined the EU in 1973. In: Journal of Borderland Studies 29, vol. 3, p. 353–373.

Lannoy, Pierre/Ramadier, Thierry (2007): La mobilité généralisée: formes et valeurs de la mobilité quotidienne. Louvain-la-Neuve: Editions Académia-Bruylant.

Martinez, Oscar J. (1994): The Dynamics of Border Interaction. New Approaches to Border Analysis. In: Schofield, C. H. (ed.): World Boundaries, Vol. 1: Global Boundaries. London: Routledge, p. 1–15.

Memory Studies, Special Issue on Nostalgia (2010): Memory Studies 3(3).

Minghi, Julian V. (1991): From Conflict to Harmony in Border Landscapes. In: Rumley, D./Minghi, J. V. (eds.): The Geography of Border Landscapes. London: Routledge, p. 15–30.

Pascual-de-Sans, Àngels (2004): Sense of Place and Migration Histories. *Idiotopy* and *Idiotope*. In: Area 36, no. 4, p. 348–357.

Reichert-Schick, Anja (2017): *Rural Gentrification* an der Obermosel? Eine Fallstudie zu internationaler Wohnmigration und den Herausforderungen für die Dorfentwicklung. In: Europa Regional 24, p. 77–94.

Rolshoven, Johanna (2009): Kultur-Bewegungen. Multilokalität als Lebensweise. In: Österreichische Zeitschrift für Volkskunde 63, no. 3, p. 285–303.

Schnuer, Gregor (2014): Circulating in places and the spatial order of everyday life. Human Studies 37, no. 4, p. 545–557.

STATEC (2018): Luxemburg in Zahlen. Luxemburg: STATEC, https://bit.ly/2yC9Ekt [Access: 19/102018].

Stock, Mathis (2009): Polytopisches Wohnen. Ein phänomenologisch-prozessorientierter Zugang. In: Informationen zur Raumentwicklung, no. 1–2, p. 107–116.

Strüver, Antje (2005): Spheres of Transnationalism within the European Union: On Open Doors, Thresholds and Drawbridges along the Dutch–German Border. In: Journal of Ethnic and Migration Studies 31, no. 2, p. 323–343.

Thrift, Nigel (1994): Inhuman geographies: Landscapes of speed, light and power. In: Cloke, P./Doel, M./Matless, D. (eds.): Writing the Rural: Five Cultural Geographies. London: Paul Chapman, p. 191–248.

Van der Velde, Martin (2012): Boring European Borders?! Integration and Mobility across Borders. In: Eurasia Border Review 3, p. 115–126.

Van Houtum, Henk/van der Velde, Martin (2004): The Power of Cross-Border Labour Market immobility. In: Tijdschrift voor economische en sociale Geografie 95, no.1, p. 100–107.

Van Houtum, Henk/Eker, Mark (2015), Redesigning Borderlands: Using the Janus-Face of Borders as a Resource. In: Brambilla C./Laine, J./Bocchhi, G. (eds.): Borderscaping: Imagination and Practices of Border Making. London: Ashgate, p. 41–51.

Van Houtum, Henk/Gielis, Rubin (2006): Elastic Migration: The Case of Dutch Short-Distance Migration in Belgian and German Borderlands. In: Tijdschrift voor economische en sociale geographie 97, no. 2, p. 195–202.

Weichhart, Peter (2015): Multi-Local Living Arrangements—Terminology Issues. In: Weichhart, P./Rumpolt, P. A. (eds.): Mobil und doppelt sesshaft. Studien zur residenziellen Multilokalität. Abhandlungen zur Geographie und Regionalforschung 18. Wien: Institut für Geographie und Regionalforschung der Universität Wien, p. 61–82.

Wille, Christian (ed.) (2015): Lebenswirklichkeiten und politische Konstruktionen in Grenzregionen. Das Beispiel der Großregion SaarLorLux: Wirtschaft – Politik – Alltag – Kultur. Bielefeld: Transcript.

Wille, Christian/Schnuer, Gregor/Boesen, Elisabeth (2014): Beyond Luxembourg. Raum- und Identitätskonstruktionen im Kontext grenzüberschreitender Wohnmigration. In Wille, C./Reckinger, R./Kmec, S./Hesse, M. (eds.): Räume und Identitäten in Grenzregionen. Politiken – Medien – Subjekte. Bielefeld: Transcript, p. 333–346.

About the author

Elisabeth Boesen | University of Luxembourg | Campus Belval, Maison des Sciences Humaines | UR IPSE / Institut d'Histoire | 11, Porte des Sciences | 4366 Esch-sur-Alzette | Luxembourg | T +352 46 66 44 6350 | elisabeth.boesen@uni.lu

Elisabeth Boesen is a senior researcher at the Institute for History at the University of Luxembourg. Prior to this, she worked at the University of Bayreuth, the Ludwig-Maximilians University in Munich and the Centre for Modern Oriental Studies in Berlin. She holds a Ph.D. in cultural anthropology from the University of Bayreuth. Her work centers on issues of spatial mobility and rural change in the West African Sahel, where she did fieldwork among nomadic pastoralists, and in the Greater Region SaarLorLux. Currently her research centers on mobility and dwelling in cross-border regions and on immigration from Lusophone countries to the Grand Duchy of Luxembourg and the Greater Region.

Epistemic border struggles: exposing, legitimizing, and diversifying border knowledge at a security conference

Dominik Gerst

Abstract

In this chapter, a concept of border knowledge is introduced. After an overview of the relationship between borders and knowledge within border studies and beyond, an ethnomethodological and conversation analytical perspective is deployed. Raising the question of how border knowledge in action is used as a resource to articulate border experiences and thus deal with border complexity, this chapter conducts an analysis of the epistemic border struggles at the border event *Security Conference: Eight years of an open German–Polish border. An inventory* shows how border knowledge is exposed, legitimized, and diversified. The chapter closes with a characterization of border knowledge, highlighting its multi-perspectival and processual features.

Keywords

Border knowledge, German–Polish border, membership categorization analysis, border security

1. Introduction

This chapter focuses on a concept of *border knowledge* and a perspective on the relationship between borders and knowledge in general. It brings together results from two independent yet intertwining arguments regarding contemporary border research. On the one hand, a lack of discussion about the epistemic dimension of borders is identified. Even though theoretical and conceptual developments, e.g. *borderwork* (cf. Rumford 2008), *bordering practices* (cf. Parker/Adler-Nissen 2014), *borderscapes* (cf. Brambilla et al. 2016) *border complexities* (cf. Gerst et al. 2018), or *border textures* (cf. AG Bordertexturen 2018) implicitly refer to the connection between borders and knowledge, a conceptual explication is still desirable. On the other hand, empirical accounts of border experiences regularly deal with questions about what people know about borders and how this knowledge is produced and used under different circumstances, regardless of methodology and method of elicitation. But surprisingly, hardly any study treats these "data" as knowledge in its own right, as a border-related epistemic phenomenon. Border knowledge is "seen but unnoticed" (Garfinkel 1967, p. 118) and consequently does not get much attention in contemporary border studies.

Therefore, this chapter seeks to contribute to exploring this gap in three steps. It starts with a cursory overview of how the relationship between borders and knowledge has been grasped within border studies and beyond. Section 2 culminates in a call for a fine-grained analysis of the varied ways in which border knowledge is made relevant situationally. In section 3, a perspective informed by ethnomethodology and conversation analysis is deployed. It suggests taking peoples' own reasoning about borders seriously, which means being sensitive toward the methodical articulation of border knowledge performed through categorial ordering work in interaction. This perspective resonates with methodological considerations, which on the one hand call for analysis based on the actual "borderliness" of border phenomena, and on the other hand center on the question of how border complexity is accomplished in practice. The section prepares for an analysis of the border event *Security conference: Eight years of an open German–Polish border. An inventory*. In section 4, I will show how the panel discussion of border security experts becomes an arena for epistemic border struggles. As the event evolves, those taking part in the discussion constantly negotiate what a border is and how it works, how different perspectives on that border are bound to different membership categories, and how these are connected to specific knowledge resources and forms of articulation. My analysis will concentrate on three dimensions of border knowledge: first, how the exposition of border knowledge is performed via an essentializing account; second, how the legitimization of border knowledge is connected to epistemic authority and the negotiation of membership categories such as *expert;* and finally, how the diversification of two conflicting knowledge repertoires—namely *objective security situation* and *subjective feeling of safety*—is established. The chapter will conclude in section 5 with a sketch of a concept of border knowledge that highlights the multiperspectival and processual characteristics of border-related knowledge in action.

2. *Knowledge in border studies (and beyond)*

In this section, I want to discuss conceptual approaches to the relationship between borders and knowledge, a relationship which is fundamental, since borders have an epistemic characteristic *per se*, as Vasilache (2007) shows. Thinking *about* borders is always about simultaneously thinking *in* borders. Borders are horizons, to use another metaphor, separating the known from the unknown and/or imagined, just as they separate and connect different knowledge systems. To describe marginalized knowledge "outside of the cultural mainstream" (Rhoades 1995, p. 8), a concept of *border knowledge* has been introduced in education studies by Rhoades. In his understanding, "border knowledge is most often embraced by those situated on society's margins of race, class, gender, age, and sexual orientation" (*ibid.*, p. i). This metaphorical use of *border* designating a certain kind of knowledge which is located beyond society's cultural boundaries resonates with Mignolo and Tlostanova's (2006) concept of "border epistemology", which carries a critique of Eurocentrism and the totalization of Western epistemology. Mignolo (2002) claims that our knowledge rests on "colonial difference" and therefore has to be historicized for us to gain an understanding of how alternative knowledge is made invisible, in order to open up the possibility of making it productive. This idea of "geopolitics of knowledge" then leads to the perspective of *border thinking*, which is "the epistemology of the exteriority; that is, of the outside created from the inside; and as such, it is always a decolonial project" (Mignolo/Tlostanova 2006, p. 206). While on the one hand *border* in this understanding is mostly used as a metaphor to describe epistemic exteriority, on the other hand it carries the important note that contemporary political borders not only have a geographical but also an epistemic dimension.

Aside from metaphorical understandings of border knowledge and critical approaches to the epistemic dimension of borders, Li and Scullion (2006) analyze multinational corporations managing knowledge of highly geographically and culturally dispersed sources. Following the question of "how [...] knowledge acquisition, transfer and integration processes can be operationalized" (*ibid.*, p. 73) in specific settings across borders, they investigate "cross-border knowledge holders"—individuals or groups that possess information, experience, or understanding—on a micro level. Thus, they show how the transfer of cross-border knowledge needs to bridge distances in a geographical, institutional, and cultural sense. In a similar vein, research on cross-border cooperation has developed an interest in knowledge transfer across borders as part of ongoing regionalization and European integration processes. Miörner et al. (2017) analyze "cross-border knowledge flows" linked to innovation policies, while stating that bridging epistemic barriers produces "many beneficial outcomes, ranging from new combinations of knowledge and competencies to complementarities and synergies that could be capitalized on through such linkages" (*ibid.*, p. 2). In their understanding, the flow of cross-border knowledge is facilitated through practices such as buying patents, building innovation partnerships, increasing labor and student mobility, and others.

Especially since the *practice turn* (cf. Schatzki et al. 2001) entered border studies and related fields, knowledge has increasingly become a topic in theorizing borders. While most of the literature about bordering and bordering practices conceals the role of knowledge in these processes (cf. Newman 2006), Wille (2015) explicitly refers to the practical knowledge at the heart of an analysis of "spaces of the border" via practices such as commuting. Against an essentialist understanding of knowledge, which e.g. characterizes the interest in cross-border knowledge flows discussed above, he claims that

> it is not knowledge as a feature of cross-border commutings [sic] or a spatial range of validity for specific knowledge structures either side of a national border that is the central question here, but rather which knowledge can take effect, be actualised and produced or reconstructed in social practices (*ibid.*, p. 66).

In line with this situational understanding of knowledge, Baird (2017) investigates how knowledge of security practices is produced, shared, and consumed at security fairs. Replying to Frowd's (2014, p. 230) statement that "there is very little work explicitly theorizing tacit or overt knowledges of border control", knowledge in his view is conceptualized as "the routinized rationalities, logics, and norms practiced while working as an (in)security professional […] an expression of constructed cultures of border security" (Baird 2017, p. 2). In his event on ethnography, he emphasizes the situated relevance of knowledge of practice in highly commercialized and geographically dispersed fairs, and concludes that "border security consists of contradictory practices and knowledges that, rather than being resisted, are reproduced through commercialized events" (*ibid.*, p. 14).

Finally, another strand of border research focusing on the discursive and narrative construction of borders has gained insights into the variability of meaning-making in the context of borders. While only implicitly explicating the links between meaning, sense, perception, and knowledge, narrative accounts of borders, for example, deal with the lexical specifics of *border talk* (cf. Pickering 2006), *border rhetoric* (cf. DeChaine 2012), ways of articulating border change (cf. Laube/Roos 2010), and in general people's "way of making sense of their border-related social world" (Doevenspeck 2011, p. 129). In her examination of border narratives in the US press, Pickering (2006, p. 45) notes:

> How that border is narrated in public discourse [...] tells us how we routinely inscribe borders with meaning that serve to reinforce particular border imaginations [...]. Borders are performed to multiple audiences and produce not only a range of words, languages and codes to communicate their location and function, but also the border itself.

She concludes that border narratives are partly contradictory and partly concur, and thus their simultaneous existence legitimizes a state's policing practices. Her lexical analysis stands out especially because she can show how narratives can be analyzed as organized ways of producing, circulating, and thus implementing knowledge about borders and related phenomena. In a similar vein, Meinhof and Galasinski (2002, p. 78–79) deal with cross-generational constructions of identity in the German–Polish borderland, and formulate an interest in "the complex and fluid ways in which people construct and confirm identifications at discursive level through the lexico-grammatical choices that they make in talking and narrating themselves". They hence examine self- and other-categorizations and emphasize that using collective identity categories across a range of scalar possibilities depends on border-related contextual specifics as well as the researchers' methods of eliciting narrative accounts.

The concepts reviewed thus show how the relationship between borders and knowledge is discussed in border studies and beyond. They raise awareness of how the epistemic dimension of borders is crucial, even if they follow a transcending understanding of *border* which is either metaphorical or underdeveloped, or essentializes in highlighting the process of crossing a border. By contrast, recent border studies focusing on bordering practices as well as border-related narratives and discourses offer conceptual suggestions, which specify an interest in borders as subjects in their own right and which can be made useful, as they highlight the practical and thus situational conditions under which border knowledge is made relevant. Against this background, in the following I will suggest an analytic perspective that grounds border knowledge in specific border phenomena. Therefore, I adopt a sociological perspective to shed light on the detailed ways in which border knowledge is situationally established and dealt with.

3. *Investigating border knowledge: methodological remarks*

To shed light on situated border knowledge, I follow a perspective that can be described as a sociology of knowledge, mainly influenced by ethnomethodology (EM) and conversation analysis (CA). EM, according to Garfinkel (1967, p. vii f.), is interested in

> learning how members' actual, ordinary activities consist of methods to make practical actions, practical circumstances, common sense knowledge of social structures, and practical sociological reasoning analyzable, and of discovering the formal properties of commonplace, practical common sense actions, "from within" actual settings, as ongoing accomplishments of those settings.

CA brings this interest to the field of social interaction and seeks to identify the doings that constitute interaction *in situ*. Whereas CA has developed into a somehow technical discipline with an interest in the "machinery" of interaction (Sacks 1992), another stock of research—rooted in the beginnings of CA—labeled "membership categorization analysis" (MCA) deals with the interactional categorial ordering work that is done by members of society in the mundane business of sense-making of the world. According to Housley/Fitzgerald (2015, p. 3), "[t]his focus on the use of routine ordinary common-sense knowledge to competently navigate society [is] to be found in people's descriptions of their social world."

Thus, if we follow a line of research in border studies that is interested in *border interactions* (cf. Martínez 1994) and the everyday relevance of borders and the ways people deal with them (cf. Jones/Johnson 2014), descriptions of borders are understood first and foremost as members' phenomena (cf. Francis/Hester 2004), and any analysis must show how accounting for a border is achieved in practice. MCA is thus not a fully elaborated methodology, but rather an "analytic mentality" (Hester/Eglin 1997, p.1) toward the fine-grained specifics of "taken-for-granted knowledge-in-action" (Fitzgerald 2012, p. 305). This praxeological approach points out that practical knowledge embraces both a *knowing that* and a *knowing how* (cf. Ryle 1945). An analysis that follows this argumentation goes beyond a content analysis, in that it is interested in the methodical use of border knowledge, that is, its characteristic of being grounded in border-related common sense and its situational relevance. In this way, it matches all the requirements for a methodology that is appropriate for the subject of borders, which, according to Mezzadra and Neilson (2013, p. 7–8) should be sensitive toward "situation[s] where many different knowledge regimes and practices come into conflict," which "involves negotiating the boundaries between the different kinds of knowledge that come to bear on the border".

A research strategy that is sensitive toward border knowledge and its characteristics may be oriented toward methodological principles formulated to guide qualitative border research (cf. Gerst/Krämer 2017). The first principle suggests "think[ing] from the border" when carrying out border research. Such a position is directed against two opposing yet recurrent tendencies in border studies and related fields, whose methodological consequences have not been fully reflected on: on the one hand, *borderism*, which describes a tendency to relate various phenomena with borders without showing how exactly this relationship is established and where the border comes in—voiced prominently in Balibar's (2004) famous phrase "borders are everywhere." On the other hand, a perspective of *borderlessness*, which states that borders have lost their significance—as proposed in the "borderless world" paradigm (cf. Ohmae 1990)—or should be seen as a secondary phenomenon of wider social processes. Thinking from the border demands an analysis that starts with the concreteness of a border and how it is made relevant, thereby being able to show the processual *borderliness* of a phenomenon, along with its conditions and consequences. A second principle suggests focusing on the ordering effects of borders. Borders are complex phenomena as they gather different dimensions, elements, actors, practices, and discourses (cf. Gerst et al. 2018). From the vantage point of border knowledge, this complexity produces and is the product of specific orders of knowledge, as a border is the place and time where these are put into some kind of epistemic contact situation, as Amilhat-Szary and Giraut (2015, p. 1) note:

> While knowledge about borders is growing steadily, their constant evolution invites scholars and practitioners alike to continue to revise ideas about what they represent for us and what they do to our lives.

And most strikingly, borders facilitate negotiations about what counts as border knowledge. Taken together, these methodological considerations converge in a situated understanding of borders and articulations of border knowledge.

In the following, I will turn to the case at hand: the *Security Conference: Eight years of an open German–Polish border. An inventory* and, in doing so, will thereby follow Radu's (2010, p. 410) insight that "borders as processes involve a diversity of actors, practices and discourses that can be [...] better grasped through events." I will illustrate the situational occurrence and organization of border knowledge in what can be characterized as a *border event* (cf. Radu 2010), while a perspective focusing on the epistemic dimension might describe the processes constituting this border event as ongoing engagement in an *epistemic border struggle*. Mezzadra and Neilson (2013) coined the term *border struggle* to refer to a border's capacity to provoke the articulation of the border, thereby producing multiple subjective positions and thus viewpoints on borders. While the concept of border struggle seems appealing as it centers on negotiations and positionalities, I want to diverge slightly from this understanding. Instead of making it a *political* question and thus emphasizing the production of political subjectivities through these struggles, I want to make it a *sociological* question and ask for the social organization of knowledge resources and interactional settings in the course of struggles concerning the reality of borders.

4. Dimensions of border knowledge: exposition, legitimization, diversification

In February 2016, the youth organization of a German political party organized a public event, which was announced as a *Security Conference*, bringing together five experts on a podium to discuss the topic *Eight years of open German–Polish border. An inventory*. An auditorium of about thirty people followed the discussions, which took place in the German part of a twin city (cf. Joenniemi/Jańczak 2017) located on the German–Polish border. Security-related issues of border crime, matters of urban security in the border region, the development of crime rates, the establishment of cross-border cooperation in the field of security, and the visibility of border controls were discussed—issues that are a constant topic of public discussion in the border region. While border scholars have long emphasized that matters of security are central to understanding historical as well as contemporary border formations (cf. Brunet-Jailly 2007; Côté-Boucher et al. 2014), this is especially true of the German–Polish border, whose complexity is centrally built around matters of security and related aspects such as economic disparities (cf. Schwell 2008).

The event was announced as an *inventory* or a *retrospective*, tracing the developments since and the effects of Poland's accession to the Schengen Agreement and thus the opening of the German–Polish border in 2007. Until Poland joined the European Union in 2004 as part of the eastward enlargement of the EU, the German–Polish border marked an EU external border, characterized by a strict border regime. When Poland became an EU member state, the border transformed into an internal border, which indeed increased its permeability. But it was only Poland's accession to the Schengen Agreement that brought about the abolition of border controls and free movement between Poland and Germany. At that time, public discussion was divided. While on the one hand the opening of the border was seen as opening up economic, social, and political possibilities, on the other hand it was said to increase danger and threat (cf. Buraczynski 2015). Setting up this specific spatiotemporal frame, stretching from the historical turning point to the present, the participants were engaged in collaboratively "doing history" (Willner et al. 2016) of the border, as experts and the public were brought together to share, discuss, and confront perspectives about *how things have evolved*. Thus, this border event forms part of a public discourse, which contributes to a common-sense understanding of what the border is and was, and how it should be characterized.

The event was clearly processual (cf. Deppermann/Günthner 2015). The *interaction order* (cf. Goffman 1983) of the security conference showed a structure that opened up specifically designed slots, which shaped *what* could be said about the border, *how*, and *at which point in the event*. Five *experts* were invited to share their experiences and perspectives: a member from the administration of the university where the event took place, the former mayor of the border town, a local prosecutor, a representative of the state office of criminal investigations, and a local politician. Finally, an auditorium of *visitors* followed the discussions. While they remained silent listeners most of the time, they got the chance to direct questions to the experts toward the end of the event. Their mostly passive co-presence made the security conference a *public event*, this public character ensuring linkages to a general discourse about the topics discussed. As I will demonstrate, these speaker identities articulated knowledge resources which are category-bound and which are built upon different visions of the border; as Laine and Tervonen (2015, p. 66) conclude: "the same border may look simultaneously very different and be given different value at different contexts, different levels sectors, and by different actors. The border is not one but many." As I will show, these visions are brought into a—sometimes conflictual—contact situation.

In general, the event took two-and-a-half hours and had a structure that was announced by the moderator at the beginning and collaboratively implemented by all participants over the course of the event (cf. Meyer 2014). After an introduction from the moderator, the experts introduced themselves by stating their professional border-related background, thus legitimizing their expert status. Thereupon, all experts gave short statements, responding to the main theme of the event and the slogan *economy top, security flop*, which the moderator had introduced in his opening sequence. This was followed by rounds of questions, consisting of question-and-answer sequences between the moderator and each expert. The questions were designed in such a way as to tease out the very specific perspective of every expert. At the end, the audience asked their questions, before the moderator closed the event. In general, the speeches by the participants were rather monologic compared to everyday conversations. This might be seen as one of the genre's affordances, as the podium discussion sought to create a space for accounts of the border, which meant shared anecdotes and unfolding perspectives, as well as displaying epistemic authority (cf. Patrona 2012).

4.1 Exposition of border knowledge: the methodical essentialization of the border and why security matters

The security conference revolved around the question of how the accession of Poland to the Schengen Agreement affected the German–Polish border especially regarding matters of security. Such an undertaking requires participants to either reach an implicit understanding or to expose an explicit articulation of accounts that tackle the question of what the border basically *is*. Considering this as an interactional problem, the variable indexicality of *the border* itself and the various ways in which it could be made sense of becomes a major concern. In the analysis of the following extract, I want to show how one of the expert participants—a state prosecutor, working at an office of public prosecution at the German–Polish border—makes sense of the border in a way that is common to the institution he works for and the public discourse around the relationship between economic disparities between the two countries and phenomena of border crime. In doing so, on the one hand he meets the interactional requirement imposed by the moderator of responding to the slogan *economy top, security flop* and to deal with the question of *where the priorities lie* and *what can be said about them from a security-related viewpoint*. On the other hand, the prosecutor meets the requirement of formulating a workable understanding of the border and thus reduces its basic complexity.

Extract 1: The border to Poland is still a prosperity gap

State prosecutor:

Economy top, security flop, provocative sentence. Maybe it
looks like this: the border to Poland is still a prosperity gap. In
recent years this has been leveled, but this prosperity gap
is a fact and as long as this prosperity gap is there, a certain
kind of border crime will always be there. Two months ago, I
was in the Netherlands, in Belgium, and Luxembourg and at the

prosecution in Aachen, and I looked around at how they deal with border crime. And you won't believe it, but I can say that basically these border states have the same worries as we have. A colleague from Luxembourg said to me: "We have a prosperity gap with France, in Luxembourg we have domestic burglaries committed by French gangs, we have car thefts by French and domestic perpetrators." That means if you live in a border region which is characterized by a prosperity gap relative to its neighbors, you will have to live with a higher level of crime; that is the sober truth in my opinion.

In the extract, we can see how the prosecutor performs a fundamental equation, that of the border *being* a prosperity gap (2). The verbal form is remarkable here as it carries an ontological description of the border: neither does the border mark, represent, or stand for a prosperity gap, it *is* this principle of economic disparities, regardless of academic accounts which either promote the diagnosis of a prosperity gap or consider such a characterization inappropriate[1]. The speaker wraps his account of the border in a temporal account, which describes a process of slight *leveling* (3), stating that the prosperity gap is *still* relevant and as such characterized as a *fact* (4). As I will elaborate on a little more in the third part of this section, in the course of the security conference, the security professionals in particular, the prosecutor being one of them, emphasized that *facts* are the main basis for their action. Facts are data-driven, assured knowledge that both states truth and makes reality workable for professionals (see extract 5). Here, it is used to *essentialize* the economic dimension of the border: Sohn (2016, p. 183) emphasizes that the term *border* frequently carries a "reduced understanding" that is "akin to a synecdoche, a figure of speech in which a part is used for the whole or the whole for a part". In a similar vein, Haselsberger (2014, p. 6) suggests conceptualizing *the border* as a unique arrangement of boundaries, which demarcate single facets of the border. She claims that borders become decodable by understanding them as aggregated "boundary sets". In the extract, we can see how this reduction of the border is made productive under practical circumstances. Although in the field of cross-border security, the border can *be* various kinds

1 A close examination of the literature on this subject suggests that the diagnosis of a prosperity gap is crucial for discourses related to matters of security, while it is relativized in economic interrelations (e.g. Blaneck 2005, p. 46). This points to the multiperspectival character of borders: different (cross-)border motifs produce and are built on different forms of common sense and knowledge.

of demarcations (e.g. a *language barrier*, a *legal limitation, a spatial area*), following the slogan of the conference, the prosecutor makes the economic boundary relevant as part of a complex boundary set called the German–Polish border. In terms of conversation analysis, this act of *preference organization* (cf. Bilmes 1988) not only structures the conversational flow, as the other participants have to react to this characterization of the border, but opens a unique semantic field, or area of knowledge, which becomes specified when the prosecutor strongly connects the existence of a prosperity gap with phenomena of border crime. Strikingly, border crime is presented as causally connected to the prosperity gap (if a then b), as its existence is bound to the persistence of economic disparities (4–5). The explication of this account is performed as a proof procedure when the prosecutor reports a visit to the borders between the Netherlands, Belgium, Luxembourg, France, and Germany, and thereby strengthens the established connection, claiming that *these border states have the same worries as we have* (9). The inserted sequence contains the *look around*-experiences (7) of the prosecutor and the quoted speech of a colleague from Luxembourg, and leads to an epistemic transformation of the connection between economics and border crime: from a current *fact*—which characterizes the temporally marked (*still, as long as*) state of the German–Polish border—to a generalized *sober truth* (16) that holds for all border regions characterized by a prosperity gap.

To sum up, the extract exemplifies how methodically achieved knowledge in action about what the German–Polish border is is designed to fulfill interactional as well as epistemic requirements. The border is essentialized regarding its economic dimension, and thereby the connection between economics and security is established. In the next part, I will demonstrate that accounting for the border under these conditions evokes the necessity to explicitly negotiate expert status.

4.2 Legitimization of border knowledge: negotiating expert status

Even though this was not an explicitly formulated topic, the constellation of participants and the process of discussions made it necessary for epistemic authority to be constantly displayed and negotiated throughout the whole security conference. The event was characterized by a *participant framework* (cf. Goffman 1981) that was built around three membership categories. The *moderator* guided the discussions as he constantly initiated question-and-answer sequences tailored to the *experts*. He thereby asked for and enabled the unfolding of diverse perspectives that were bound to specific stocks of border knowledge. On the one hand, these were placed on a socio-spatial scale, for example when he addressed single discussion participants to speak about the *Brandenburgian perspective* or the *communal viewpoint*. On the other hand, *professional status* was used to initiate articulations of professional viewpoints. As we will see, expert status is not a stable attribute which motivates fixed categorization, but is subject to negotiation. In the opening remarks, the moderator addressed all the participants as *experts*, a membership category which is built around a differentiation between members based on topically oriented knowledge resources that they can or do draw on—or cannot draw on, which would make them *laypersons* (cf. Hitzler et al. 1994). As Mondada (2013, p. 598) pointed out, "epistemic authority can be challenged, competed with and negotiated in a flexible way within situated activities and evolving sequential contexts." This holds true for the security conference: the participants acted differently in response to the categorization by the moderator, which led to the display and negotiation of *epistemic status* and *epistemic stance* (cf. Heritage 2012) and—as I will show in the last part of this section—a diversification of knowledge. Whereas epistemic status describes the positioning of members toward a specific knowledge domain through access to and distribution of this knowledge, epistemic stance grasps the "moment-by-moment expression" (Mondada 2013, p. 600) of this positioning, which is designed according to interactional flow. The next extract shows how one of the participants, a member of the administrative staff of the university where the conference took place, rejected the category *expert* while simultaneously establishing a common-sense understanding of what constitutes a security expert. After the moderator had asked all the participants to introduce themselves to the auditorium, the administration staff member was the first in line to do as requested:

Extract 2: I am probably the one who can contribute least to the discussion

Administration staff member:

Well, my name is [name] and I have been a member of the administration of this institution for fourteen months. First and foremost, I have already joined a talk about the topic by [name of the prosecutor who is also participating in the security conference] and I bow down before the factual knowledge of others participating in this panel discussion. Well, regarding the factual area of what happens within border crime and security I can hardly contribute, but I can say something general about this institution, about

Europe's open borders and Schengen, and in the first place, I expect more information from the experts about how the situation actually evolves. If I remember the talk by [name of the prosecutor] correctly, it was surprising to me that whereas one could expect the crime rates to explode, at that time this seemed not to be the case. So, I would be very interested in the facts, and regarding the facts I am probably the one who can contribute least to the discussion.

The extract starts with an introduction in its most basic form, giving the speaker's name and affiliation (17–18). In contrast to all the other participants, who use the following sequence to positively demonstrate why they are part of the panel discussion by displaying epistemic authority, the member of the administration staff produces an account that answers the question of what he could *contribute to the discussions* (34), while rejecting the category *expert*. The administration staff member does so by referring to a talk held by the prosecutor who has also joined the panel discussion. He shows himself to be highly appreciative of the *factual knowledge* which he suspects *others participating in this panel discussion* (22–23) might have. Taking the prosecutor as an example of the group of *others*—a category which, in the following, is transformed into the category *experts* (28)—he separates himself from this group and thereby confirms that having *factual knowledge* (22) is to be seen as a *category-bound predicate* (cf. Reynolds/Fitzgerald 2015) of the category *expert*. He shows that his self-categorization does not embrace this predication, by explicitly differentiating the *expert* topic of *border crime and security* from the *general* topic of *Europe's open borders and Schengen* (26). He then formulates his expectations regarding the panel discussion. This brings him closer to the auditorium following the discussion, who the moderator had categorized as *visitors* or *guests*, and who might be characterized as being "the public" to be *informed* by the event. Thus, he expects the experts to deliver *more information about how the situation actually evolves* (28). Referring again to what he remembers from the talk by the prosecutor, he emphasizes that he is *interested in the facts* (32), a kind of knowledge which is presented throughout the conference to give detailed information about the reality of the border since its opening. As he points out, not only is access to this particular knowledge restricted, as it is bound to expert status, but it might also be counterintuitive; whereas mundane reasoning suggests a connection between increasing crime rates and opening borders (30–31), the *actual situation* (28) seems to have been different.

To sum up, this extract shows how the university staff member positions himself within the group of participants regarding epistemic status and stance. Given the topic "border security," this is not done through a direct rejection, e.g. expressing that *I am not an expert*, or the establishment of another candidate category, but through an account which on the one hand differentiates border knowledge into different resources, as he demonstrates what he does and does not know, and on the other hand breaking the categorial equation of panel participant = expert by explaining who else he thinks might fulfill the requirements of the category *expert*. In the next abstract, I want to show how another panelist, the local politician, also deals with the question of epistemic status and stance in his introduction. While he does not reject the category *expert*, he certainly raises the question of what kind of knowledge is bound to expertise.

Extract 3: We can hear a lot from the perspective of experience during the evening

Local politician:
My name is [name], I am thirty-six and I come from
Eisenhüttenstadt […]. I have been in local politics
Along the Oder and Neiße for a few years and I was on
the local council in Neißemünde. Of course, you can trust
statistics only if you faked them yourself, but I do believe
that we should move away from the technical and the
feeling of what numbers can and cannot tell. Because I
think basically it is all about the feeling of safety of the
people who still are here and want to live here in the
next ten, twenty, fifty years and that they don't have to
look every time something has been stolen again. We
can hear a lot from the perspective of experience during
this evening and I am just looking forward to seeing the
great men here and maybe me as a counterpoint.

In his introduction, the local politician immediately starts to claim local expertise. In contrast to the administration staff member, he chooses not to open his account with his age and current affiliation, but with his age and place of birth (36), a town close to the German–Polish border. He continues to mention career stages in relation to the border, thus formulating this reference to the border in spatially localized terms, as the German–Polish border is marked by the rivers Oder and Neiße (37). Only implicitly, this short introduction follows the moderator's categorization, in the sense that it demonstrates good reason for him to be part of the panel discussion: a longstanding engagement in local politics. He then challenges an understanding of factual knowledge as being informative about the topic. He claims that *statistics* (38) and *numbers* (41), which—as I will show in the third part of my analysis—are candidates in the class of elements that constitute the category *factual knowledge*, are characterized as too *technical* (40) and lack reflection on their explanatory scope (41). He initiates his skepticism about this certain kind of knowledge by quoting a widely-known phrase in Germany—*do not trust statistics you did not fake yourself* (38–39)—which is commonly ascribed to either Winston Churchill or WWII Nazi propaganda, while its origin is still an unsolved question (cf. Barke 2004). In contrast to the member of the administration staff who claimed general knowledge which excluded him from the experts (see extract 2), in the following, the local politician introduces another repertoire of knowledge bound to the category *perspective of experience* (46), which marks a different stance toward *what* can be known about the border and *how* and—as I will show in the next section—is established as a different mode of knowing. Central to this alternative understanding of expertise is the predicate of *feeling of safety* (42), which e.g. can be tackled by being the victim of burglary (44–45). In the last part of his account, the politician transfers this general differentiation between types of knowledge into the framing of the panel discussion. While his *perspective of experience* embraces both the stance of the politician due to his local expertise as well as the reported stance of *the people* he refers to (42), within the group of panelists this makes him a *counterpoint* (48). Strikingly, he sees the relation to the other experts as an asymmetrical one, as he denotes them as *the great men* (47), claiming a somehow marginalized position for his counterpoint perspective. He thereby emphasizes his position to speak on behalf of those who have experienced border crime.

Closing this section, we have seen how the articulation of border knowledge is bound to the categorial ordering work by all participants, either claiming membership or dealing with other-categorization. Central to the security conference is the display, predication, and negotiation of the category *expert*, as are struggles about what kind of knowledge is bound to this category. In the last part of this analysis, I will elaborate a little more on how these two repertoires, *factual knowledge* and *experience*, are continuously confronted throughout the conference. I will show how they are key elements in establishing a diversification of border knowledge, built around a diagnosis of the current state of security issues at the German–Polish border, which is either described as an *objective security situation* or a *subjective feeling of safety*.

4.3 *Diversification of border knowledge: objective security situation and subjective feeling of safety as two modes of border knowledge*

The analysis so far has shown that talking about border security at the conference brought up the necessity to negotiate what border knowledge *is*. I want to dedicate this final section to a fundamental epistemic differentiation that can be traced throughout the discussion. As we will see, these two are not only perspectives but repertoires and modes of knowledge whose transferability is continuously negotiated. One of the participants, the former mayor of the border town where the security conference was taking place, mentions this fundamental differentiation early on and asked for an integrated discussion.

Extract 4: The feeling of safety and the security situation are two separate things

Former mayor:

[The] feeling of safety and the security situation are two separate things, and someone who has been a victim of theft and has been harmed feels very differently than the statistician who looks at data about how many police are needed, because that costs tax money, and whether we could once again cut another few hundred to save tax money. That is a wholly different perspective. If we manage to bring these perspectives together, I would call this evening a success.

In the extract, the former mayor identifies a *feeling of safety* and the *security situation* (49) as two perspectives on how to account for the topic *eight years of open German–Polish border*. Furthermore, he produces a contrasting device to elaborate on the difference. The categories *victim* (of theft and harm) (50) and *statistician* (52) are contrasted to show how border crime is dealt with from these perspectives. Whereas the statistician *looks at data* to figure out *how many police are needed* (52) and thus contributes to economically motivated reasoning, the victim has been *harmed* (50) by theft and in this way—as the local politician stated above—*experienced* border crime.

Bringing these perspectives together (55) turned out to be a rather hard task, as the repertoires that serve as resources to articulate those perspectives were established in opposition. On the one hand, the repertoire of the objective security situation is mainly used by the prosecutor, the representative of the state office of criminal investigation and the former mayor, and consists of a class of epistemic categories like *data*, *statistics*, (case) *numbers*, *quotas*, and *facts*, which can be *compared* and *put into relation*. Thus, how the accession of Poland to the Schengen Agreement affected the border is measurable, and therefore only retrospectively explicable. The last eight years are described as a *development* of increasing and decreasing numbers and as part of an *overall development* which goes back to the establishment of the German–Polish border. Based on this knowledge, *measures* and *decisions* are taken concerning legal adjustments, institutional cross-border cooperation, reorganization of the police, control practices, etc. On the other hand, the repertoire of the *subjective feeling of safety* is used by both the local politician and the member of the university administration. It is expressed in *experiences* and *opinions*; thus, the history of the open border is not a linear one, but one that can be articulated via stories, anecdotes, descriptions of involvement, and (real or imagined) scenarios. The consequences are *actions* and calls for action. The emotions of those talked about, as well as emotional articulation, play a crucial role.

The juxtaposition of these different epistemic repertoires is the mainspring of constant epistemic border struggles. These repertoires are situationally used stocks of knowledge which, at their heart, result from reasoning that is grounded in different border realities. In the last extract, the prosecutor closes a rather long contribution to the discussion, explicating the development of crime rates in the border region since the 1990s, and directly addresses the problem of commensurability.

Extract 5: I can only stick to the numbers

State prosecutor:

Thus, the assessment of the situation concerning the level
has decreased; in fact, what is apparent is that the
population's subjective feeling about the level of crime has
increased. I can't explain that, I am not a psychologist, I
don't know, I can only stick to the numbers and the
numbers are relatively clear in this respect.

After the prosecutor states that the level of crime rates has decreased by a third over the last 25 years, the extract shows that he recognizes an increase in the subjective impression of the level of crime level (58–60). In an insisting sequence, he remarks that he is *not a psychologist* (60), which renders him unable to *explain* (60) this inconsistency in perception. Invoking the category of psychologist points to the individual and subjective dimension of border knowledge, to which, from his viewpoint, he has no access. Rather, numbers are established as a unit of knowledge which are able to speak *relatively clearly* (62) about the situation.

5. Discussion: a characterization of border knowledge

The analysis here has shown how the exposition, legitimization, and diversification of border knowledge in action was methodically accomplished at the security conference. Exposing border knowledge demands a reduction in border complexity by facilitating ordering work framed by epistemic and interactional constraints. Legitimizing border knowledge means negotiating epistemic authority based on ongoing self- and other-categorization by all the participants, and implicitly or explicitly establishing connections between membership categories and attributed border knowledge. Finally, the diversification of border knowledge rests upon different visions and experiences of the border, which not only lead to coexisting repertoires of knowing, e.g. objective situation and subjective feeling, but to epistemic border struggles.

Conceptualizing border knowledge can be helpful for a praxeological analysis of (linguistic) border work which pays attention to the professional and mundane doings that constitute borders *in situ*. Any analysis must make these knowledge resources a topic of description to gain an understanding of border knowledge as highly situational knowledge in action and to shed light on borders as an ongoing achievement. Rather than seeing border knowledge as fixed and stable, the argument is to see it as situated knowledge. According to Laidi (1998), bordering in its most basic form should be understood as a process of creating spaces of meaning—which implies an epistemic connotation. This has culminated in the call for *multiperspectival border studies* (Rumford 2012). Questioning the idea that borders are consistently visible to everybody and that the state is the principal actor engaged in borderwork, the multiperspectival study of borders aims to take into account the multiplicity of actors, experiences, perspectives, and meaning-making via border narratives that make up the complexity of borders. Consequently, and as my analysis has shown, border knowledge is diverse but still ordered, linked to specific membership categories, and bound to professional as well as mundane perspectives on the border.

As the analysis of the panel discussion has shown, border knowledge is processual in two respects. On the one hand, not only do perspectives of a border constantly change, but the border itself is in permanent motion, as Nail (2016) has shown. Either this change of the border *gestalt* is conceptualized as the outcome of external processes, e.g. historical transformation, for instance securitization, or of internal processes, e.g. changing interactions of border dimensions or evolving mobilities. Consequently, as the border changes, so does the knowledge that produces and/or is the product of this change. On the other hand, the articulation of border knowledge is not only bound to epistemic changes, but to the situational affordances of border interactions. Articulating the border within interaction is thus a process of mutual adaption between interaction order and border complexity, so that the border can be told.

Finally, a detailed analysis of border knowledge is crucial in order to understand the commonplace that every border is unique. Kleinschmidt (2014) explains that the search for a core meaning—or a stable and fixed stock of knowledge—of a generalized understanding of *the border* must fail. Rather, we should be aware of the ambivalences of the semantic profile of the border, which are generated by the historical and social conditions under which borders are put into place. These in turn lead to various routinized ways of *making sense* of the border. To borrow a widely-known Foucauldian term: a border creates an idiosyncratic knowledge-related *space of possibilities* which is situationally established and dealt with.

References

AG Bordertexturen (2018): Bordertexturen als transdisziplinärer Ansatz zur Untersuchung von Grenzen. Ein Werkstattbericht. In: Gerst, D./Klessmann, M./Krämer, H./Sienknecht, M./Ulrich, P. (eds.) (2018): Komplexe Grenzen. Themenschwerpunkt Berliner Debatte Initial 29, no. 1, p. 73–83.

Baird, Theodore (2017): Knowledge of practice: a multi-sited event ethnography of border security fairs in Europe and North America. In: Security Dialogue, p. 1–17.

Balibar, Etienne (2004): We the people of Europe? Reflections on transnational citizenship. Princeton: Princeton University Press.

Barke, Werner (2004): “Ich glaube nur der Statistik, die ich selbst gefälscht habe...” In: Statistisches Monatsheft Baden-Württemberg 11, p. 50–53.

Bilmes, Jack (1988): The Concept of Preference in Conversation Analysis. In: Language and Society 17, no. 2, p. 161–181.

Blaneck, Andrea (2005): Netzwerke und Kooperationen an der deutsch-polnischen Grenze. Untersuchungen zum wirtschaftlichen Milieu in der Grenzregion an der Oder. Münster: LIT-Verlag.

Brambilla, Chiara/Laine, Jussi/Scott, James W./Bocchi, Gianluca (eds.) (2016): Borderscaping. Imaginations and Practices of Border Making. London/New York: Routledge.

Brunet-Jailly, Emmanuel (ed.) (2007): Borderlands. Comparing Border Security in North America and Europe. Ottawa: University of Ottawa Press.

Buraczynski, Radoslaw (2015): Die Herstellung von Sicherheit an der EU-Außengrenze. Migrations- und Grenzpolitik in der polnischen Region Karpatenvorland. Wiesbaden: Springer.

Côté-Boucher, Karine/Infantiano, Federica/Salter, Mark B. (2014): Border security as practice: An agenda for research. In: Security Dialogue 45, no. 3, p. 195–208.

DeChaine, Robert (ed.) (2012): Border Rhetorics. Citizenship and Identity on the US–Mexico Frontier. Alabama: The University of Alabama Press.

Deppermann, Arnulf/Günthner, Susanne (eds.) (2015): Temporality in Interaction. Amsterdam/Philadelphia: John Benjamins.

Doevenspeck, Martin (2011): Constructing the border from below: narratives from the Congolese–Rwandan state boundary. In: Political Geography 30, p. 129–142.

Eigmüller, Monika (2016): Der duale Charakter der Grenze. Bedingungen einer aktuellen Grenztheorie. In: Eigmüller, M./Vobruba, G. (eds.): Grenzsoziologie. Die politische Strukturierung des Raumes. Wiesbaden: Springer, p. 49–68.

Fitzgerald, Richard (2012): Membership categorization analysis: wild and promiscuous or simply the joy of Sacks? In: Discourse Studies 14, no. 3, p. 305–311.

Francis, David/Hester, Stephen (2004): An invitation to ethnomethodology: Language, society and interaction. London: Sage.

Frowd, Philippe (2014): The field of border control in Mauritania. In: Security Dialogue 45, no. 3, p. 226–241.

Garfinkel, Harold (1967): Studies in Ethnomethodology. Englewood Cliffs/New Jersey: Prentice-Hall.

Gerst, Dominik/Klessmann, Maria/Krämer, Hannes/Sienknecht, Mitja/Ulrich, Peter (eds.) (2018): Komplexe Grenzen. Themenschwerpunkt Berliner Debatte Initial 29, no. 1.

Gerst, Dominik/Krämer, Hannes (2017): Methodologische Prinzipien einer allgemeinen Grenzsoziologie. In: Lessenich, S. (ed.): Geschlossene Gesellschaften. Verhandlungen des 38. Kongresses der Deutschen Gesellschaft für Soziologie in Bamberg 2016.

Goffman, Erving (1981): Forms of Talk. Oxford: Blackwell.

Goffman, Erving (1983): The Interaction Order, in: American Sociological Revue 48, no. 1, p. 1–17.

Haselsberger, Beatrix (2014): Decoding borders. Appreciating border impacts on space and people. In: Planning Theory & Practice, DOI: 10.1080/14649357.2014.963652.

Heritage, John (2012): Epistemics in action: action formation and territories of knowledge. In: Research on Language and Social Interaction 45, p. 1–25.

Hester, Stephen/Eglin, Peter (1997): Membership Categorization Analysis: An Introduction. In: Hester, S./Eglin, P. (eds.): Culture in Action. Studies in Membership Categorization Analysis. Washington: International Institute for Ethnomethodology and Conversation Analysis & University Press of America, p. 1–24.

Hitzler, Ronald/Honer, Anne/Maeder, Christoph (eds.) (1994): Expertenwissen. Die institutionalisierte Kompetenz zur Konstruktion von Wirklichkeit. Opladen: Westdeutscher Verlag.

Housley, William/Fitzgerald, Richard (2015): Introduction to Membership Categorization Analysis. In: Fitzgerald, R./Housley, W. (eds.): Advances in Membership Categorisation Analysis. London: Sage, p. 1–22.

Joenniemi, Pertti/Jańczak Jarosław (2017): Theorizing Town-twinning. Towards a global perspective. Journal of Borderlands Studies 32, no. 4, p. 423–428.

Jones, Reece/Johnson, Corey (2014): Placing the border in everyday life. Farnham: Ashgate.

Kleinschmidt, Christoph (2014): Semantik der Grenze. In: APuZ 63, no. 4/5, p. 3–8.

Laidi, Zaiki (1998): A world without meaning: the crisis of meaning in international politics. London/New York: Routledge.

Laube, Lena/Roos, Stefan (2010): A "border for the people"? Narratives on changing eastern borders in Finland and Austria. In: Journal of Borderlands Studies 25, no. 3–4, p. 31–49.

Li, Shenxue/Scullion, Hugh (2006): Bridging the distance: managing cross-border knowledge holders. In: Asia Pacific Journal of Management 23, p. 71–92.

Meinhof, Ulrike H./Galasiński, Dariusz (2002): Reconfiguring East–West identities: Cross-Generational discourses in German and Polish border communities. In: Journal of Ethnic and Migration Studies 28, no. 1, p. 63–82.

Meyer, Christian (2014): Die soziale Praxis der Podiumsdiskussion. Eine videogestützte ethnomethodologische Konversationsanalyse. In: Angermüller, J./Nonhoff, M./Herschinger, E./Macgilchrist, F./Reisigl, M./Wedel, J./Wrana, D./Ziem, A. (eds.): Diskursforschung. Ein interdisziplinäres Handbuch, vol. 2. Bielefeld: Transcript. p. 404–432.

Mezzadra, Sandro/Neilson, Brett (2013): Border as method, or, The multiplication of labor. Durham: Duke University Press.

Mignolo, Walter D. (2002): The Geopolitics of Knowledge and the Colonial Difference. South Atlantic Quarterly 101, no. 1, p. 57–96.

Mignolo, Walter D./Tlostanova, Madina V. (2006): Theorizing from the Borders: Shifting to Geo- and Body-Politics of Knowledge. In: European Journal of Social Theory 9, no. 2, p. 205–221.

Mondada, Lorenza (2013): Displaying, contesting and negotiating epistemic authority in social interaction: descriptions and questions in guided visits. In: Discourse Studies 15, no. 5, p. 597–626.

Nail, Thomas (2016): Theory of the border. New York: Oxford University Press.

Newman, David (2003): On borders and power: A theoretical framework. In: Journal of Borderlands Studies 18, no. 1, p. 13–25.

Newman, David (2006): Borders and Bordering. Towards an Interdisciplinary Dialogue. In: European Journal of Social Theory 9, no. 2, p. 171–186.

Ohmae, Kenichi (1990): The Borderless World. Power and Strategy in the Interlinked Economy. New York: Harper Collins.

Parker, Noel/Adler-Nissen, Rebecca (2014): Picking and Choosing the 'Sovereign' Border: A Theory of Changing State Bordering Practices. In: Parker, Noel/ Vaughan-Williams, Nick (eds.): Critical Border Studies. Broadening and Deepening the 'Lines in the Sand' Agenda. London/New York: Routledge, p. 47–70.

Patrona, Marianna (2012): Journalists on the news: The structured panel discussion as a form of broadcast talk. In: Discourse & Society 23, no. 2, p. 145–162.

Pickering, Sharon (2006): Border Narratives. From talking security to performing borderlands. In: Pickering, S./Weber, L. (eds.): Borders, Mobility and Technologies of Control. Wiesbaden: Springer VS, p. 45–62.

Radu, Cosmin (2010): Beyond border-'dwelling': temporalizing the border-space through events. In: Anthropological Theory 10, no. 4, p. 409–433.

Reynolds, Edward/Fitzgerald, Richard (2015): Challenging Normativity: Re-Appraising Category Bound, Tied and Predicated Features. In: Fitzgerald, R./Housley, W. (eds.): Advances in Membership Categorisation Analysis. London: Sage, p. 99–122.

Rhoades, Robert A. (1995). Critical Multiculturalism, Border Knowledge, and the Canon: Implications for General Education and the Academy. In: Journal of General Education 44, no. 4, p. 256–273.

Rumford, Chris (2008): Introduction: Citizens and Borderwork in Europe. In: Space and Polity 12, no. 1, p. 1–12.

Rumford, Chris (2012): Towards a Multiperspectival Study of Borders. In: Geopolitics 17, no. 4, p. 887–902.

Ryle, Gilbert (1945): Knowing How and Knowing That: The Presidential Address. In: Proceedings of the Aristotelian Society 46, p. 1–16.

Sacks, Harvey (1992): Lectures on Conversation. Vol. I and II. Edited by Gail Jefferson. Malden: Wiley-Blackwell.

Schatzki, Theodore/Knorr-Cetina, Karin/von Savigny, Eike (eds.) (2001): The Practice Turn in Contemporary Theory. London/New York: Routledge.

Schwell, Alexandra (2008): Europa an der Oder. Die Konstruktion europäischer Sicherheit an der deutsch-polnischen Grenze. Bielefeld: Transcript.

Sohn, Christophe (2016): Navigating borders' multiplicity: the critical potential of assemblage. In: Area 48, no. 2, p. 183–189.

Wille, Christian (2015): Spaces of the Border — a Practice-theoretical Cultural Studies Perspective in Border Studies. In: Europa Regional 21, no. 1–2, p. 60–71.

Willner, Sarah/Koch, Georg/Samida, Stefanie (2016): Doing History. Performative Praktiken in der Geschichtskultur. Münster: Waxmann.

About the author

Dominik Gerst | University of Duisburg-Essen | Institute for Communication Studies | Universitätsstraße 12 | 45141 Essen | Germany | T +49 201 183 3340 | dominik.gerst@uni-due.de

Gerst, Dominik, MA, sociologist, research associate at the Institute for Communication Studies, University of Duisburg-Essen; research interests: border & boundary theories and methodologies, sociology of knowledge, ethnomethodology & conversation analysis.

Acknowledgements

All extracts cited in this chapter were originally in German. This chapter emerged from research as part of the Ph.D. project *Border knowledge in the German–Polish security field*. The research was funded by a Ph.D. scholarship provided by the Viadrina Center B/ORDERS IN MOTION from 2014–2016. I am thankful to Concha Maria Höfler for her valuable comments on this chapter.

Border Experiences: Communication and Languages

Digital media practices as digital border experiences among French cross-border commuters in Luxembourg

Corinne Martin

Abstract

The purpose of this chapter is to analyze the impact of a digital border on the digital media practices of French cross-border commuters in Luxembourg, and how this contributes to the construction of their border experiences. An outline is given of the typology of media practices, and put into perspective with the social representations of the border, the Greater Region, and the position of the cross-border commuters in the social, professional, and cultural space. The methodology is qualitative: semi-directive interviews (N=20, 10 women, 10 men) addressed all the media practices of the respondents (traditional media, digital media, and social networks via smartphones/computers/tablets) and their real-life experiences as cross-border commuters.

Keywords

Border, digital border, cross-border commuters, digital media, digital practices

1. *Introduction: the circulation of news in the media in the Greater Region*

Our study aims to highlight the impacts of the digital border on the digital media practices of French cross-border commuters working in the Grand Duchy of Luxembourg. Firstly, our project is mainly within the current of studies on domestication, the sociology of uses, and media sociology in analyzing digital media practices (Silverstone/Haddon 1996; Jouët 2000; Jouët/Rieffel 2013). Secondly, we developed our research in the context of the Infotransfront project[1] (2010–2014) initiated at the CREM (*Centre de Recherche sur les Médiations*) and supported by the MSH (*Maison des Sciences de l'Homme*) at the University of Lorraine, in partnership with the Franco-

1 Project headed by Vincent Goulet.

German University, the University of the Saarland, CIERA (*Centre Interdisciplinaire d'Etudes et de Recherches sur l'Allemagne*), and LISER (Luxembourg Institute of Socio-Economic Research, formerly CEPS-INSTEAD). The aim of the Infotransfront project was to analyze the circulation of media information in the Greater Region (Goulet/Vatter 2015). More particularly, it involved gaining an understanding of how, in the context of the construction of a cross-border area (Hamman 2005; Goulet/Vatter 2013; Koukoutsaki-Monnier 2014; Hamez 2015; Durand 2015; Amilhat Szary 2016), a regional cross-border media field (Goulet/Vatter 2015) could emerge—or not.

In this context, the aim of our own study was to gain an understanding of practices of consulting media news on a smartphone (and/or tablet)—in other words, digital and mobile media practices—among French cross-border commuters in the Grand Duchy of Luxembourg, compared with the more traditional practices of consulting the media (printed press, radio, television), in order to measure all the specific and complementary features of this method of consulting news reports in the digital age (Granjon/Le Foulgoc 2010; Granjon/Le Foulgoc 2011; Jouët/Rieffel 2013). Thus, one of the first questions we sought to answer was: does being a cross-border commuter and traveling every day encourage—or discourage—the consultation of news on a smartphone? And if it did encourage consultation, what type of news was consulted? More particularly, what place did local news—i.e. that relating to the Greater Region—occupy[2]? In other words, are the residents of one country interested in what happens on the other side of the border? What hybridization takes place between the digital media and the traditional media to compensate for the reported absence of cross-border information in the latter type?

The empirical survey carried out in 2012–2013[3] (cf. *infra*) very quickly revealed the existence of what we have qualified as a real digital border: in the field of mobile communications, roaming charges between the various countries of Europe were introduced as soon as mobile phones emerged (in the mid-1990s), resulting in not inconsiderable charges for mobile communications billed to cross-border commuters. Therefore, cross-border commuters were compelled to disconnect[4] (cut off from their French net-

2 For a detailed analysis of the characteristics of the Greater Region, cf. Belkacem/Pigeron 2012.

3 The survey was carried out well before the European Union put an end to roaming charges in June 2017.

4 As opposed to the claim of the right to disconnect, analyzed by the sociologist Francis Jauréguiberry (2014).

work) exactly at the moment they crossed the border to enter the area of the Grand Duchy. How was their border experience constructed, being associated with that cut-off every morning to go to work? How did they manage to maintain communication with their relatives who remained in France during the whole working day? We propose the hypothesis that this economico-technical apparatus—the roaming charges—shaped (Cardon 2010) their border experiences and made their digital practices specific. Is it possible to analyze this digital border in the context of the phenomena of re-bordering?

We were able in this way to highlight three major repertoires of usage covering the routines and practices of consulting news. These repertoires of usage have been linked to their sociability and cultural practices (Donnat 2009), and their everyday experiences—including their border experiences—in the tradition of studies on the domestication and sociology of uses (Jouët 2001; Jouët/Rieffel 2013). It is these three repertoires of usage that will be presented.

The methodology is qualitative, inspired by the tradition of the non-directive interview that gives prominence to the participant's viewpoint (Blanchet, 1985; Blanchet/Gotman, 1992). Twenty non-directive interviews were carried out (with 10 men and 10 women, aged between 23 and 48, interview lasting one to two hours), all transcribed in full; they constitute our corpus. We are able to state that this sample is sufficiently diversified, particularly in terms of the socio-professional and cultural origin of the respondents. Similarly, our work was guided by the comprehensive interview method developed by Jean-Claude Kaufmann (1996). This is justified by grounded theory: instead of drawing up prior hypotheses, we attempted to construct hypotheses on the basis of the information gathered in the field, and our initial analysis after the interviews had been held led us to posit the hypothesis of a real digital border. This is what we shall cover in this paper's first section, before presenting the three repertoires of usage.

2. *A digital border that promotes re-bordering phenomena*

While it was easy to understand *a priori* that mobile phone communications between the countries of the European Union were restricted by their not inconsiderable cost[5], the field survey revealed just what a massive impact this phenomenon had on the cross-border commuters we met and on their everyday mobile communications, from the introduction of the mobile phone (mid-1990s) to June 2017 (the end of roaming charges; it should be recalled that the field survey was carried out in 2012–2013, see above). Everyone mentioned the surprising phenomenon that occurred at a specific place, very close to the place they crossed (by car or in a train) the geographical border between France and the Grand Duchy: conversations were interrupted, pages stopped downloading, and there was no signal. Mobile phones were put away in pockets by all those users who only had subscriptions to a French network. We have qualified this cut-off point as a real digital border, in as much as it was a reminder of the demarcation line of the borders which are no longer materially visible in this cross-border area. This digital border even affected cross-border commuters with high purchasing power. Nearly all deplored or criticized this state of affairs; it is interesting to see the various impacts this technico-economic apparatus had on these cross-border commuters and their use of mobile devices for more than twenty years. Most of the respondents had in fact learned to filter incoming calls, only answering occasionally, assessing the calls according to the identity of the caller and the degree of urgency, and as a result they postponed looking at their mobile communications with their acquaintances until they returned to France at the end of the working day. It should also be said that their contacts had also evidently learned to avoid calling during the day (except in an emergency). It is therefore interesting to note that there was an impact not only on practices but also on the social imaginary associated with the invention of the mobile phone (ubiquity, the ability to call from anywhere at any time), which had in fact completely disappeared for many cross-border commuters. On the other hand, a number of respondents in our sample—those whose job required management of client relations (mainly in the liberal professions)—found themselves obliged to equip themselves with a second phone (or a second SIM card, for use in a special dual-SIM phone) in order to have access to the Grand Duchy's network. This was the case for Angélique (self-employed in the complementary medicine sector, 37 years old), a professional coach in contact with her clients for appointments, who halved her phone bill by acquiring a second phone; she was now paying 250 euros per

5 The matter of the cost of using mobile phones before the invention of plans including unlimited communications—and the end of roaming charges—was a fundamental issue.

month instead of the 500 euros she had been paying previously, when she had a single phone and a lot of out-of-plan communications. Lastly, a very small number of respondents in our sample had opted for a specific plan, such as a plan including one hour of calls to landlines in the Grand Duchy, but they remained very much a minority. To end this section, we should also point out that the large majority of respondents had learned to apply ruses and practices to bypass the apparatus of the digital border, thereby developing new "ways of operating" ("*manières de faire*" defined by Michel de Certeau (1998)) that may be assimilated to instruction manuals. Thus many of the respondents made use of a number of free apps, both for downloading content (including Instapaper and Flipboard, the latter being included by default on some smartphones) and for free messaging WhatsApp. But there were significant constraints: the user still needed a Wi-Fi connection to be able to use WhatsApp—thereby excluding the possibility of communicating during the commuter journey—and, particularly for Instapaper, the need to anticipate and download while the user was still connected to the network.

This was the case for Charles (a computer specialist, 26 years old), who discovered Instapaper and used it to download and, more particularly, save a few articles to read offline on his smartphone during the journey by train and bus to Luxembourg City. For his IT thesis he was required to carry out an information watch, which made him a "big consumer of information", and he developed a quasi-routine. He made a note of articles of interest (he subscribed to a number of RSS feeds from pre-selected sites) the night before or during the day while working on the computer he was using to prepare his thesis, then synchronized them onto his iPhone and downloaded them in the morning as he stood on the platform waiting for his train, using Instapaper. As Charles pointed out, however, there was one major constraint: "you have to plan ahead".

Another interesting case was that of Anaïs (a management assistant, 25 years old), whose interview revealed nothing short of a re-bordering phenomenon in her management of calls to and from her network of Luxembourgish and Belgian acquaintances and co-workers. Before making any call from her workplace, she would always consider where the other person might be geographically, and the type of mobile phone plan they had (French or Luxembourgish network), and the time of day (still at work or already back home in France or Belgium)—her aim being to make the best use of the cost of her two mobile phones:

> I have a Belgian friend [a Belgian cross-border commuter; we used to work together when I had a previous job in the Grand Duchy] so I

> know she'll be in Belgium, so I always use my Luxembourg mobile phone to text her since it's cheaper than using my French mobile phone. I know French people working in the Grand Duchy too, so I have to think about it... for instance, given the time it is now, is he going to be in France [laughter], in which case I'll use my French mobile phone because I've got unlimited text messaging? Or is he in the Grand Duchy at the moment, in which case I'll use my Luxembourg phone? But if I'm in France and using my Luxembourg phone, is that going to be cheaper or more expensive than if I were in the Grand Duchy? Well, it was a real disaster [laughter] [...] well, it was all about making it cheaper but in fact, er *well, it was a bit cheaper, but it was more complicated than it was worth, really.*

The cognitive cost was indeed far from negligible, and Anaïs eventually lost her Luxembourg mobile phone. To sum up, the digital practices of the respondents in our sample were all impacted in one way or another by this digital border. We shall now move on to describe and analyze in the next three sections the three repertoires of usage we were able to identify on the basis of the empirical survey.

3. *The "tunnel" effect*

Economists call employees who travel backwards and forwards between the place where they live and the place where they work, and who are a feature of large metropolises, commuters or 'pendular migrants': the imagery is very clear (cf. Foucault's pendulum, 1861). Every morning, they cross a border to get to work, and cross back again in the opposite direction in the evening to go back home. The blogger Sylvie Neidinger[6] has added a bit of humorous wordplay (in French) to the purely statistical approach by describing in her own way the people she calls "cross-border pendular travelers" ("*les pendulaires frontaliers*"): the cross-border commuter is compared to "a ping-pong ball that two states send backwards and forwards at fixed times in a faultless mechanical fashion". In the qualitative approach we adopted, the image of a "tunnel effect" stood out quite obviously. We shall deal with this in the next section.

6 Sylvie Neidinger posted a blog about commuters. http://duboutduborddulac.blog.tdg.ch/archive/2011/12/23/les-pendu-laires-2-2.html; Retrieved on April 21, 2018.

3.1 The geographical border: a new border between private life and work?

In this section, we will demonstrate how the geographical boundary becomes a metaphor for the boundary between work and private life on a daily basis and thus contributes to the construction of border experiences.

3.1.1 Exacerbated pendular migration

Why have we referred to a tunnel effect? The narratives of many of the cross-border commuters in this group with this experience of pendular migration as they described it evoked the metaphorical image of a tunnel: it is as if they were being teleported through a tunnel to their place of work, either in a train or in a car stuck in a long traffic jam. Florence (a psychologist, 38 years old) gave an excellent description of this image of long rows of workers, which even reminded her of workers leaving the factory in her childhood (her father was such a worker):

> So when I think of a cross-border commuter, I see myself in the morning on my way to the station. I park, get out of the car, and there's this mass of people walking in silence towards the station. I say to myself, "Well, it's not a factory, is it?" But sometimes I tell myself that anyone watching us must think we're really…, well, stupid, because it's really… We're all traveling to work half-asleep; yes, that's what it is. It's the train, and the people… Well, that's what I see in the phrase 'cross-border commuter'.

Does the idea of this "mass" of people correspond to a crowd as Gabriel de Tarde means it? (Moscovici 2005). Is it a mass of "stupid" people who have lost their freedom of will and their critical faculties? At any event, they stay grouped together; they are not responsive—in fact, they seem submissive, like automatons, but the scene taking place at six o'clock in the morning makes the experience of these pendular migrants relatively similar to that of the inhabitants of major metropolises, such as Paris or elsewhere.

So why have we mentioned the extreme dimension of this pendular migration? Because it is as if these cross-border commuters were going through a "tunnel"—wearing blinkers that prevented them from seeing what was happening on the spot, in the Grand Duchy. They never stayed on in the evening after work, never came back at the weekend, never pursued any leisure, sport, or cultural activities in the geographical area of the Grand Duchy, and took little or no interest in what was going on locally. Their media practices guided them towards the French/international news since, as far as they were concerned, "local news" remained the news of their place of residence or the area in which they lived. Lastly, they developed almost no sociability with people living in the Grand Duchy and they stayed "among themselves" and did not mix, since they were working in companies that mainly recruited cross-border commuters like themselves. And they were quite simply keen to get back home in the evening, since a cross-border commuter's day is long enough as it is, particularly because of the time spent traveling. The interviewer's question: "As a cross-border commuter, do you have any activities in the Grand Duchy apart from your work?" elicited a negative reply from many of the respondents in this group; at best, their reply was "not very often". One aspect involved here was the amount of time "lost" traveling[7], time that ceased to be available for leisure activities. As a result, many of the respondents reported a kind of hermetic separation between work and "everything else", i.e. their private lives and leisure activities, the latter being only very rarely carried out in the Grand Duchy. The case of Jean-Pierre (an administrative agent, 46 years old) shed light on this:

> No, because afterwards I'm quite happy to… er, once the day's over… I don't stay on […] I don't stay, no, of course I don't stay […] so, well, er, I don't know, I'm interested, it's not that I'm not interested [defensively], but I mean, er; I'm glad the day's over so that's it, it's finished, you know? […] no, no, after the Grand Duchy… I work there, it doesn't go further than that… you know? [laughter] […] but, since I live near Metz, I don't know, er… I've had enough of being in the same place as I work, and it doesn't go any further than that, I don't do any more afterwards, I don't come back… here… you could say, my working life is here, and everything else is in France.

Jean-Pierre was very clear on this point: he separated his working life from "everything else", meaning his private life, which was almost unlimited—not finite, in any case. In contrast, working time had to be limited, constrained, regulated—"it doesn't go any further than that"—and after work he was "glad the day's over"; the expressions "I've had enough of being in the same place as I work", "I don't stay on", and "I'm not interested" are very clear. As for weekends, he remembered returning to the Grand Duchy on no more than one occasion, bearing in mind that he had been working

---

7 Some spend between two and three and a half hours in a bus every day; the time spent in a car is equally long (because of the inevitable daily traffic jams on the single motorway into the Grand Duchy).

in the Grand Duchy for ten years. Many cross-border commuters in this group managed to make a clear dividing line between work and their private lives.

3.1.2 *Reconstructing a border between work and private life*

It did indeed seem that these cross-border commuters managed to gain some kind of secondary advantage (in the psychological sense) from their daily migration: after rationalizing and hence inverting the negative mental charge into a quasi-positive charge, traveling time was used as a real "decompression chamber" after work, and the geographical border was symbolically requalified and mentally reconstructed, becoming a new border dividing work and private life. This is a not inconsiderable advantage, given the problems many employees experience in relation to the increasing porosity of the border between work and the private sphere, as a result of the intensive use made of digital technologies and the new relationship with time and urgency they have promoted in our contemporary societies (Jauréguiberry 2014; Aubert 2010). Angélique (self-employed in the complementary medicine sector, 37 years old) explained very clearly her need to raise a "barrier" after work, which occurred almost magically at the exact moment she crossed the geographical border:

> If I stay on in the Grand Duchy, I always have the impression that it's more for the work environment, because there's a different atmosphere and ambiance [...] you feel as if you're still in the work sphere with its pressures, er... [...] but when you cross the border, I don't know, there's something happens and it's not the same [smile] that [...] you get the feeling: once you cross the border [exhaled breath] that's it, you've left it behind you... you know, I see so many people here who are stressed, who are all sorts of things, so I know I mustn't store it all up; I have to put up a barrier, so it's not, well it's not... you have to deal with it somehow [...] that's it, because you get the impression you're still at work [...] so crossing the border means leaving all that behind [...]. That's the feeling I have, I leave, so I get back to France, I [deep exhaled breath] I relax.

It should be noted that Angélique was self-employed in the complementary medicine sector, offering services (not refunded by the official health scheme) in the field of relaxation, fitness, and nutrition. Her clients were therefore highly stressed people, and she consequently "stored up" their stress; she therefore had a strong need to prevent it happening to her—I have to put up a barrier"—and it occurred "when you cross the border, I don't know, there's something happens". She put everything behind her, all the negative affective burden, leaving it in the geographical area of the Grand Duchy; it ceased to affect her, the pressure was off: "[*deep exhaled breath*] I relax". It should also be said that she was not affected by the rush-hour traffic jams, not only because she had chosen to live in France close to the border (she had previously lived much further away in the southern part of Lorraine), but above all because she left early in the morning and returned home late in the evening (her timetable was dependent on appointments with clients).

Thus while the cross-border commuters in this group practiced what we have qualified as "tunnel" migration and were in a hurry to get back to their homes in France in the evening after a long day's work (a working week of 40 hours with abundant overtime at every level), what about their media practices? Did they make any attempt to obtain information and keep abreast of news connected with the Grand Duchy? These are the questions we shall deal with in the next section.

3.2 *Media practices focused on France and international affairs, paying relatively little attention to the Grand Duchy*

What all the members of this group had in common was the fact that they had little interest in news in the Grand Duchy, and reading the daily newspaper *L'Essentiel*—if they actually did—was quite sufficient. It should be noted that *L'Essentiel* is a free Luxembourg daily newspaper, part of whose audience is made up of cross-border commuters: it addresses the interests and particularities of cross-border commuters and, at the same time, gives a brief overview of local news in the Grand Duchy. In 2011–2012, during our survey, *L'Essentiel* took part in setting up the democratic debate on the Luxembourg government's plan to abolish family allowances for cross-border workers (Lamour 2015). There were some differences nevertheless, since the media practices of individuals remained considerably diversified (Granjon/Le Foulgoc 2011; Jouët/Rieffel 2013). We therefore felt it pertinent to consider two categories of media practices within this "tunnel effect" group.

Firstly, those cross-border commuters who were not particularly interested in the news in general and/or those whose main sources of information on current affairs were still the traditional media (particularly the evening news on television, watched on returning to France after work, or the radio in the morning, before leaving for work) were not going to be particularly interested in the news in the Grand Duchy, the country where they were working. At best they would skim through *L'Essentiel*, but not systematically. Some of the respondents said they only read it occasionally, while others, including Karine (a director in the complementary medicine sector, 28 years old), hardly ever looked at it: "I don't have to read it; I don't take the time to do it."

Secondly, one set of cross-border commuters in this group was more interested in news, but it should be noted that their practices in terms of consulting news reports had evolved; they made less use of the traditional media supports (the printed press, television news programs, radio) and more of apps on their smartphones, which enabled them to select both the type of media and the topics of interest to them.

The next case was that of Arnaud (a computer specialist, 28 years old), who described his quasi "addiction" to the news, which he needed in order to clear his mind during his lunch break and instead of a cigarette break. Whereas he had always read the paper version of *L'Essentiel* previously, he had since downloaded the News Republic[8] app on his smartphone (smartphone provided by his employer in IT maintenance). "I look at my phone while I'm eating". His main centers of interest selected in the app were "world news", "France", and "high-tech", including all the news on video games. He also often listened to the France Info radio station, sometimes even when he was at work. From this, it transpires that he had very little appetite for news about the Greater Region, except perhaps for minor news items, things happening "nearby", news items concerning the Greater Region that he had been quite happy to come across in *L'Essentiel*. However, he went on to acknowledge quite freely that he had stopped reading that newspaper on a daily basis since he had started reading the news on his smartphone.

Summing up, we have shown how little interest these respondents in the "tunnel effect" group showed in news in the Greater Region. Even in this last case, *L'Essentiel* was quite sufficient: no other daily Luxembourgish newspaper in French, free or otherwise, was ever consulted, even when they were at home, although they were quite keen on French/world news or news items connected with their personal centers of interest. So why did they not feel the need to go any further? Why did they not seek more

---

8 News Republic is actually an aggregator for mobile devices, with links to the content of many traditional media outlets (e.g. The Guardian, Huffington Post, 20 Minutes, etc.).

detailed information about the country in which they were working? We now need to look at their cultural and social practices.

3.3 *Few cultural and social practices carried out in the Grand Duchy*

We have given an ample description of the "tunnel effect" which led these cross-border commuters to want to engage in their leisure and cultural activities near their place of residence, near their places of sociability, and not want to stay on or come back to the geographical area of the Grand Duchy. As we have seen, there were many reasons for this, connected with not only constraints involving trains and buses but also their affective desire to clearly draw a dividing line between their work and their private lives. The case of Jean-Pierre (an administrative agent, 46 years old) may be recalled; he returned to the Grand Duchy for leisure activities just once in ten years of working there, apart from the traditional annual end-of-year meal with his co-workers. It should not be forgotten, however, that in most cases the co-workers of these cross-border commuters were cross-border commuters themselves, and although a certain level of sociability developed because of their work, they were able to meet up outside the work environment at their place of residence. Occasionally, they would go out with co-workers after work (for a drink or a meal, for example) on the spot in the Grand Duchy, but very few cases were reported to us. The only person in the entire sample to have mentioned "evening parties" at the homes of co-workers living in the Grand Duchy was Arnaud, who was also one of the very few to work in an environment with a majority of Luxembourgish co-workers (sub-contracted to a public service).

In conclusion, these cross-border commuters who experienced the "tunnel effect" had reconstructed—in the place of the former geographical border—a sort of new and more symbolic border between work and their private lives, and had every intention of developing their social and cultural lives in the place where they lived. Their media practices were focused on seeking information on French and international news in general, and reading the free daily newspaper *L'Essentiel*—if they did—was more than sufficient to assuage their meagre appetite for local news connected with the Grand Duchy. The second group from the sample should now be described; we have labelled them "the ambivalents".

4. The ambivalents

This small group contains those cross-border commuters who were active in the liberal professions and residents (former cross-border commuters) who had developed a limited degree of anchorage in the Grand Duchy. This juxtaposition may appear surprising; it nevertheless came about firstly because of their common desire to integrate—more or less intensively—and, as a result of this desire to integrate, because of the pervasiveness of the many paradoxes scattered throughout most of their utterances, which show how difficult it had become for them to situate themselves, as if they were to some extent torn between the two countries, between rational demands (becoming integrated into a new country) and more affective demands (retiring comfortably into a known environment/world, their country of origin). Although the group was small in number, the issue characterizing them seemed an interesting one to identify. Moreover, the "ambivalence" or the dilemma the migrants experience in their everyday lives is well-known in Migration Studies (Bolzman 2016). To attempt to understand the origin of this ambivalence, we shall explore the media, cultural, and sociability practices of these respondents.

4.1 A strategic desire for integration but a paradox-filled discourse

The members of this small group were residents, plus one cross-border commuter active in a liberal profession (a lawyer, who spent much of his time in the Grand Duchy). All shared one essential concern: that of wanting/having to integrate *a minima* in the Grand Duchy. The case of Jonathan (a lawyer in a private practice, resident, 29 years old) will serve as a paradigmatic example to illustrate this ambivalence. His desire to integrate was extremely strategic: after studying law in Nancy, he completed his qualification as a lawyer in the Grand Duchy, since there were a number of advantages not available to him in France (he received a grant for the six months the training lasted, followed by a paid placement with a firm of lawyers, which is not the usual practice in France). He said he had not been alone in taking this path (some 150 lawyers graduate each year in the Grand Duchy, and there are about 2,000 lawyers in practice throughout the country, which is a very high proportion of lawyers in the population—much higher than in the Nancy metropolitan area, despite its historic Law Faculty). He opened his own office and became a resident, thereby displaying a marked desire to integrate: "I'm completely integrated here: I've done it by choice … [a few minutes later] this is the country that provides me with a living, so I live here."

Jonathan was even considering the possibility of acquiring dual nationality[9] in two years' time, so that he could have access to "certain professions that are reserved for Luxembourgers" (Pigeron-Piroth 2009) in the legal field, particularly in the public sector. And yet it quickly appeared that his discourse was full of paradoxes, revealing a manifest ambivalence: Jonathan wanted to keep open the possibility of returning to France one day. He was very happy with the idea of dual nationality recently introduced by the Luxembourg government, since he was overcome at the mere thought of losing his French nationality and thus having the status of a "foreigner" if ever he wanted to return to live in France—a door he wanted to keep open. But it quickly appeared that this ambivalence was making it difficult for him to feel settled in the country and his neighborhood (cf. *infra*), and he went on to describe himself as a "weekend cross-border commuter". The expression is an interesting and very significant one; he was commuting differently, returning to France every weekend. As for the other residents in this small group, the relative ambivalence regarding their integration was in fact correlated to their restricted local social life in the Grand Duchy.

4.2 In the end, very limited local social life and local anchoring

It is a fact that the local sociability of the respondents in this group was very limited. They did not attempt—or did not manage—to truly participate in the life of the village or neighborhood where they lived. Jonathan described himself as a "weekend cross-border commuter", meaning that, resident in the Grand Duchy for the previous five years, he spent all week at his place of work in the Grand Duchy, that he participated "very little in local life here" but took advantage of the weekend to go back to France, to meet up with his friends, to go out, saying that he had very few Luxembourgish friends, and just a few Belgian friends.

The case of Christophe (a computer specialist, resident, 39 years old) is equally interesting. He also felt very torn. Although he had raised a family in the Grand Duchy (two young children) with a woman of Polish origin who had been living there for "more than twenty years" and had acquired Luxembourgish nationality, he still expressed deep ambivalence with re-

9 See the Act of 23 October 2008 for dual nationality.

gard to integration, since he refused to exclude the possibility of returning to live in France: "I'm thinking about... not coming back... in fact, I don't really know... so, er... [...] well I go there nearly every weekend as it is, so, er..."

He had been living in the Grand Duchy for fourteen years and stated clearly that his family and friends had all stayed in northern Lorraine: he still remained very attached to the area, and went to visit them every weekend. But although his children had been born in the Grand Duchy, had always lived there, and had attended a school in the Luxembourg education system (he was proud that they were able to speak the country's three languages, plus Polish with their mother), he was aware of the difficulties the future might bring. His home town in northern Lorraine "isn't home for them" [his children], so he was looking to the future with some anxiety: "And I expect when they're grown up it will be the same [not home for them], so I'm going to be a bit torn between the two..."

What was he to do if on the one hand his children wanted to stay in the Grand Duchy, in the country where they were born and had always lived, and on the other he wanted to go back to Lorraine? It would be a real dilemma. To overcome this, Christophe went on, just seconds later, to manifest a certain degree of denial—"in fact I don't feel torn between the two because there's so little distance"—while at the same time carrying out nothing short of territorial reunification—"personally, I don't see any border between the two, in fact." Thus the Greater Region made it possible for him not to have to make a choice—he could be in both countries at once since they were part of a single territory: the borders had almost ceased to exist—he had just abolished them. The same applied to all those for whom "the Greater Region has a meaning"; it is a very strong meaning, as it brings the economic and affective dimensions together. It seems that the case of these residents, who were formerly cross-border commuters, might raise questions relatively similar to those sociologists used to ask about migrants, or those that psychologists are asking today, with the benefit of hindsight, with regard to the alternating custody of children: how is it possible to live, integrate, put down roots, and construct one's identity in two different geographical places with the idea of alternating and the possibility of returning always at the back of one's mind? Whatever the case, ambivalence and paradox constituted fundamental characteristics of this group, whose integration into the new country was to some extent limited by their still very strong attachment to their country of origin, as if it were impossible to make a definitive choice (Kaufmann/Jemelin 2008). In the following section, we shall analyze the media practices of this group, which will reveal their lack of interest in local news with regard to the Grand Duchy.

4.3 Media practices turned toward France/the world

It appears that the media practices of this small group were, ultimately, not that different from those of the first group; they were not particularly interested in local news in the Grand Duchy and, if they were, reading *L'Essentiel* was quite sufficient for them. They did not read any other Luxembourgish newspaper. Thus, in general their media practices remained oriented toward France and international news. There was only one significant difference in the third group (cf. *infra*).

The case of Philippe (a partner in a firm of lawyers, 43 years old) is interesting: while he was the only person in the entire sample to subscribe to *Le Quotidien* (a French-language printed daily newspaper in the Editpress/Le Républicain Lorrain joint venture) for professional reasons (he said he needed to take an interest in local news for the sake of his local clients), he admitted that he never actually read it, because he was actually not interested in Luxembourg news.

> Otherwise, that interests us as well… not much what happens… so in the Grand Duchy, well… but we need to know for our work […] you have to take a bit of an interest in the country where you work.

His utterance is full of ambiguity (need to take an interest vs. lack of real/actual interest), revealing once again the ambivalence of this group. Thus, Philippe preferred to consult the *Le Monde* app (with alerts), or Google News. Jonathan, who considered himself a "weekend cross-border commuter", said he was only receptive to local news when he returned to the village of his childhood in southern Lorraine, because at least there he knew the names of the surrounding villages, which was not the case in the Grand Duchy, where he was not involved in local life. And Christophe still entered the postcode of the town where he was born in northern Lorraine when he consulted Google News, and did not read any of the Luxembourgish daily newspapers.

To sum up, the media practices of the respondents in this group were, in the end, not so very different from those of the members of the first group. Their sociability and their involvement in local life were also relatively limited, but the essential difference was that their desire to integrate into the Grand Duchy was particularly evident in their discourse, and also sometimes in their actions (particularly by their decision to live in the

Grand Duchy), although this desire remained imbued with ambivalence. We have called them "the ambivalents", since they were torn in this way between their various discursive positions and their acts, the latter not necessarily exactly reflecting the former. This means that there was an increased risk of cognitive dissonance; the ambivalents expressed their difficulties in positioning themselves not only in the social space but also in the territorial/geographical and even linguistic and cultural spaces. Let us now analyze the last group.

5. The Greater Region as a reservoir of cultural resources

We have placed in this group those respondents who, unlike the other groups, appeared to benefit from their particular geographical situation, considering the Greater Region to be a real reservoir of resources, mainly in cultural terms. The Greater Region may also be perceived as a resource for consumer goods, but this was extremely secondary in our survey. Thus, they differed from the previous two groups in their cultural practices, which were more substantial, and consequently in terms of the greater differentiation in their media practices, in as much as they were focused, in additional to general news, on seeking cultural information relating to the whole of the Greater Region.

5.1 Occupying the territory of the Greater Region via cultural practices

Cultural practices seemed to be the most discriminating dimension for characterizing this group: they chose to carry out their outside cultural activities (shows, music, lectures, etc.) throughout the Greater Region. A law of cumulation (Donnat 2007, 2009), well-known in the cultural field, operates here: these respondents were already describing more substantial and more frequent cultural practices than the other members of the sample, who mainly stayed close to home for their outside cultural activities. There may also be a "distinction" effect (Bourdieu 1979) in them seeking to occupy the territory to take advantage of all its resources. These respondents had understood the reality of the resources available in the Greater Region; the only condition was being mobile throughout the territory. Thus, they were not discouraged by the idea of traveling long distances after work, staying on in the evening, or coming back to the Grand Duchy at the weekend. Louis (a computer specialist, 25 years old) explained what the

Greater Region meant to him: it is a roughly rectangular area (approximately 50 kilometers across and 100 kilometers from top to bottom), centered on Metz, and he was prepared to travel anywhere within it for all his outings. Mobility was also a feature for Charles, who realized, with his wife, what area was at his disposal:

> And indeed we took a bit of time… […] it's a… a mindset you need to have, it took us a while to say to ourselves… "We're just being stupid about this! It doesn't make any difference if it's in Luxembourg or Metz, there are loads of things going on".

Having decided to live in Thionville meant being aware of being halfway between Luxembourg and Metz, two culturally attractive cities which were considered and represented in a single mental universe and in a single territory; this virtually erased any ideas of borders and separation. But it also supposed a certain "mindset" since "you have to make the effort to get out of … well, staying in a purely French environment". Charles went on to refer to "loads of things going on" in "the European capital", citing 'Hamlet' at the Grand Théâtre and a concert by the philharmonic orchestra in Luxembourg City, at the *Kulturfabrik*, or even at the *Rockhal* (two concert venues in Esch-sur-Alzette); his wife (not a cross-border commuter) joins him after work: "we have something to eat and go back home after the show." The same was true of the other respondents in this group: it appears that their cultural practices were frequent and substantially above the average for our sample. Let us now look at their media practices.

5.2 Additional media practices, turned toward looking for cultural information

The media practices of members of this group with regard to general and political news were not basically any different from those of the other cross-border commuters. They read *L'Essentiel*, just like the others, but their discourse seemed to point toward greater openness and, above all, their media practices were very different, focusing on cultural news. Because in order to be able to engage in their cultural activities throughout the Greater Region, it was necessary for them to have full information on the shows, concerts, lectures, etc. taking place throughout the territory. And it was there that digital devices came to the fore, facilitating their active effort to seek specific topical information. Firstly, these cross-border commuters looking for cultural information used to subscribe to the various newsletters and alerts available from institutions organizing shows and/or the traditional media. This was explained by Louis, a subscriber to alerts from *L'Essentiel.lu* in order to obtain the information he needed to be able to travel throughout the Greater Region, which he referred to as his "action area", for his outings and leisure activities:

> Well, for instance there I've got the news in the Grand Duchy [via *L'Essentiel*]; yesterday I got a number of alerts telling me "right, the Schueberfouer has started in the middle of Luxembourg"; it might be worth going. I've read a few articles about it, including some minor news items ... I saw there was going to be a presentation at the garden in Wiltz ... a bit of a special evening, very arty, with lanterns, on 10 September, I've penciled in the date already.

Secondly, some of the respondents in the group used social networks, particularly Twitter, which enabled them to forgo traditional media to some extent, and thus have access to cross-border information that was not systematically taken up in the traditional media.

The case of Charles was interesting: he had discovered Twitter three years earlier (he was an early adopter of it at the time of the survey) and he talked about the information consumption dimension, not without humor, explaining in great detail how it had taken some time but he had managed to get the hang of and finally make the most of using Twitter to carry out a real information watch for his Ph.D. thesis: the people on the list of his followers supplied information in the same way as a browser (Cardon 2010; Stenger/Coutant 2011). He subsequently decided to follow a number of institutional accounts circulating cultural information about the Greater Region, such as those of local authorities (Metz city, the Regional Council, the Council for the *département*) and a number of cultural institutions (the tourist board, the 'Pompidou Metz' Centre, concert halls in Lorraine and the Grand Duchy, including *L'Atelier* and the *Rockhal*). He ended by quoting the media on his list, including the France 3 and Mirabelle TV television channels—he was holding on to a few Tweets on cultural news topics—but his analysis was absolutely clear. It was indeed his use of Twitter which, by putting him in direct contact with the institutions and local authorities, etc. concerned, was enabling him to be almost certain of gathering all the available cultural information about the Greater Region, almost exhaustively because he had cumulated and crossed his sources of information. This new "way of operating" ("*manière de faire*") (de Certeau 2004) was combined with severe criticism of the traditional media regarding their inability to circulate cross-border information:

> I think it's because of the borders... er... I was going to say the geographical borders... artificial borders, rather... that are upheld by, er... I was going to say particularly by the traditional press, or even beyond that... that... information, or cultural information, at least yes, that's it, about cultural events that might be going on circulates, I'd say, with more difficulty and I think that by using the, the....well, everything that's new, the communication technologies... it's possible to get rid of all that!

The phrase was out—"it's possible to get rid of all that!" The criticism was clear and incisive—the traditional local and regional media (press, TV, radio) did not circulate information beyond national borders, particularly cultural information, and this new freedom (for that is what is at stake) had been won thanks to digital devices and social networks. This result was associated with a deep and more general criticism of the traditional media. Thus, for example, Louis mentioned the "lack of depth" to the information he was able to find in *L'Essentiel*, which was unsatisfactory for someone like him who was carrying out a specialized information watch. That was why he only read *L'Essentiel* occasionally and not systematically —"I've already got all the information options"; if there was an important event in the general news, he preferred to consult major media sites such as *Le Monde* for an in-depth critical analysis.

To conclude, we feel that this question of criticism of the media corresponds to an intensive use of Twitter. Quentin (a computer specialist, 26 years old) said nothing different when he explained how he decided whether or not to follow a person on Twitter:

> It's the information they choose to share; you decide to follow them for that as well, because it's... the person, the idea, [...] you're not dependent on an editorial line any more, we've even managed to get rid of that.

What Quentin was looking for in the information he collected via Twitter (and in the information circulated by journalists) was the person's "own words" or "opinion"; he felt that carried more weight than if it was relayed by an "entity" or media institution. And he made the same strong demand for freedom expressed by Charles: "we've even managed to get rid of that [editorial line]." How should we understand Quentin's discourse? Our hypothesis is in line with the thoughts developed by Guillaume Caseaux (2014) on the individualization of information in the context of digital media practices.

6. *Conclusion*

To sum up, a genuine digital border was identified on our completing this survey in 2012–2013: for more than twenty years, several tens of thousands of French (approximately 75,000) cross-border commuters were unable to use their mobile phones (for voice and data) as soon as they crossed the border every morning, unless they paid out-of-plan charges or equipped themselves with a second mobile phone. It has been possible to confirm our hypothesis by showing how this socio-technico-economic apparatus (roaming apparatus) may have configured the usage by and the practices of the cross-border commuters and *de facto* their daily border experiences. We witnessed some rather surprising examples of re-bordering, revealing discontinuities when the mobile phone was supposed to provide seamless communication. We have been able to construct a typology, dividing the cross-border commuters into three groups according to their media, cultural, and sociability practices, and their border experiences and social representations of that border.

The first group—the "tunnel effect" group—comprised those commuters who tended to reconstruct a border between their work and their private lives. In fact, the digital border fosters this divide between professional and private life and thus constructs their border experiences; their life in the area of the Grand-Duchy is linked to work and only to work. They developed virtually no social life in the Grand Duchy after work, apart from a few links with their commuter co-workers, and their cultural life was firmly rooted near their place of residence. Their media practices were thus centered on French and international news. Reading the *L'Essentiel* free newspaper was more than sufficient for them, providing them with a little local news about the Grand Duchy.

The second group—the "ambivalents"—comprised members of the independent professions who were mainly residents in the Grand Duchy. They were characterized by their ambivalence and paradoxes, expressing a real integration strategy. They were nevertheless "torn", as they had not broken their links with France, and some of them practiced a form of debordering, which meant that they did not have to make a choice between the two areas. Moreover, their ambivalence meant that they still often felt they were foreigners in the geographical area of the Grand Duchy, and their social, cultural, and media practices were ultimately not all that different from those of members of the first group, i.e. devoid of involvement in local life.

Lastly, the members of the third group perceived and experienced the Greater Region as a real reservoir of essentially cultural resources. Their cultural practices fell within a law of cumulation (Donnat 2007) and they had no hesitation in traveling anywhere in the territory for their outings after work or at the weekend. Their media practices differed from those of the other two groups mainly because they needed to look for cultural information. And we may say without fear of contradiction that this is fostered by digital devices and social networks, including Twitter, which made it much easier for them to find this cross-border information. Seeking information while bypassing the traditional media also led them to develop a critical discourse on the subject of the media; in the end, they were not unhappy to have managed to forgo it.

The results presented, on the basis of a qualitative sample of twenty people, however diversified it may be, cannot claim to be of any general value. They may, however, constitute areas for further thought, particularly as some of our respondents could be considered pioneers, at the time the survey was carried out, in their use of digital devices and social media. With this empirical survey, we tested the influence of the economico-technical apparatus of roaming on the digital media practices of cross-border commuters; it would be relevant to conduct an equivalent survey, to observe the impacts of the abolition of roaming charges since June 2017. Have the digital media practices of border residents increased since the end of the disconnection at the border? And in what way? With the network in France and/or also with the network of colleagues, particularly in the area of the Grand-Duchy? Has their experience of the border evolved towards broader forms of de-bordering, close to transnationalism, fostered by the Internet, digital media and social networks? We may hypothesize that it is more continuous and approaches seamless communication, which was the social imaginary of the ubiquity associated with the very first mobile communications.

References

Amilhat Szary, Anne-Laure (2016): La frontière au-delà des idées reçues. In: Revue internationale et stratégique 2, no. 102, p. 147–153.

Aubert, Nicole (2010): Le culte de l'urgence. La société malade du temps. Paris: Flammarion.

Belkacem, Rachid/Pigeron-Piroth, Isabelle (eds.) (2012): Le travail frontalier au sein de la Grande Région Saar-Lor-Lux. Pratiques, enjeux et perspectives. Nancy: Presses universitaires de Nancy.

Blanchet, Alain (1985): L'entretien dans les sciences sociales. L'écoute, la parole et le sens. Paris: Dunod.

Blanchet, Alain/Gotman, Anne (1992): L'enquête et ses méthodes: l'entretien. Paris: Nathan.

Bolzman, Claudio/Gakuba Théogène-Octave/Minko Siboney (2016): Résidents inattendus: trajectoires, dilemmes et situations de vie des Africains et latino-américains âgés en Suisse francophone. In: Vie Sociale 4, no. 16, p. 79–90.

Cardon, Dominique (2010): La démocratie internet. Promesses et limites. Paris: Seuil.

Cazeaux, Guillaune (2014): Odyssée 2.0. La démocratie dans la civilisation numérique. Paris: A. Colin.

Certeau de, Michel (1998): L'invention du quotidien. Tome 1. Arts de faire. Paris: Gallimard.

Donnat, Olivier (2009): Les pratiques culturelles des Français à l'ère numérique. Enquête 2008. Paris: Ed La Découverte/Ministère de la culture et de la communication.

Donnat, Olivier (2007): Diversité culturelle et combat contre la loi du cumul. In: Revues Plurielles.org, no. 148, access: http://www.revues-plurielles.org/php/index.php

Durand, François (2015): Theoretical Framework of the Cross-border Space Production – The case of the Eurometropolis Lille – Kortrijk – Tournai. In: Journal of Borderlands Studies, 30, no. 3, p. 309–328, DOI: 10.1080/08865655.2015.1066701.

Granjon, Fabien/Le Foulgoc, Aurélien (2010): Les usages sociaux de l'actualité. In: Réseaux "Presse en ligne" 2, no. 160–161, p. 225–253.

Granjon, Fabien/Le Foulgoc, Aurélien (2011): Penser les usages sociaux de l'actualité. In: Réseaux "Actualités et citoyenneté à l'ère numérique" 6, no. 170, p. 17–43.

Goulet, Vincent, Vatter/Christoph (eds.) (2013): Champs médiatiques et frontières dans la "Grande Région" SaarLorLux et en Europe. Mediale Felder und Grenzen in der Grossregion SaarLorLux und in Europa. Nancy: Presses universitaires de Nancy.

Goulet, Vincent/Vatter, Christoph (eds.) (2015): Grenzüberschreitende Informationsflüsse und Medien in der Großregion SaarLorLux. La circulation transfrontalière des informations médiatiques dans la Grande Région Saar-Lor-Lux. Baden-Baden: Nomos.

Hamez, Gregory (2015): Pour une analyse géographique des espaces transfrontaliers. Mémoire HDR, Université de Rouen.

Hamman, Philippe (2005): Les travailleurs frontaliers en Europe. Mobilités et mobilisations transnationales. Paris: L'Harmattan.

Jauréguiberry, Francis (2014): La déconnexion aux technologies de communication. In: Réseaux "La Déconnexion" 4, no. 186, p. 15–49.

Jouët, Josiane (2001): Retour critique sur la sociologie des usages, In: Réseaux 18, no. 100, p. 487–521.

Jouët, Josiane/Rieffel, Rémy (eds.) (2013): S'informer à l'ère numérique. Rennes: Presses universitaires de Rennes.

Kaufmann, Jean-Claude (1996): L'entretien compréhensif. Paris: Nathan.

Kaufmann, Vincent/Jemelin, Christophe (2008): La motilité, une forme de capital permettant d'éviter les irréversibilités socio-spatiales? In: Sechet, R./Garat, I./ Zeneidi, D. (eds.): Espaces en transaction. Rennes: Presses universitaires de Rennes, DOI : 10.4000/ books.pur.432.

Koukoutsaki-Monnier, Angeliki (ed.) (2014): Identités (trans)frontalières au sein et autour de l'espace du Rhin supérieur. Nancy: Presses universitaires de Nancy.

Lamour, Christian (2015): La presse gratuite comme vecteur d'une métropolisation transfrontalière? In: Goulet, V./Vatter, C. (eds.): Grenzüberschreitende Informationsflüsse und Medien in der Großregion SaarLorLux. La circulation transfrontalière des informations médiatiques dans la Grande Région Saar-Lor-Lux. Baden-Baden: Nomos, p. 79–103.

Martin, Corinne (2004): Représentations sociales du téléphone portable chez les jeunes adolescents et leur famille. Quelles légitimations des usages? Doctoral thesis, Sciences de l'information et de la communication, Université Paul Verlaine-Metz. http://docnum.univ-lorraine.fr/public/UPV-M/Theses/2004/Martin.Corinne.LMZ0413.pdf.

Moscovici, Serge (2005): L'âge des foules. Un traité historique de psychologie des masses. Paris: Fayard.

Pigeron-Piroth, Isabelle (2009): Le secteur public. In: Économie et statistiques 34, p. 1–34.

Silverstone, Roger/Haddon, Leslie (1996): Design and the domestication of information and communication technologies: technical change and everyday life. In: Mansell, R./Silverstone, R. (eds.): Communication by Design: The Politics of Information and Communication Technologies. Oxford: Oxford University Press, p. 44–74.

Stenger, Thomas/Coutant, Alexandre (eds.) (2011): Ces réseaux numériques dits sociaux. In: Hermès, no. 59.

About the author

Corinne Martin | University of Lorraine | Centre de Recherche sur les Médiations | Ile du Saulcy | F–57045 Metz Cedex 1 | France | T +33 6 84 30 66 12 | corinne.martin@univ-lorraine.fr

Corinne Martin is a sociopsychologist. She obtained her Ph.D. in Information and Communication Sciences in 2004, and is an Associate Professor at the University of Lorraine (France)/ *Centre de Recherche sur les Médiations* (CREM, ÉA 3476). She has worked on digital practices, mobile culture (mobile phones/smartphones), digital media, and social networks, and has extended her research to digital culture within different territories (e.g. third places). She is also participating in the "13-Novembre" program, a cross-disciplinary research program (2016–2028) on the construction and evolution of individual and collective memory after the terrorist attacks in Paris in 2015.

Betweenness and the emergence of order

Florian Dost, Konstanze Jungbluth, Nicole Richter

Abstract

Experiencing betweenness is quite frequent in border spaces where liminal spaces arise. Our case studies range from Belgian Walloon/Belgian French/ Dutch virtual encounters to German/Russian/English chat communication and to Polish/German face-to-face conversations. In these contexts, people's perceptions are of a fleeting nature, reflecting the dynamics of the b/ order in question. In contact with one another across borders and languages, they challenge their own ways of evaluating products or speech; unconsciously, they accommodate themselves to their interlocutors or show divergence from some of them. Sometimes they start to create shared forms of expression.

Bridging economics and linguistics, our research confirms the notion that experiencing betweenness is contiguously related to the liminal space. Either this transitional phenomenon suffers a setback and fades away, or a well-ordered system arises, inevitably accompanied by the emergence of a new order.

Keywords

Border, order, betweenness, business sciences, linguistics, microeconomics, language contact, perception studies

1. *Experiencing betweenness of B/Orders*

The motto of our interdisciplinary approach to border experiences embedded in business, social and cultural sciences may be called *economics meets linguistics*. Strongly committed to empirical data, and its analysis and interpretation, we aim to show that plurilingual encounters, face-to-face or virtual, should be considered liminal spaces (Turner 1998). People of different linguistic and cultural backgrounds experience betweenness along fading borders, where the flux of the orders belonging to either part allows crossings and the creation of new combinations, which may or may not be positively evaluated. Our case studies range from Belgian Walloon/Belgian

French/Dutch virtual encounters to German/Russian/English chat communication and to Polish/German face-to-face conversations. Our survey on value perception among consumers in Belgium and the Netherlands—some of them Dutch–French bilinguals—shows that language barriers determine the access to additional information and consumers' possible re-evaluation of products.

Choices not only form parts of economic contexts, but also determine language use. Speakers are always forced to accommodate their way of speaking to the needs of their interlocutors, but in contexts of plurilingual communities, these choices of items and their combination, for words and grammar, have an even stronger impact. There are different constellations of productive or receptive bilingualism which must be taken into consideration in order to understand the moves of interlocutors in an ongoing conversation. We argue that members of bilingual language communities in border regions and others, engaged in virtual communication, are experts in plurilingual dialogue (German–Polish, Russian–German–English) who masterfully exploit the full potentialities of language contact. In the first phase, experiencing borders may lead to convergence between the codes involved. In the second phase, code-mixing may be observed. Finally, fused forms may become more and more frequent, indexing an emerging new system with the potential to become routinized, later conventionalized, and finally generalized by a community upgrading their way of expressing themselves into the coining of a new language variety.

Experiencing the former borders as constructed and changeable leads to an in-between state which must be considered temporary. How do social actors (re-)establish well-defined borders, and which steps in this process can we observe in our data? More precisely, we focus on individual and collective behavior, showing the integration of forms or features in contact due to the different perspectives and practices present in the ongoing interaction. Which circumstances favor the emergence of a codified new order? From a dynamic perspective, betweenness characterizes the transdifferent states on the move experienced by social actors directly at the borders between old and upcoming new orders (Lösch 2005; cf. 5 below).

2. *Experiencing the emergence of new orders*

When contact along these borders happens, social actors experience the differences on either side of the old border, but from the perspective of neither side. As a result, the actors involved feel pressure to resolve and dissolve the inherently borderless state. Betweenness is, thus, a pressing, fleeting perceptual phenomenon, as it becomes resolved in the dynamics of the b/order (Schiffauer et al. 2018). Betweenness can be temporary, in that the undefined and undecided transdifferent state dissolves into a modified border and order (see Figure 1). However, betweenness may also develop into emerging new borders with a defined and codified liminal space that extends temporally in a stable state into the future, thus representing a new order.

A: Temporary betweenness and modified (new) order

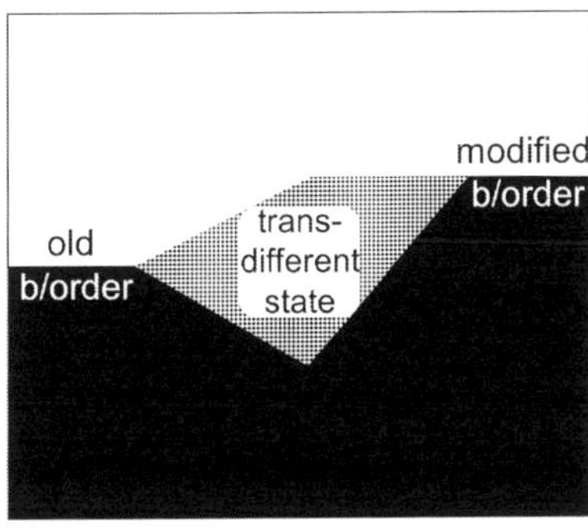

B: Betweenness and the emergence of a codified new order

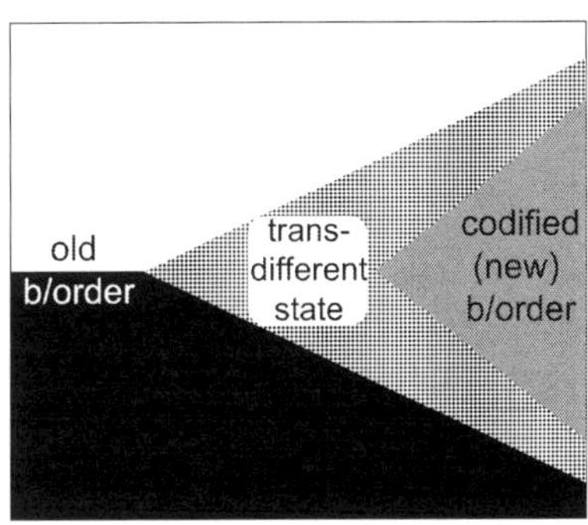

Figure 1: Betweenness of old and new orders and the emergence of new borders

We argue that this concept of betweenness can help to explain the dynamics of b/orders and the formation of new orders in many fields of social science. It is therefore an important, yet also elusive concept for describing border regions in social perception, cultural orders and processes, complex social systems, linguistic phenomena, and communication. We outline, demonstrate, and discuss betweenness (in its individual experience and through external observation across disciplines) from the unlikely perspective of business sciences and economics, and link it back to the concept in linguistics, which is itself rooted in ethnology (Turner 1998).

3. *Experiencing betweenness in decision-making*

3.1 *Experiencing betweenness in individual social actor decision-making*

Social actors experience betweenness at many perceived and socially constructed borders, including those most fundamental to the business sciences and microeconomics: borders in decision-making or choice. In classic economic theory, choice behavior involves trade-offs of expected utility versus monetary sacrifice. Almost all economics textbooks define the border as being at the point of equilibrium betweem utility and sacrifice, i.e. the border(s) between choice or no choice—stated in monetary terms as the reservation price. Yet between choice and no choice—directly at the border—there exists a "range of reservation prices" (Wang/Venkatesh/Chatterjee 2007) where choice is undefined and uncertain. This range of reservation prices then marks betweenness in the classic economics notion of choice. Experiments studying consumers and product demand simulations have shown that disregarding this instance of betweenness in choice, and thereby sticking to the single-border concept of reservation price, leads to inferior predictions of actual consumer purchase behavior (Wang/Venkatesh/Chatterjee 2007; Dost/Wilken 2012). This betweenness in choice extends beyond monetary settings; similar betweenness can be observed in the willingness to contribute time to a local public good in a non-monetized, small-scale community in Papua New Guinea (Pondorfer/Rehdanz 2018).

Similarly, betweenness occurs in general judgments and evaluations, for example when judging distances, lengths, or counts (Krüger et al. 2014). Betweenness in evaluations becomes particularly pronounced when social actors enter a psychological state of high-level construal, characterized by abstract and psychologically distant (e.g. temporally distant) mental processing. The more abstract and future-oriented the way in which a social actor processes a current border, the wider the related betweenness extends into the space of seemingly different orders. Conversely, with more concrete or present-oriented mental processing, the sharper and more distinct the border seems to be. Incidentally, the same effect of pronounced betweenness from more abstract processing has been experimentally confirmed in a consumer-choice setting with reservation price ranges (Isaak/Wilken/Dost 2015).

Betweenness in reservation prices marks an indecisive state of decision makers (Dost et al. 2014; Schlereth/Eckert/Skiera 2011). In this state, decision makers are under a perceived pressure to update their preferences with all available information, potentially shifting and modifying the old border(s) of choice, and thus arriving at a modified order (i.e. a new reservation price; Wathieu/Bertini 2007). Similarly, when integrating information from the liminal space, new, temporally stable, and distinct choice options can be manifested in the perception of the decision maker (Dost/Wilken 2014). It has been shown, for example, that after consumers are exposed to an unexpected state of betweenness in their choice of coffee, "fair trade" is increasingly perceived as a distinct category of coffee with a higher perceived value, commanding a higher monetary sacrifice. Conversely, at prices well outside the range of reservation prices (i.e. on either side of the old order), consumers initially evaluated fair trade coffee as just another coffee variant, and therefore, no temporally stable new category for fair trade coffee is formed (Wathieu/Bertini 2007). We argue that experiencing betweenness will typically exert pressure on social actors; it is this pressure that drives the onset of the dissolution of old borders, the modification of bordering orders, or the emergence of a new liminal space in a new order.

3.2 *Experiencing betweenness in topic or issue formation*

With its relevance for perception and valuation, betweenness occurs in communication processes such as the emergence of new topics, issues, or trends. Topics between related networks and systems of meaning which are distinct from either existing order—and are thus in-between—hold the most promise for forming persisting new networks of meaning and forms of communication. For example, Barron et al. (2018) found, in an information–theoretical analysis of the French revolution national assembly records, that new topics or new modes of delivery ("patterns of heteroglossia") were more likely to change the subsequent form and content of discourse when they managed to relate to existing word patterns, while also being radically novel. When new delivery does not codify into a new order, it disappears quickly, contributing just minor modifications to the existing forms (Barron et al. 2018). Similarly, in online social network communication, the existing orders offer a "trellis" (Bail 2016) to support the codification of the new topics or forms of communication as a distinct new order. Trending topics in the news cycle are those that bridge existing orders and topical networks (Bail 2016). Many similar observations have been made regarding the persistence and success of new scientific ideas that fall between existing fields and networks of knowledge (Borrett/Moody/Edelman 2014) and regarding the language and word patterns to describe these ideas (Vilhena et al. 2014). In all these instances, betweenness shapes the dynamics of communication and discourse.

Subsequently, we provide an empirical case from marketing communications that involves an emerging betweenness in the communication among consumers, pressure from experiencing betweenness in one consumer group, and the dissolution of betweenness without a stable change in old orders.

We analyzed survey perception data on an emerging product perception issue in the context of marketing a product through a consumer community in three regions and two languages (Flemish/so-called 'Belgian Dutch' and Walloon in Belgium, Dutch in the Netherlands). Here, betweenness enters consumers' product value perceptions in the form of an ecological issue with the product arising in the Dutch part of the consumer community. The ecological issue is picked up by the Dutch-speaking Flemish part of the community, and much later by the French-speaking Walloons, leading to a transdifferent state in their product valuations as well as increased pressure to resolve their in-between valuation.

The study follows the introduction of a new cleaning product by means of a so-called product seeding or micro-influencer campaign (Haenlein/Libai 2017). In such marketing campaigns, everyday consumers are equipped with a new product and asked to test it. The participating consumers enter a campaign-related online community platform to network and communicate with each other as well as the product manufacturer. Businesses hope that the consumers involved will spread product recommendations and word-of-mouth information to their peers (Dichter 1966; Berger/Schwartz 2011).

In our case, 913 consumers across the Netherlands, and the Flemish and Walloon regions of Belgium participated in the campaign for five weeks. Every week, a list of the most prevalent positive or negative topics or issues was compiled using the online platform communication of the three consumer groups. Here, we focus on the top three negative issues per week (see Figure 2). In addition, a weekly survey asked all consumers for product valuations and their cognitive involvement in a possible purchase decision on commonly used Likert-type scales (rescaled to 0: lowest and 1: highest). The averages for all three consumer groups are plotted in Figure 2 as well.

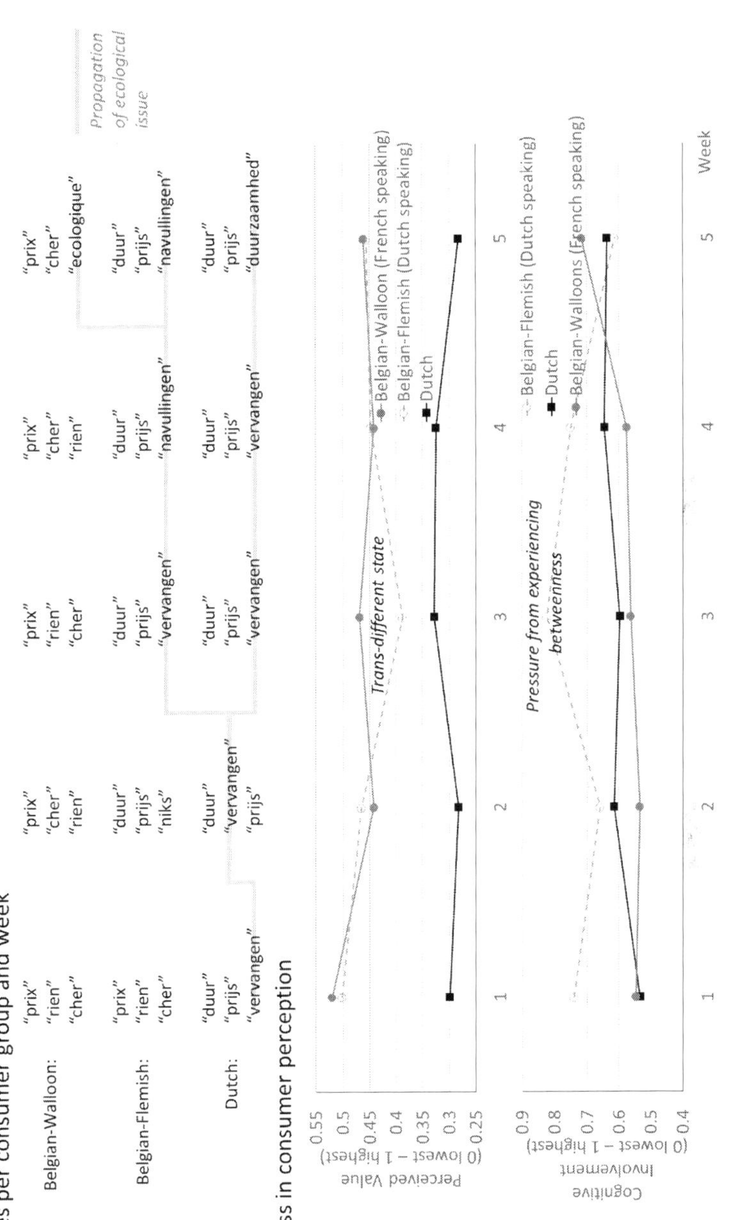

Figure 2: Experiencing betweenness in product valuation across language barriers

In the first week, following the product's introduction, a negative issue came up among the Dutch consumers. While all consumers in all regions perceived the cleaning product to be expensive (marked by trending topics "cher" and "prix" in Walloon, and "duur" and "prijs" in Flemish parts of Belgium and the Netherlands), the Dutch consumers also spotted an ecological downside to the product: They discussed how the cleaning product requires frequent refills ("verwangingen" or "verwangen"), thus generating additional waste. This issue was picked up in week three by the Dutch-speaking Flemish ("navulligen", "vervangen"), and only entered the discussions of the predominately French-speaking Walloons in week five ("ecologique"). The corresponding aggregate product evaluations from the weekly surveys demonstrate the betweenness experienced by the Flemish consumers, as their evaluations drop to a level between their Dutch and Walloon counterparts. Before week three, Dutch consumers started with lower product evaluations than Belgian consumers, possibly due to the perceived ecological issue. As Flemish consumers are often bilingual and can read both the Dutch and French comments of their fellow participants, they picked the issue up in week three. At the same time that their product evaluations drop to an in-between level, Flemish consumers' average cognitive involvement reaches the highest level observed across the consumer groups and weeks. We attribute this increase to the perceived pressure to resolve the experienced betweenness in the discussed social consensus on product perceptions and evaluations. After a week of discussions, mainly among the Flemish participants, the betweenness dissolves, but without establishing a new order, even though the issue is finally picked up by the Walloon consumers as well.

3.3 Findings and their effect on betweenness

In this example from a consumer-generated marketing communication context, betweenness enters cleaning product evaluations of a consumer group that can perceive two distinct discourses about the product. When the consumer group (the Flemish consumers) picks up the discourse in Dutch, their evaluations approach those of their Dutch consumer counterparts. Concurrently, betweenness starts exerting pressure in the form of higher cognitive loads. We argue that this pressure leads the Flemish consumers to resolve their in-between evaluation and return to evaluations similar to their French-speaking peer group, the Walloon consumers. This example illustrates the inherent instability of an emerging betweenness in communication.

The discourse about this cleaning product happened in a virtual border space, an electronic communication platform, where geographic barriers are less meaningful, but language barriers may remain. The example shows the importance of social actors capable of bridging these remaining barriers, such as in the case of bilinguals in border regions. The following examples will investigate the role of bilinguals for betweenness in language and discourse from a deeper, linguistic perspective.

4. Experiencing betweenness in situations of language contact

4.1 Language contact in plurilingual encounters

Borders are no longer lines, but liminal spaces between two centers. This is true for border regions such as the *Greater Region SaarLorLux* spanning across Saarland and the Rhineland-Palatinate in Germany, the Grand Duchy of Luxembourg, the French region of Lorraine, and finally Belgium's Walloon region, where French is spoken, as well as the German-speaking community in Belgium. Furthermore, such liminal spaces may develop twin cities like Frankfurt (Oder) (D)/Słubice (POL), Görlitz (D)/Gorzelec (POL), or Euroregions such as Brandenburg (D)/Lubuskie (POL). In these spaces, new markets emerge between the centers already established in the past, e.g. Berlin (D) and Poznań (POL), favoring plurilingual encounters. People meet in these spaces to exchange goods and enjoy their leisure time, among other activities.

Their bi- and plurilingual language use facilitates communication among speakers of different first languages (L1 speakers). The interlocutors learn to express themselves and understand others in their second and third languages and beyond (L2 speakers, L3 speakers etc.). When they meet more and more frequently, these encounters become conventionalized and the groups involved form bi- and plurilingual communities of practice (Wenger 1998; Wille 2008). They create routines which are sometimes reciprocally used as internal identity markers among their members. Their particular language use is recognized by outsiders, thus assuming an external importance. Similar language routines may be observed in the language use among migrants and their children or grandchildren, residents of certain suburban areas shared by members of first, second, and third generations, or among people living in diaspora (on Brazil, cf. Jungbluth 2016; on Georgia, cf. Höfler forthcoming; on Germans in the former Russia, cf. Baumgärtner 2018). All of them use several languages—spoken or written—to communicate with each other from time to time, more or less regularly.

In these spaces of betweenness, new (urban) dialects may emerge (for example: Kiez-Deutsch, cf. Wiese 2006, 2012a, 2012b; ARTE 2012; Singlish: Vogelsang 2014; Schneider 2017). Some of them may be considered (proto-)creoles, a process which recalls the emergence of Romance languages roughly one thousand years ago, when the varieties of Latin spoken in the different parts of the Roman Empire underwent a process of emancipation and developed their own spoken and later on written forms, e.g. French, Spanish, Catalan, Portuguese, Romanian, and Italian, among others.

These changes characterizing the underlying processes take place in three phases: first, acceptance of variants by bi- or plurilingual individuals; second, the selection of some forms deemed by members of certain groups as identity markers; and third, the reduction of the forms when their use spreads, is generalized, and finally becomes the norm for all citizens (residents of the respective neighborhood; group members living in that space; people of a state: "imagined communities"; cf. Anderson 1983). Though language change happens in all language settings, plurilingual speech communities often exhibit an extraordinarily strong drive. A temporal dimension is also added to spatial belonging when the latter stage takes the floor right at the moment when a self-confident new language community arises.

Observing the language use of bilingual speakers offers a detailed picture of the processes of language production when two (or more) languages are involved. The tendency to choose one language (in the first place), then also to include the other language if necessary, has been described by many scholars in linguistics (cf. Muysken 1995, Clyne 2000, Lüdi 2004, Jungbluth 2012). In this article, we will focus on how borders are perceived by interlocutors in language use, and how they are established or dissolved in discourse. In discussing these phenomena, we emphasize a three-phase process of betweenness.

4.2 Experiencing betweenness: accepting new forms

Examples of bilingual language use—Russian in contact with German and English:

Whenever speakers make use of code-mixing, they demonstrate that two more or less equal polylingual forms exist in the first place. In the following, some examples will be presented, showing that users in bilingual chats communicate within their group quite naturally. In doing so, they not only establish this community of practice but also repeatedly confirm their form of expression. Even if we are dealing with so-called typed communication, it still reminds us of oral communication phenomena where codemixing is typical amongst bilingual speakers. Of course, this technique is usually used when all participants in a conversation have access to the languages involved.

Example (1) is taken from a trilingual online chat (Chit-Chat within russen-chat.de) and contains German elements within a Russian utterance (cf. Schreiner 2010).

(1) *dlja tex kto po angliski ne* sprech-*ujet*
for those who in English not speak (3.P.Sg.Pres.)
(Rus/Ger/Eng online chat *russen-chat.de, date: 06/09/2010*)

The word-like element *sprechujet* consists of a German word stem *sprech-* (ENG: *speak*) that transfers the semantics of the "word", and the Russian flectional ending *u-jet* is added onto the German stem. When looking at the whole sentence, we see that this flectional ending is correct from the Russian perspective. From the speaker's (or user's) perspective, this form could be defined as a spontaneous neologism. It is spontaneous because it is not generally known as a neologism, but it is easily understood. One potentially interesting research question arises here: namely, whether bilinguals would immediately notice that the "other language" has been inserted. However, in this article we concentrate on how these examples show betweenness.

As discussed by Pavlenko (2002) for Russian–English bilinguals, the uttering of mixed forms seems to be a common technique. Pavlenko reports a study that consists of examples of English and Russian emotional oral communication and narratives. She additionally refers to an example introduced by Andrews (1999), where an English word is inserted into a Russian utterance:

(2) *Oni budut ochen'* eksaited*!* Andrews (1999, p. 100)
they will be very excited (Russian *vzolnovannyj*)

As compared to (1), there is no morphological marking showing integration into the matrix language. An interesting discussion concerning the differing semantics of the two lexemes *excited* (ENG) and *vzolnovannyj* (RUS) is suggested by Pavlenko; focusing on the inserted adjective *eksaited*, "the translation is only an approximate one, as the Russian word contains a negative element of worry or nervous agitation, absent from its English counterpart" (Pavlenko 2002, p. 71). So, the consequence here is that a bilingual who wants to focus on the encouraging or promising semantics has chosen to, according to Pavlenko, "appeal to lexical borrowing and code-switching". (2002, p. 71) One could also label this form as a spontaneous neologism due to its semantic difference.

While code-switching is frequent, forms of code-mixing below the word level are less common (examples 3 & 4), and abbreviations are a way to bridge the liminal space on the one hand, and to establish an insider jargon on the other. The latter, which can indicate identity-marking, will be discussed in the next part.

Examples of the first phase are the following:

(3) *Jades do* op-*yi* om-*y*. (Jańczak 2013, p. 180).
Go you to grandpa-CASEand grand-ma-CASE
You go to your grandparents.

(4) *Nie ma* zug-*u*. (Jańczak 2013, p. 179)
Nois train-CASE
There is no train.

These examples show that the bilingual users, members of a bilingual German–Polish speech community, frequently integrate German nouns into their predominantly Polish sentences. They even do not hesitate to attach flectional morphology, treating the words as if they were Polish nouns—as described for the Russian–German examples in (1). Sometimes, even native words are replaced with neologisms: *Zitron* (German: "Zitrone") instead of Polish *cytryna* (Meise 2008, p. 124). The reciprocal acceptance of producing and listening by the interlocutors—in short, the shared licensing of these forms of expression and their evaluation as legitimate language use—reflects the conventionalized form of practice established and performed again and again among its members.

4.3 Experiencing betweenness: emergence of new forms indicating identity

Examples of bilingual language use—Russian in contact with German and English:

As noted above, discussing examples surrounding the concept of the border does not have to involve a physical geographic division. Rather, it can be located in the individuals themselves when online communication is the object of study. For Russian–German bilinguals, the border is between languages, language families, and communicative conventions.

From a sociolinguistic perspective, we can see that the pure use of bilingual mixed forms shows that these forms are understood and accepted in a community. The question arises whether mixing phenomena can also be interpreted as a marker of identity for an individual who has produced the forms, and further as an identity marker for a whole community.

Russian–German bilinguals are faced with borders on several levels, borders between the two languages that only partly share morphological forms and morphological marking. Other levels may concern language families or different cultures. In the online conversations mentioned above, the reference to identity can be observed in the use of special nicknames or user screen names symbolizing bilingualism. Some examples of these names are: Xx-Sonza-xX, Sladkij2008 or RUSSLANDDEUTSCHER (cf. Schreiner 2010). The word *sonza* in the first screen name shows that the Russian pronunciation of the middle consonant [ts] is represented by the letter <z>, its typical realization in German orthography. Thus, bilingualism is demonstrated at the outset in the name itself. The second name, Sladkij, is a Russian adjective (Eng. 'sweet'), and can thus imply the user's Russian identity. The third example, 'Russlanddeutscher' (Russian German), is a German word and a clear symbol that inserts the category *Russian German* directly into the conversation. We, of course, do not speak of the identity of the individuals themselves, but these names are cited as examples symbolizing bilingualism, which is emphasized in the communication at hand.

Similar frames in the morpho-syntactic structure of the languages allow the interlocutors to easily switch between languages and insert words or even morphemes into the other language. By doing so, the speakers and users show some part of their (communicative) identity, which can be described as being in-between—or at least the language that they use shows equivocal elements of betweenness.

Examples of language use in the liminal space of the border region:

Of course, examples of typical markers of insider talk are not limited to the aforementioned use of abbreviations (studied in the context of outlaws, e.g. Rotwelsch in Kluge (1987), Yenish in Ehlich (2010), or criminal gangs). The use of abbreviations is motivated by the desire to disallow or at least to reduce understanding/comprehension for outsiders—in the cases discussed here, representatives of society such as police officers, judges, or other members of the respective speech community. During adolescence, the exclusion of parents, teachers, and peers from certain topics (and their evaluation discussed by the adolescents (cf. 'liminal' Turner 1998) and young adults) is one of the motives for using abbreviations or cryptic forms of expression. Meaning can be further obscured by applying processes of change in the linear sequence of parts of speech, as in the example of speaking backwards (cf. the French argot is known for using the technique of *Verlan* characterized by replacing the word order of syllables in French vernacular speech, *opposé au "parler correct"*).

First, residents of Frankfurt (Oder), and even many students of the European University Viadrina, are not familiar with the term *offa*, an abbreviation or acronym used by the previously discussed bilingual student group in several of their cohorts to refer to German 'öffentliches Recht' *public law*. Second, among other identifiers, the naming of their insider-talk as *Viadrinisch ('Viadrinic')* reveals that their form of expression has become a marker of their belonging to the place, to the institution, and particularly represents their being part of the inter-year classes at different levels studying German and Polish Law, generation by generation, one following the other.

In the context of Denmark, Quist (2005, p. 146) states that the variety of Danish used among the adolescents in Copenhagen should be considered a new linguistic resource—a variety of Danish in its own right, confirming, among other things, their new identity ('act of identity'; cf. Le Page/ Tabouret-Keller 1985). In doing so, she rejects negative assessments calling it "incorrect Danish" or devaluations declaring their language use as "uncompleted second language acquisition" (cf. Wiese 2006).

The adolescent informants themselves exhibit a well-defined self-awareness of belonging on several levels: "In the end we [people from the quarter] are Kreuzbergers—Berliners—German[er]s—Cosmopolitans." (*Im Endeffekt sind wir Kreuzberger – Berliner – Deutschländer – Weltbürger!* cf. Corpus Kiezdeutsch; Wiese 2012b).

4.4 Experiencing betweenness: emerging new language communities

This third phase is represented here by the special case of Russian–German–English virtual online communities. These communities may develop into communities in the "real world" if the communication is extended to the offline domain (on establishing communities, cf. Androutsopoulos 2006, Brehmer 2013). The first two phases can be seen as the basis for a new language community. As has been explained, linguistic markers can be interpreted as symbols of identity for both the individual speaker and for speech communities consisting of speakers (and users) using these mixed forms.

In today's world of global communication, the spread of what may have been considered to be cryptic insider talk may end up as a new dialect (cf. Kiezdeutsch: Wiese 2012a). The use of the aforementioned French argot developed in the *banlieues* (Eng. "quarters"), and is no longer restricted to its former speakers, but has been imitated by teenagers from other social groups and is also used in the media. There are even suggestions about integrating this way of speaking French into the German-speaking classroom in Switzerland (Nacro 2001, and educational recommendations there). One is not required to follow this proposal, but one must be aware that new language communities may be the outcome of an early state of betweenness.

In contrast to the neologisms integrated into a speech act reflecting the first phase, where the interlocutors may accept or refuse their use, and the second phase characterized by upgrading certain practices into a speech style indicating a certain group identity, the third phase is characterized by an ongoing conventionalization of the use of fused forms observed by the members of a speech community as a whole. This expansion of use as part of the social dimension is accompanied by a change in the forms of expression themselves. The high variability of expressions during the earlier phases solidify into one or two forms. Some of them still show their dual origins and may be characterized as transparent with regard to the languages involved in their becoming a word (cf. Bachmann 2005 & forthcoming), but others represent fused forms. These lemmas are more or less opaque, but they are definitely no longer the arbitrary combination of two languages, as they have undergone a profound change; rather than demarcating a clear line of division, they show an extended overlapping space which may belong to either language.

(5) wyräumuj
DER V IMP 2.P.Sg
clear out (the dishwasher)

This order shows a fused form, as there are two Polish affixes—one of them of a derivational (wy-), the other of flectional nature (-uj: IMP 2.P.Sg.)—surrounding a German root (Zinkhahn-Rhobodes 2016, p. 204–205).

(6) ten Prüfung cały
DET N ADJ
This whole exam

The superficial impression that the two languages are used in a well separated way is misleading, as two of the lexical items forming part of the nominal phrase, the demonstrative pronoun *ten* ("this") and the adjective *cały* ("whole"), obviously show agreement with the noun *Prüfung* ("exam") with regard to number: singular, gender: masculine, and case: accusative. The latter may be derived from the (possibly left out) verb *mieliśmy* ("we had") (colloquial) and its regimen. The choice of the gender may follow either the rules of gender in Polish, which in the case of a consonant ending designate it as masculine, or by referring to the Polish masculine counterparts: *egzamin* ("exam") or *sprawdzian* ("test"). This kind of language use is only possible by routinized bilingual speakers toward equally well-trained listeners. There is no doubt whatsoever about the fused character of the nominal phrase (Zinkhahn-Rhobodes 2016, p. 185–187).

Wiese (2012a) emphasizes the positive evaluation of the way former migrants speak German in some neighborhoods of Berlin by identifying this restructured form of expression in German as an emerging new urban dialect. In doing so, she also recognizes its function as an identity marker, and as a symbol of belonging to a certain community of practice, possessing its own customs and its particular way of speaking.

Again, the borders here are not strictly geographic—certainly much less so than the former Iron Curtain—but the shared experience of talking to one another in the language of the host country, which is the second or third language for most of the inhabitants of these districts. The migrants came from distant areas where a wide range of languages are spoken. The majority of this speaker group is third-generation immigrants, who have learned to speak German fluently, and use it to communicate regularly with one another. However, their word choice and syntax are not the same as in areas where the majority of the residents is of German ancestry. Their way of speaking German has been influenced by language contact as well; in informal contexts, most of them speak a German variety flagged by a more or less openly marked German dialect representing their regional belonging.

For all these users, language contact is not restricted to two languages, even less to two language varieties. Every single day they are in contact with people belonging to different language communities and use several languages. In line with Auer/Muhamedova (2005, p. 52–53), we must rethink the still well-established methods of researching language contact based on the languages which we assume to be in contact. However, the data and the way the interlocutors perform suggest that we should start from their concrete utterances:

> We wanted to argue for an approach to code-mixing utterance as the starting point, rather than the monolingual 'codes' which these mixed

> utterances seem to refer to. Our examples demonstrate that often, there is no monolingual code which can be taken as the point of reference. This conclusion is also reached by Myers-Scotton in her 2002 theory with respect to the matrix language; here she insists that the matrix is not identical to any single 'monolingual' language but is just an abstract construct. [...] The conclusion, however, is inevitable: bilingual talk cannot be analysed as a mixture of two monolingual codes (Auer/ Muhamedova 2005, p. 52–53).

In the broader context of border studies, Lösch (2005) has proposed leaving behind binary theories of cultural differences. He proposes using the term *transdifference* instead (for a recently published application cf. Gaio 2018).

5. *Experiencing transdifference and research perspectives*

Similar to the larval stage of insect development, transdifference refers to an in-between phase—it is a transitional state in the liminal space. This phase is unsteady, but people may decide to develop its structure further. In doing so, they establish a new routine, e.g. a shared practice of valuation or a new language use, which may become shaped as a recognized form. A new order emerges and the new variety becomes more and more stable, limited by its own borders becoming more and more durable during this process. The term "transdifference" offers us the opportunity to analyze the phases of betweenness from different perspectives: they can be heard in the conversations between speakers and their interlocutors, overheard, documented, and transcribed in our linguistic data, and also observed in the behavior of consumers, as shown by the survey data in the first part of this article.

Examples in modern times of former creole languages, such as *kreyòl ayisyen* in Haiti, Papiamento in the ABC islands (Bachmann 2005 & forthcoming), or the emergence of the Romance languages a thousand years ago, show that a community's way of speaking may develop into a fully-fledged language that can be used in all domains of society.

The data and our analysis convincingly show that liminal spaces are characterized by betweenness. We argue that betweenness is an essential concept for social perception, language communication, and processes in border spaces where experiencing in-betweenness is frequent. Research on transitional stages questioning and sometimes overcoming former borders should therefore be encouraged and employed in interdisciplinary research, in order to gain a deeper understanding of the particular cultural contexts which favor or discourage the transition toward new behavior in any kind of social environment.

By bridging economics and linguistics, particularly pragmatics and perception studies, our aim was to boost the concept of betweenness in the broader context of border studies. The perspective of betweenness as a shared point of reference in interdisciplinary research has the potential to enable discussion of the data belonging to different data types, and to scaffold a comparative analysis. At best, this proposal may encourage other researchers in the field to continue interdisciplinary border studies.

References

Anderson, Benedict (1991 [1983]): Imagined communities: reflections on the origin and spread of nationalism. London: Verso.

Andrews, David (1999): Sociocultural Perspectives on Language Change in Diaspora: Soviet Immigrants in the United States. Amsterdam/Philadelphia: John Benjamins.

Androutsopoulos, Jannis (2006): Multilingualism, diaspora, and the Internet: codes and identities on German-based diaspora websites. In: Journal of Sociolinguistics 10, no. 4, p. 520–547.

ARTE (2012): Banlieues: le parler des cités. www.youtube.com/watch?v=txLQl_jPXMA, 29/01/2019.

Auer, Peter/Muhamedova, Raihan (2005): 'Embedded language' and 'matrix language'. Insertional language mixing: Some problematic cases. In: Italian Journal of Linguistics / Rivista linguistic 17, no. 1, p. 35–54.

Bachmann, Iris (2005): Die Sprachwerdung des Kreolischen. Eine diskursanalytische Untersuchung am Beispiel des Papiamentu. Tübingen: Narr.

Bachmann, Iris: Creoles becoming Languages: A History of Creole Studies [revised and expanded edition of the German book (2005)]. London: Palgrave Macmillan (forthcoming).

Bail, Christopher (2016): Combining natural language processing and network analysis to examine how advocacy organizations stimulate conversation on social media. Proceedings of the National Academy of Sciences 113, no. 42, p. 11823–11828.

Barron, Alexander/Huang, Jenny/Spang, Rebecca L./DeDeo, Simon (2018): Individuals, institutions, and innovation in the debates of the French Revolution. In: Proceedings of the National Academy of Sciences 115, no. 18, p. 4607–4612.

Baumgärtner, Edgar (2018): Sprachtod = Spracherwerb rückwärts? Zu (grammatischen) Entwicklungstendenzen I der deutschen Sprachinsel der Altai-Region. MA dissertation [unpublished manuscript]. Frankfurt (Oder): EUV.

Berger, Jonah/Schwartz, Eric (2011): What drives immediate and ongoing word of mouth? In: Journal of Marketing Research 48, no. 5, p. 869–880.

Borrett, Stuart/Moody, James/Edelmann, Achim (2014): The rise of network ecology: maps of the topic diversity and scientific collaboration. In: Ecological Modelling, no. 293, p. 111–127.

Brehmer, Bernhard (2013): Sprachwahl und Sprachwechsel in slavisch-deutscher bilingualer Internet-Kommunikation. In: Franz, N. et al. (eds.): Deutsche Beiträge zum 15. Internationalen Slavistenkongress Minsk. München/Berlin: Sagner, p. 79–88.

Clyne, Michael (2000): Constraints on code-switching: how universal are they? In: Wei, L. (ed.): The Bilingualism Reader. London/New York: Routledge.

Dichter, Ernest (1966): How word-of-mouth advertising works. In: Harvard Business Review 44, no. 6, p. 147–160.

Dost, Florian/Wilken, Robert/Eisenbeiß, Maik/Skiera, Bernd (2014): On the edge of buying: a targeting approach for indecisive buyers based on willingness-to-pay ranges. In: Journal of Retailing 90, no. 3, p. 393–407.

Dost, Florian/Wilken, Robert (2012): Measuring willingness to pay as a range, revisited: when should we care? In: International Journal of Research in Marketing 29, no. 2, p. 148–166.

Dost, Florian/Wilken, Robert (2014): Verhaltensorientierter Ansatz zur Erklärung von Preisreaktionen bei Commodities und Empfehlungen für die Preissetzung auf Commodity-Märkten. In: Enke, M./Geigenmüller, A./Leischnig, A. (eds.): Commodity Marketing. Wiesbaden: Springer Gabler, p. 119–134.

Ehlich, Stefan (2010): Verschriftlichung von Sondersprachen in Internetforen am Beispiel des Jenischen. BA dissertation. Frankfurt (Oder): EUV.

Gaio, Mario L. M. (2018): Etnicidade Linguística em Movimento: Os Processos de Transculturalidade Revelados nos Brasileirítalos do Eixo Rio de Janeiro-Juiz de Fora. Bern/Frankfurt a.M./Berlin: Peter Lang.

Haenlein, Michael/Libai, Barak (2017): Seeding, referral, and recommendation: creating profitable word-of-mouth programs. In: California Management Review 59, no. 2, p. 68–91.

Höfler, Concha Maria: Identifying as Greek and belonging to Georgia: processes of (un)making boundaries in the Greek community of Georgia. Baden-Baden: Nomos (forthcoming).

Isaak Karina/Wilken Robert/Dost, Florian (2015): The Influence of Psychological Distance on Consumers' Willingness to Pay. In: Proceedings of the 2015 NeuroPsychoEconomics Conference, June 18–19, 2015 Copenhagen, Denmark.

Janczak, Barbara Alicja (2013): Deutsch-polnische Familien: Ihre Sprachen und Familienkulturen in Deutschland und in Polen. Frankfurt a.M.: Peter Lang.

Jungbluth, Konstanze (2012): Aus zwei mach eins: switching, mixing, getting different. In: Janczak, B./Jungbluth, K./Weydt, H. (eds.): Mehrsprachigkeit aus deutscher Perspektive. Tübingen: Narr, p. 45–72.

Kluge, Friedrich (1987 [1901]): Rotwelsches Quellenbuch Rotwelsch. Quellen und Wortschatz der Gaunersprache und der verwandten Geheimsprachen. De Gruyter: Berlin.

Krüger, Tobias/Fiedler, Klaus/Koch, Alex Stefan/Alves, Hans (2014): Response category width as a psychophysical manifestation of construal level and distance. In: Personality and Social Psychology Bulletin 40, no. 4, p. 501–512.

Le Page, Robert B./Tabouret-Keller, Andrée (1985): Acts of Identity. Creole-based approaches to language and ethnicity. Cambridge: Cambridge University Press.

Lösch, Klaus (2005): Begriff und Phänomen der Transdifferenz. Zur Infragestellung binärer Differenzkonstrukte. In: Allolio-Näcke, L./Kalscheuer, B./ Manzeschke, A. (eds.): Differenzen anders denken. Bausteine zu einer Kulturtheorie der Differenz. Frankfurt a.M.: Campus, p. 26–49.

Lüdi, Georges (2004): Codeswitching. Tübingen: Niemeyer.

Meise, Agnieszka (2008): Vier Wochenstunden Polnisch in einem deutschen Kindergarten – was bringt das? Eine Studie am Projekt "Frühstart in der Nachbarsprache." MA dissertation [unpublished manuscript]. Frankfurt (Oder): EUV.

Muysken, Pieter (1995): Code-switching and grammatical theory. In: Milroy, L./ Muysken, P. (eds.): One Speaker, Two Languages: Cross-disciplinary Perspectives on Code-switching. Cambridge: Cambridge University Press, p. 177–198.

Myers-Scotton, Carol (2002): Contact Linguistics. Oxford: Oxford University Press.

Nacro, Fanta Regina (2001): Relou (short movie). (Pas d'histoires! 12 regards sur le racisme au quotidien). www.filmeeinewelt.ch/deutsch/pagesnav/framesE4.htm?../pagesmov/40141.htm&KA, 11/06/2018.

Pavlenko, Anna/Barbara C. Malt (2011): Kitchen Russian: cross-linguistic differences and first-language object naming by Russian–English bilinguals, In: Bilingualism: Language and Cognition no. 14, p. 19–45.

Pavlenko, Aneta. (2002): Bilingualism and emotions, In: Multilingua, no. 21, p. 45–78.

Pondorfer, Andreas/Rehdanz, Katrin (2018): Eliciting Preferences for Public Goods in Nonmonetized Communities: Accounting for Preference Uncertainty. In: Land Economics 94, no. 1, p. 73–86.

Quist, Pia (2005): New speech varieties among immigrant youth in Copenhagen—a case study. In: Hinnenkamp, V./Meng, K. (eds.): Sprachgrenzen überspringen. Sprachliche Hybridität und polykulturelles Selbstverständnis. (Studien zur deutschen Sprache 32). Tübingen: Narr, p. 145–161.

Schiffauer, Werner/Koch, Jochen/Reckwitz, Andreas/Schoor, Kerstin/Krämer, Hannes (2018): Borders in Motion. Durabilität, Permeabilität, Liminalität. Working Paper Series B/Orders in Motion, vol. 1, Frankfurt (Oder): Europa-Universität Viadrina.

Schlereth, Christian/Eckert, Christine/Skiera, Bernd (2012): Using discrete choice experiments to estimate willingness-to-pay intervals. In: Marketing Letters 23, no. 3, p. 761–776.

Schneider, Edgar W. (2017): Perspectives on Language Contact. In: Brinton, L. J. (ed.): English Historical Linguistics. Approaches and perspectives. Cambridge: Cambridge University Press, p. 332–359.

Schreiner, Jana (2010): Deutsch-russische computervermittelte Kommunikation: Eine Analyse von Chat- und Forenbeiträgen im Hinblick auf Sprachkontakt. MA dissertation [unpublished manuscript]. Jena: Fr. Schiller University.

Turner, Victor W. (1998): Liminalität und Communitas. In: Belliger, A./Krieger, D. J. (eds.): Ritualtheorien. Ein einführendes Handbuch. Opladen: Westdeutscher Verlag, p. 251–264.

Vilhena, Daril/Foster, Jacob/Rosvall, Martin/West, Jevin/Evans, James/Bergstrom, Carl (2014): Finding cultural holes: How structure and culture diverge in networks of scholarly communication. In: Sociological Science 1, DOI 10.15195/v 1.a15, p. 221–239.

Vogelsang, Sara (2014): Language, Borders and Identity in Singapore. MA dissertation [unpublished manuscript]. Frankfurt (Oder): EUV.

Wang, Tuo/Venkatesh, R./Chatterjee, Rabikar (2007): Reservation price as a range: An incentive-compatible measurement approach. In: Journal of Marketing Research 44, no. 2, p. 200–213.

Wathieu, Luc/Bertini, Marco (2007): Price as a stimulus to think: The case for willful overpricing. In: Marketing Science 26, no. 1, p. 118–129.

Wenger, Etienne (1998): Communities of Practice: Learning, Meaning, and Identity. Cambridge: Cambridge University Press.

Wiese, Heike (2006): "Ich mach dich Messer" – Grammatische Produktivität in Kiez-Sprache ("Kanak Sprak"). In: Linguistische Berichte 207, p. 245–273.

Wiese, Heike (2012a): Kiezdeutsch. Ein neuer Dialekt entsteht. München: C.H. Beck.

Wiese, Heike (2012b): http://www.kiezdeutsch.de (last access: 11/06/2018).

Wille, Christian (2008): Zum Modell des transnationalen sozialen Raums im Kontext von Grenzregionen. Theoretisch-konzeptionelle Überlegungen am Beispiel des Grenzgängerwesens. In: Europa Regional 16, no. 2, p. 74–84.

Wille, Christian (ed.) (2015): Lebenswirklichkeiten und politische Konstruktionen in Grenzregionen. Das Beispiel der Großregion SaarLorLux. Bielefeld: Transcript.

Zinkhahn-Rhobodes, Dagna (2016): Sprechen entlang der Oder: der Charakter der sprachlichen Grenzen am Beispiel der deutsch-polnischen Sprachroutine. (Sprachliche Konstruktion sozialer Grenzen, vol. 1). Bern/Berlin: Peter Lang.

Abbreviations

ADJ	adjective
DER	derivation
ENG	English
GER	German
IMP	imperfect
L1, L2, L3	[speaker of] first, second, third language
N	noun
Pl	plural
POL	Polish
Pres.	presence
RUS	Russian
Sg	singular
V	verb
2.P.	second person
3.P.	third person

About the authors

Florian Dost | Alliance Manchester Business School | Management Sciences and Marketing | Booth Street West | Manchester M156PB | United Kingdom | T +4401612756540 | florian.dost@manchester.ac.uk

Florian Dost is a Senior Lecturer (Associate Professor) in Marketing at the University of Manchester. He studied industrial engineering at TU Berlin and obtained a Ph.D. in Business Administration from ESCP Europe. Florian researched at several Universities, and worked at a word-of-mouth marketing firm, before continuing to his present position. His research is interdisciplinary in nature and wide in scope, covering consumer decision processes, communication phenomena, and emergent properties in complex socioeconomic systems.

Konstanze Jungbluth | European University Viadrina | Faculty of Social and Cultural Sciences | 15230 Frankfurt (Oder) | Germany | T +49 335 5534 2740 | jungbluth@europa-uni.de

Konstanze Jungbluth lectures at the Faculty of Social and Cultural Sciences at Frankfurt (Oder) and researches on border issues, pragmatics, and language contact, particularly in the context of (Ibero-) Romance languages. At the university campus, she experiences the Polish–German border, but she is also curious about contact among Europeans and Africans in Europe, on the Cape Verde islands and in West Africa in early modern times.

Nicole Richter | European University Viadrina | Collegium Polonicum | Linguistics | Große Scharrnstraße 59 | 15230 Frankfurt (Oder) | Germany | T +49 335 5534 166845 | nrichter@europa-uni.de

Nicole Richter teaches Multicultural Communication (Slavonic and English Linguistics & Language Use) at the European University Viadrina and Collegium Polonicum. In her research, she focuses on oral communication, pragmatics, and contrastive linguistics. The main languages she studies are Russian, English, Czech, and German. She obtained a Ph.D. in Slavonic Linguistics from Friedrich Schiller University Jena.

Researching forced migrants' trajectories: encounters with multilingualism

Erika Kalocsányiová

Abstract

This contribution is concerned with the impact of multilingualism on forced migrants' trajectories. Drawing on a corpus of linguistic ethnographic data that was collected over a two-year period, it focuses on the experiences of two individuals who were granted international protection in Luxembourg. Key events and anecdotes are used to reconstruct their sociolinguistic trajectories, learning histories, and mobile aspirations before and after settling in the Grand Duchy. Despite having similar linguistic repertoires, "Ahmad" and "Patrick" reported disparate experiences. This chapter provides unique insights into how linguistic integration is understood and experienced in multilingual societies.

Keywords

Repertoires and trajectories, forced migration, multilingualism, linguistic integration, (im)mobility

1. *Introduction*

Investigating border experiences is a continuing concern in sociolinguistic studies. Borders represent a crucial angle from which to examine the many ways in which mobility intersects with nation-state politics of language and integration. Migration/displacement across borders entails a change in the linguistic environment with whose practices, discourses, and rules a person is familiar (cf. Busch 2017). Language thus constitutes a powerful means of self-affirmation in new sociocultural milieus. Given its rich migration history, the Grand Duchy of Luxembourg provides a fascinating setting for exploring how individuals (re)create, sustain, and contest borders through languages. New arrivals to Luxembourg are expected to integrate into a society that is structured around the widespread circulation of people and their linguistic repertoires. This raises crucial questions: What are the politics of language and integration in settings of complex linguistic diversity? How do these policies shape and/or inflect immigrants' sociolinguistic trajectories? What types of individual trajectories emerge? This chapter addresses each of these questions in more detail. More specifically, it focuses on the struggles and accomplishments of two men, Ahmad and Patrick (pseudonyms), who sought refuge in Luxembourg. The chapter builds on the findings of a two-year ethnographic research project that addressed the impact of multilingualism on forced migrants' trajectories. The use of the term "forced migrant" in this context is meant to acknowledge both refugees and people who are forced to migrate due to factors that are not spelled out by the 1951 Refugee Convention (e.g. conflicts, natural or environmental disasters, famine, broader human rights violations, and development projects).

The first subchapter is devoted to the relationship between language, migration, and national borders (cf. Canagarajah 2017; Van Avermaet 2009; Newman 2006; Stevenson 2006). Next, a summary of major methodological influences is provided (cf. Busch 2017; Juffermans/Tavares 2017, Stevenson 2014). The section concludes with a brief overview of the sociolinguistic situation and integration debates in Luxembourg. The purpose of the second subchapter is to describe the research methods used and to contextualize the participants' stories. In part three, key events are used to reconstruct the research participants' language (hi)stories *vis-à-vis* their migration experience to Luxembourg, their learning trajectories in their new sociolinguistic environment(s), and their future mobile aspirations. The chapter ends with a discussion and concluding remarks.

2. *Language, migration, and the nation state*

The language–migration nexus has recently attracted considerable attention: in parallel to what Faist (2013) described as the "mobility turn", the last decade also saw a substantial proliferation of scholarly work devoted to the intersection of language, borders, and human (im)mobility (cf. Canagarajah 2017). To index the forms of communication and contact that transcend bounded, territorialized, and separated languages, scholars have adopted multiple terms, some of which are "translanguaging" (cf. Creese/Blackledge 2010; García/Li Wei 2014), "metrolingualism" (cf. Otsuji/Pennycook 2010), "polylingualism" (cf. Jørgensen et al. 2011), and "truncated multilingualism" (cf. Blommaert 2010). This body of research drew attention to, among other things, the complex patterns of language use that arise as people move across borders and spaces where multiple languages are in use. While there is a growing acknowledgement of migration-driven diversity in Europe, commonly discussed under the rubric of super-diversity (cf. Vertovec 2007), linguistic integration studies are still largely shaped by ethno-national approaches (cf. Grzymala-Kazlowska/ Phillimore 2018) and methodological nationalism (cf. Glick Schiller 2009). In policy terms, there are many indications of essentializing tendencies, evidenced by the new (or renewed) language requirements that multiple EU member states have imposed on those seeking citizenship, residency or even entrance to their territories (cf. Van Avermaet 2009). Arguments asserting that insufficient knowledge of state-mandated/national languages constitutes an obstacle to integration and is a cause of violence and social conflict often go uncontested. Meanwhile, the real-life complexities faced by forced migrants seeking asylum across Europe remain an under-researched area.

Linguistic differences have traditionally served as means of creating a sense of distinction between the "us here" and the "them there". In Burke's view, the social changes of the late eighteenth century turned language into an "instrument of the cult of the nation", which "both expresses and helps to create national communities" (2004, p. 171). By way of illustration, let us consider the example of the Grand Duchy of Luxembourg. The symbolic boundaries between nineteenth-century Luxembourg and its larger neighbors were established through distinctive patterns of language use, i.e. the use of German and French as written languages along with the spoken use of one distinctive code, currently known as Luxembourgish. This boundary-drawing mechanism has been exploited to legitimize the existence of independent Luxembourg for two centuries (cf. Horner/Weber 2008, p. 85). Sociolinguistic and linguistic anthropological research has long recognized language as a powerful (semiotic) resource implicated in processes of group formation (cf. Heller 1987) as well as the construction of identities and the delimitation of space (cf. Irvine/Gal 2002). Another fundamental aspect of language is "its capacity for generating imagined communities, building in effect particular solidarities" (Anderson 1991, p. 133).

Despite the intensification of migration flows that cut across borders and continents, linguistic traits continue to play a key role in constructing and maintaining multiple boundaries; being unable to speak a particular language (or combination of languages) places restrictions on one's ability to communicate and—by extension—to identify with any territorial, ethnic, and/or national identities that language is associated with. For the eminent theorist of borderlands, David Newman, language "remains the one great boundary which, for so many of us, remains difficult to cross, in the absence of a single, global, borderless form of communication" (2006, p.

148). Linguistic differences are often drawn upon to rationalize (im)mobility, and, as Park (2014, p. 84) has pointed out, "it is through language that people on the move imagine and construct themselves as migrants." It is also important to remember that, in the context of the intensifying commodification of languages (cf. Heller 2010), language is increasingly seen as an economic/marketable resource that immigrants can acquire like any other skill (cf. Duchêne/Heller 2012). Entire projects of mobility within and across national borders often come to be structured around complex networks of ideological associations between different language(s) and spaces. An example of this phenomenon is discussed in Gogonas and Kirsch's paper (2016) about Greek migrant families in Luxembourg.

Adopting the perspective of super-diversity, numerous scholars of multilingualism—some of whom were mentioned earlier—have disputed the alleged "boundedness" of languages and made visible the fluidity and messiness of everyday languaging. According to Silverstein (2014), their observations challenge and test the states' organizational flexibility to encompass and control one or more language communities in which the people within their borders participate. Since the mid-1990s, the politicization of migration has set in motion a series of amendments to residency, citizenship, and immigration laws. The prominent position of language among these new standards has led some observers to interpret this trend as "linguistic nationalism" (cf. Stevenson 2006). A growing body of research conducted in this field has linked languages to re-bordering processes across Europe (cf. Baba/Dahl-Jørgensen 2013; Van Avermaet/Rocca 2013). As Shohamy (2006) explains, in the integration machinery, the willingness to learn and use the dominant language(s) is regarded as an indicator of loyalty, belonging, inclusion, and membership. Despite the focus on language, these reflections do not claim that language is the sole variable in the equation; it is, however, a powerful means through which forced migrants (could) reflect, position, and affirm themselves in their old/new sociocultural milieus.

Research into super-diverse environments is not well served with *a priori* notions of "language", "native speaker", and "mother tongue". Instead, sociolinguists—especially in linguistic ethnography—now generally work with the notion of linguistic repertoires. As explained by Blommaert and Backus (2013), repertoires bear traces of a person's biography, reflecting the spaces, niches, and networks in which s/he has operated. For Busch, who also revisited the concept recently (2012; 2017), a linguistic repertoire "not only points backward to the past of the language biography, which has left behind its traces and scars, but also forward, anticipating and projecting the future situations and events we are preparing to face" (2017, p.

356). Repertoires are therefore as much indexes of people's pasts as of their aspirations/desire for mobility (cf. Carling/Collins 2018). In her latest contribution to the debate, Busch (2017) is concerned with the relationship between individual life stories and what she defines as *Spracherleben* or "the lived experience of language". Her approach builds on a speaker-centered biographical perspective, which I adopt here in order to investigate how experiences of linguistic inequality/success are imprinted on forced migrants' repertoires, both in the form of explicit and implicit language attitudes and changed patterns of language use. I have also drawn inspiration from Juffermans and Tavares's (2017) research on south-north trajectories and linguistic repertoires; their work rests on a trajectory approach to migration and language which "attempts to makes sense of the practical and cognitive challenges, structural and agentive forces, and the changing subject positions in individual projects of (trans)migration, *after*, *during*, and *before* migration" (p. 104, emphases in original). A major methodological influence was research into the sociolinguistics of narrative (cf. de Fina/Tseng 2017) and Stevenson's work on language (hi)stories (2014; 2017). Accordingly, the accounts given by participants in my research are not analyzed as chronological histories but as narrations of (im)mobile and multilingual selves.

Questions of language are of fundamental importance to integration debates in Luxembourg. The Grand Duchy has the highest proportion of foreign-born population in the EU: non-Luxembourgish passport holders account for 47.8 percent of the total population of 602,005 (as of January 1, 2018; cf. STATEC 2018a); in addition, the country employs about 188,000 cross-border workers from France, Belgium, and Germany (cf. STATEC 2018b). Cross-border workers and migrants alike have brought new repertoires and practices to an already complex sociolinguistic environment, "making everyday communication in Luxembourg a highly diverse and dynamic affair" (Franziskus 2016, p. 207). Since languages are a primary factor in structuring the local labor market (Pigeron-Piroth/Fehlen 2015), the speakers of the various languages have interests to protect (de Bres 2014).

The above figures are central to understanding the specific linguistic ideas that are associated with "Luxembourgishness". Using media and government sources, Horner and Weber (2008) distinguished between two main strategies of linguistic identification: the "trilingual ideal", which entails mastery of the three languages recognized by the Language Act of 1984 (Luxembourgish/German/French), and a "monolingual identification" rooted (solely) in the Luxembourgish language. In Horner's view (2009, p. 149), these two strategies have been positioned in both complementary and conflictual relationships, "with the conflictual scenario gaining momentum since the 1970s". This shift coincided with Luxembourg's increasing reliance on immigrant and cross-border labor (cf. Beine/Souy 2016) as well as with initial attempts to foster a sense of collective European identity (cf. OP 1973). The accompanying sociolinguistic changes—reflected in the increased use of (mainly) French—stirred up discontent among some Luxembourgish nationals. Mounting concerns over the preservation of the Luxembourgish language led to the gradual implementation of language requirements and testing procedures for naturalization. Since the early 2000s, discourses of integration have positioned Luxembourgish as "an instrument of civic participation" and "the solution to the perceived problem of augmented societal and linguistic heterogeneity" (Horner 2017, p. 53). Following the 2008 and 2017 revisions to the Nationality Act, individuals aspiring to citizenship must pass a Luxembourgish language test, regardless of their proficiency in French or German, as well as a citizenship course. These measures resonate with similar forms of re-bordering legislation in Europe.

3. *Methodological approach and research participants*

Let us now move to the specific research context. This chapter draws on a corpus of ethnographic data that was collected over a two-year period. The project, which is being carried out as part of a doctorate at the University of Luxembourg, was designed as an exploratory study to uncover the complexities that define forced migrants' linguistic integration efforts in multilingual societies. Previously, I examined structured language learning tasks and broader social interactions, concluding that a multilingual pedagogical orientation creates learning spaces that help forced migrants "to see the local languages as new functional resources in their growing repertoires", a necessary and important resource for navigating local life (Kalocsányiová 2017, p. 489). The main ideological underpinnings of the integration discourse are discussed in a forthcoming publication (Kalocsányiová 2018). Here, I will focus on only two research participants, Ahmad and Patrick, both of whom applied for international protection in the Grand Duchy in 2015. Since the project's start in the spring of 2016, data collection has been dictated by the project participants' movement through different spaces, networks, and sites. Following an introductory meeting at which informed consent was obtained, the participants were invited to choose their own pseudonyms for the research. We agreed on the names "Ahmad" and "Patrick". Afterwards, I conducted narrative interviews—lasting approximately an hour—with each of them to elicit information about their repertoires, migration experiences, language learning goals, and language use in their new sociolinguistic environment. Since then, I have periodically interviewed them approximately every six months, using on occasion non-static techniques such as go-along, i.e. accompanied walks with interviewees as they go about their routines (cf. Kusenbach 2003, Lamarre 2013). In addition to formal interviews, the project also builds on information generated through informal interactions and everyday types of encounters between the researcher (me) and Ahmad or Patrick. Rodgers (2004, p. 49) refers to this approach as "hanging out" and endorses it as an ethically desirable research tool that opens a "channel for voices of forced migrants, without claiming to definitively represent them", and thus "sustain[s] a humanism in research." Ethnographic field notes and approximately 50 hours of audio-recorded interactions complement the data for this chapter.

In the following, I will present the two project participants and their language experiences prior to arriving in Luxembourg. At the time of recruitment, Ahmad was in his mid-twenties. He was born into a family of farmers in the district of Afrin in northern Syria, where he remained up until the outbreak of the armed conflict in 2012. He spoke Kurdish (Kurmanji) at home and with his childhood friends and neighbors. His mother was Lebanese; she could understand but not speak Kurdish. Because the Kurdish language was banned in schools, he received all his primary school education in Arabic. He completed nine years of schooling. Although English was part of the school curriculum, Ahmad attested to having learnt the language primarily through informal channels during his stay in Lebanon; in 2012, he fled with his family to Beirut, where he worked as an electrician for a while. As he recounts it, some of his coworkers were English speakers, and he felt he was an object of ridicule until his English skills improved. He migrated to Luxembourg following a complex route along the eastern Mediterranean route.

The second research participant, Patrick, is in his mid-thirties. He was born and raised in Kadhimiya, a northern neighborhood in Baghdad. After earning a degree in engineering, he worked at a power plant project funded by the US government in a remote region of southern Iraq. His workplace interactions included communication in both Arabic and English. For years, Patrick was eagerly looking for opportunities to expand his communicative repertoire; however, his attempts to learn French and Russian at an affordable price were fruitless. Prompted by his eagerness to learn foreign languages, he associated the efforts he had made with his aspirations for transnational mobility: "I wanted to learn these languages to maybe go to other countries and meet new cultures" (August 17, 2016). After members of his family were abducted and killed, Patrick left Iraq, fleeing first to Turkey and then to Europe, crammed on a dinghy with dozens of other people. He arrived in Luxembourg in the summer of 2015.

4. Forced migrants' trajectories and experiences with language

4.1 Early days in the Grand Duchy

Prior to them arriving in Luxembourg, the peculiarities of local multilingualism were unknown to both research participants. During our second meeting (September 17, 2016), Ahmad told an anecdote which exemplifies the initial confusion he experienced. In his imagination, Luxembourg was a German-speaking country: "I didn't know anything, I just thought it was like Germany." A couple of hours after his arrival, he and his travel companions overheard a conversation in (what they believed was) French at the refugee center. Driven by curiosity, Ahmad asked around among the other residents at the center, who gave him his first bits of information about Luxembourg's language environment. Once he corroborated that "French was everywhere", he asked in bewilderment, "What comes next?" In the local establishments, staffed (mainly) by Francophone cross-border workers, his initial attempts to communicate in English failed. His lack of familiarity with local practices, discourses, and rules became a source of discomfort. Busch (2017, p. 340) refers to similar episodes as "the underlying experience that one's own linguistic repertoire no longer fits," which, in her view, occurs not only in extreme situations but is shared by all speakers when experiencing dislocation. Shortly after presenting his asylum claim, Ahmad was relocated to Wiltz, a town of around 5,000 people in the north of the Grand Duchy. When characterizing Wiltz's linguistic texture, Ahmad alluded to a number of languages that, in addition to Luxembourgish and French, were embedded in the social fabric of local life. His accounts made frequent references to Portuguese speakers in his neighborhood, Kosovars and Bosnians in the local mosque, and Africans in his building. However, in the absence of strong social ties with the local population, the private spaces in his life remained almost exclusively monolingual (i.e. Arabic): "we don't have [a lot of] communication because we don't have French friends or *Deutsche* friends or any European friends […] we just have Iraqi and Arab friends." (August 17, 2016).

Patrick's experiences diverged from Ahmad's. His earliest accounts did not invoke moments of linguistic failure; on the contrary, he talked about the multiplicity of local languages in almost utopian terms. He used to think that multilingualism was a sign and means of cultural reconciliation, and a chance to reinvent himself as a multilingual speaker. Inspired by the example of a friend, who had once been an immigrant himself, Patrick set his sights on learning bits of the different languages surrounding him. His objective was to amass a repertoire of resources, a kind of linguistic toolbox which he could activate according to his needs, knowledge, and whims (cf. Lüdi/Py 2009). Rather than aiming for comprehensive competence in one (official) language, he wanted to develop a range of codes for a range of purposes. His approach thus exemplifies what Canagarajah and Wurr (2011) refer to as repertoire building.

4.2 Learning the ropes

When I first met them, both Ahmad and Patrick were enrolled in language courses set up by groups of volunteers. These courses were designed to provide elementary language knowledge in French in order to support learners' transition to state-sponsored language training organized by the municipalities, local associations, and the National Institute for Languages. Initially, both project participants subscribed to the view that a good command of French would provide the basis for their professional and social integration. However, as the interviews unfolded it became obvious that the "choice" to learn French was to a great extent imposed upon them: "the social agent gave me a *bon* for French[1] but I asked for Luxembourgish and she said no, you should start with French [....] I said okay, I want a *bon* for German but she said it was not possible." (August 17, 2016). The social worker's conduct could be explained by the widely held belief that French facilitates economic integration better than any other language in the local labor market (cf. Kalocsányiová 2018). Forced migrants' efforts to learn languages other than French often cause astonishment and/or are discouraged. As the above excerpt shows, Patrick expressed a strong wish to learn German (an objective shared by Ahmad). This decision was not so much related to the joint official status German enjoys in Luxembourg as to associations linking the language to the German state and its open-door refugee policy. As with Luxembourgish, both participants made efforts to learn its basics. Their initial interest in the language was spurred on by its presumed national symbolic importance; however, with the impending re-

1 Applicants for international protection receive a voucher (*bon*) to enroll in a language training course of their choice.

vision of their protection status[2], they began to see the value of Luxembourgish for their eventual citizenship applications as well as for current and future employment needs. Luxembourgish is an essential requirement in nearly half of the vacancies advertised in the Grand Duchy (cf. Pigeron-Piroth/Fehlen 2015). To give an example, Ahmad's apprenticeship application to a local HVAC contractor was formally rejected due to his insufficient competence in Luxembourgish.

The combination of French, German, and Luxembourgish indicated above also points to a desire to fit into the Grand Duchy's trilingual ideal. Both participants showed a preference for multilingual integration paths, although it must be underlined that their conscious learning efforts remained limited to the local prestige languages. Ahmad's and Patrick's interest in the other languages—ubiquitous in their immediate social environment—was rarely driven by more than common curiosity. This deserves attention for two reasons. First, because the preferred medium of communication of the people in their social circles seldom included the languages of traditional triglossia; and second, because their spontaneous language use built on elements of immigrant/minority languages that were (presumably) accumulated through informal contacts and exchanges. From the beginning of the project, both participants showed strong cross-linguistic and meta-communicative awareness. They often mentioned filling their knowledge gaps via lexical inferencing, transfers, and fluid transitions between resources that are conventionally labeled as belonging to separate languages. A promising avenue for future research would be to explore forced migrants' perception of (local) linguistic borders and their effect on processes of language acquisition. For instance, the borders that I considered relatively fixed and stable offered room for permeability and code-mixing from the participants' perspective. From our discussions, it soon became clear that it was precisely the deployment of the strategies outlined above that allowed them to engage with the multilingual social world of Luxembourg.

4.3 "Settled" life in Luxembourg

Two years after fleeing to Europe, both project participants claimed to be able to navigate local life with reasonable ease and success. In support of

2 Residence permits granted to beneficiaries of international protection are valid for five years.

his position, Ahmad cited the example of ADEM (a local employment agency) to shed light on his communication strategies. He compared his communication with public officers to riding a bicycle: after his first moves (greeting) in Luxembourgish, he moves back and forth between French and English to reduce the chances of miscommunication (September 30, 2017). After completing a 9e class[3], which is considered crucial for access to further studies and vocational training, Ahmad obtained an apprenticeship contract, and he has been working in the telecommunications sector since then. The combination of his old and newly acquired language resources allowed him to develop new contacts with locals and expatriates alike. Furthermore, he occasionally volunteered to interpret for his compatriots in refugee homes and health-care institutions, which indicates a growing level of confidence (and pride) in his language abilities. As discussed above, Ahmad's first encounters with Luxembourg's diversity were described as confusing, at times even hostile. His perspectives shifted significantly once his expanding multilingualism acquired value as economic and social capital and became a means of self-fulfillment.

Ahmad gained access to employment through demonstrating fluency in French; yet, from the picture he painted of his work environment[4], it was certainly not the only language resource he needed. His immediate colleagues change according to the shifts he works, so we can only speculate which ethnolinguistic groups he has had the most contact with. However, the two co-workers he talked about most were described as having Portuguese origins. Ahmad's occupation requires him to work in people's homes and (at the time of writing) most of his customers belonged to the indigenous population of Luxembourg. He described one of these encounters as follows:

3 9e classes correspond to the third year of secondary education. For a period of ten months, Ahmad attended daytime classes with other (forced) migrants who did not have a recognized level of education and/or whose knowledge of languages was considered insufficient to join the mainstream training system. After successfully completing the program, he received a certificate attesting, among other things, A2 level proficiency in French and English.

4 Due to ethical and practical difficulties, it was not possible to observe Ahmad's work environment.

A: When I need to explain how to use the decoder [...]
I tell to (hesitantly) I said to the client I can *explique* explain in French
he told me "I'm not good in French I cannot speak well French"
I told him don't worry, don't worry me too [either] (laugh)
I'll show you it's easy (laugh). When I explained to him
he said yeah it's easy [...] (March 17, 2018)

This excerpt shows how some members of the local community can be reluctant to speak French. Past research has also dispelled the myth that all Luxembourgers are balanced trilinguals (Horner 2004) and revealed disparate attitudes toward Luxembourg's numerous ethnolinguistic groups. After this episode, I heard Ahmad suggest that his imperfect French was to his advantage that day. Indeed, it was the fear of communicating in a language which was not their native and/or preferred one that allowed the two to engage in a dialogue and defuse potential tensions. Surprisingly, Ahmad's overall impression was that customers were more likely to switch to English than to French. This analysis clearly shows that prioritizing French for its economically integrative functions is not without its tensions.

Let me return to Patrick now. After the enthusiasm of the first months, Patrick narrated his subsequent experiences as a story of downward mobility. In April 2017, I conducted ethnographic fieldwork at a professional training course for mobile application developers that he (and ten other course participants) attended. The training was sponsored by ADEM but taught by a French *frontalier* [cross-border worker]. The data from this fieldwork provided insights into two areas of interest in my research: the role of language(s) in Patrick's labor market integration and his experience of workplace-like communication. Let us start with the latter: although the official language of the course was English, the participants shuttled between four languages (at a minimum) to achieve their communicative aims. A careful observation of their practices confirmed what other studies had also reported (cf. Franziskus/Gilles 2012; Franziskus 2016): workplace communication in Luxembourg is reminiscent of the complexities of broader societal multilingualism and entails continuing negotiations over linguistic resources. At the time, Patrick's repertoire was adequate for accomplishing most of the content-related tasks; however, it rarely allowed him to participate in moments of humor or off-task talk. In our discussions from this period, he often represented himself as an outsider, which takes us to our second topic of interest. After meeting other job seekers at the training course, his hopes of succeeding in the local labor market diminished. On multiple occasions, he positioned himself as "a refugee who doesn't speak German and French very well" and stands little or no chance against the people from Luxembourg, whom he believed to be fluent in all the languages sought after in the labor market (April 7, 2017). His fears were not unfounded: an inability to perform certain combinations of French, English, German, and Luxembourgish severely limits one's chances of being considered for positions advertised in the Grand Duchy (cf. Pigeron-Piroth/Fehlen 2015).

4.4 (Im)possibility of moving forward

Questions of language were central to Patrick's pursuit of employment, as illustrated by this excerpt from a cover letter he drafted in the spring of 2017: "*Je souhaite, afin de m'intégrer au Luxembourg, suivre des cours de luxembourgeois pour que mon activité professionnelle soit complete*"[5]. For Patrick, unemployment constituted a barrier to his language learning progress. He saw proficiency in the "right" languages as a condition for his meaningful participation in the labor market and broader social context; as a result, he felt excluded precisely from those settings where the linguistic capital he craved could be obtained. His experience resonates with Bourdieu's observation: "Speakers lacking the legitimate competence are *de facto* excluded from the social domains in which this competence is required, or are condemned to silence." (1991, p. 55, emphases in original). When asked about other avenues to expand his skills, Patrick pointed to a group of customs officers and half-jokingly remarked: "do I grab a policeman to speak with me in German? They [referring to his social circle] don't have time; everyone's taking care of their own business; this is the truth." (March 12, 2018). In his search for opportunities to practice, Patrick decided to enroll in the same adult education program that Ahmad had attended the year before. Although his degree in engineering had been recognized by the Ministry for Higher Education and Research, he suddenly found himself "studying" secondary school mathematics. In addition, he was placed in an upper elementary-level English course, which contributed to tensions between his own language use and the standard of English he and his peers were expected to orient toward. In my observations, the program accentuated mat-

5 "In order to integrate in Luxembourg, I want to attend Luxembourgish classes so that my professional activities would be completed." (This translation is an approximation aimed at representing the same structural features as the original utterance.)

ters of surface accuracy, which clashed with Patrick's (and Ahmad's) previous learning experiences, where the focus was more on meaning-making. Their language production was viewed as problematic, although both had used English for official and professional purposes before. In Blommaert's terms (2003), Patrick and Ahmad's language varieties did not "travel well"; their resources were considered functional in diverse circumstances (both before and after migration) but became dysfunctional as soon as they were placed in the context of the Grand Duchy's adult education initiatives.

Patrick's plans to move out of the refugee shelter also imploded: without an employment contract he could not apply for a lease. Instead of the upward trajectory he had hoped for (having his own place), he was again immobilized. In his reflections from this period, he circled back to the topic of languages: "everything is connected with each other, [employment] contracts and housing and languages [and] learning, sometimes I'm confused what to do, what's right" (October 28, 2017). Patrick's experience of moving downward pushes him to be active across borders and/or even remigrate within the EU. His legal status as a refugee, however, places considerable restrictions on these aspirations. Although he managed to flee to Europe, his onward movement is blocked. He is living in a state described by Carling (2002) as "involuntary immobility", which is hauntingly similar to the experiences Juffermans and Tavares (2017) documented in their research of the south–north trajectories of Luso-Africans. Patrick's wish to work, learn and move freely in Europe depends on him obtaining Luxembourgish nationality, which, as discussed earlier, requires demonstrable knowledge of the Luxembourgish language. And so, paradoxically, Patrick's escape from immobility is currently conditioned by a language the communicative reach of which is restricted to the Luxembourgish state:

P: this is the problem: if I'd have the nationality, I would
not stay here living in Luxembourg. I would go to Belgium.
R: for the moment you cannot relocate [...]
P: no I need to stay here for the rest of my life (laugh)
R: you have to stay here until?
P: yeah until I obtain the nationality, which is difficult.
How do I learn Luxembourgish to get the nationality?
This is a big problem for me [...]
it makes me exhausted to think about these things

(March 12, 2018)

In juxtaposition to French and German, the teaching and learning of Luxembourgish as a second/foreign language is fraught with complexities. For instance, the language is not used as a means of written communication by most of its speakers, except for in informal domains and new media (cf. Belling/de Bres 2014). It has also undergone major standardization in recent years, which has led to the odd situation where the Luxembourgish standard taught to immigrants (in official language courses) is not widely known among the local population. These strange circumstances severely impacted Ahmad's learning trajectory. As he showed his notes from a language course he was attending to a friend, his friend—a Luxembourger and teacher himself—labeled his laboriously acquired knowledge as incorrect, after which he "broke down and stopped" (March 9, 2017). This incident led Ahmad to withdraw from the course and discontinue his efforts to learn Luxembourgish (for a while at least). Patrick's descriptions of his learning experience with Luxembourgish revolved around the scarcity of adequate language learning tools. Recent years have certainly seen an increase in the availability of dictionaries, textbooks, and materials for self-learners, but the pool of resources is still negligible compared to the Grand Duchy's other administrative languages. Being admitted into a state-subsidized language course was not without its complications either, as the earlier discussion of Patrick's failed attempts demonstrated. In addition to being crucial for Ahmad and Patrick's citizenship applications, command of Luxembourgish also conditions access to well-paid and secure jobs in numerous domains (cf. Ehrhart/Fehlen 2011). Its significance for forced migrants' aspirations—in terms of both spatial and social mobility—indicates important directions for future research.

5. Conclusion

This contribution set out to scrutinize the impact of multilingualism on forced migrants' trajectories in Luxembourg. The chapter began by describing the language–migration nexus and discussing the role linguistic traits play in (de)constructing borders. After introducing the research context, the paper offered a detailed account of forced migrants' language (hi)stories. A careful analysis of divergent trajectories exposed the embodied efforts, emotions, and constraints inherent in constructing a new belonging, be it interpreted along linguistic, national, or personal lines. By foregrounding the participants' voices, the chapter shed light on forced migrants' experiences with the Grand Duchy's borders and their everyday enactments through linguistic differences.

The discussion focused on two people who shared similar (multilayered) linguistic repertoires but reported disparate experiences. For Ahmad, the once unsettling environment evolved into a space of self-fulfillment: his expanding multilingualism has translated into enhanced opportunities for social interaction and economic advancement. By contrast, Patrick's enthusiasm for multilingualism diminished over time; despite his extensive language learning efforts, his aspirations to progress contrasted sharply with his actual experience of moving downward. While the main focus was on Ahmad's and Patrick's language lives—i.e. how the development (and deployment) of their linguistic repertoires traces, shapes, and disrupts the flow of their lives—their narratives were often intertwined with wider social discourses on integration, social alienation, and belonging. Between them, they provided rich evidence of the complexities of integration in multilingual communities. Patrick and Ahmad are also among the first beneficiaries of international protection who will be affected by the Luxembourgish Nationality Act of 2017. Because it is still a fairly recent piece of legislation, not much is known about its impact on the individual experiences of applicants or its long-term consequences. However, it does stipulate stricter testing procedures and (from a language perspective) represents a yet further move toward a "thicker" concept of belonging and citizenship. As such, it adds to the long list of contradictions that will certainly impact Ahmad's and Patrick's subsequent trajectories.

References

Anderson, Benedict (1991): Imagined Communities: Reflections on the Origin and Spread of Nationalism (rev. edn). London: Verso.

Baba, Marietta/Dahl-Jørgensen, Carla (2013): Language policy in practice: re-bordering the nation. In: International Migration 51, no. 2, p. 60–76, https://doi.org/10.1111/imig.12048.

Beine, Michel/Souy, Bénédicte (2016): The evolution of immigration and asylum policy in Luxembourg: insights from IMPALA. In: CREA Discussion Paper Series from Centre for Research in Economic Analysis. University of Luxembourg.

Belling, Luc/de Bres, Julia (2014): Digital superdiversity in Luxembourg: the role of Luxembourgish in a multilingual Facebook group. In: Discourse, Context & Media, no. 4–5, p. 74–86, https://doi.org/10.1016/j.dcm.2014.03.002.

Blommaert, Jan (2003): Commentary: A sociolinguistics of globalization. In: Journal of Sociolinguistics 7, no. 4, p. 607–623, https://doi.org/10.1111/j.1467-9841.2003.00244.x.

Blommaert, Jan (2010): The Sociolinguistics of Globalization. Cambridge: Cambridge University Press.

Blommaert, Jan/Backus, Ad (2013): Superdiverse Repertoires and the Individual. In: de Saint-Georges, I./Weber, J.-J. (eds.): Multilingualism and Multimodality: Current Challenges for Educational Studies. Rotterdam: Sense, p. 11–32.

Bourdieu, Pierre (1991): Language and symbolic power. Cambridge, MA: Harvard University Press.

Burke, Peter (2004): Epilogue: languages and nations. In: Burke, P.: Language and Communities in Early Modern Europe. Cambridge: Cambridge University Press.

Busch, Brigitta (2012): The Linguistic Repertoire Revisited. In: Applied Linguistics 33, no. 5, p. 503–523, https://doi.org/10.1093/applin/ams056.

Busch, Brigitta (2017): Expanding the Notion of the Linguistic Repertoire: On the Concept of Spracherleben – The Lived Experience of Language. In: Applied Linguistics 38, no. 3, p. 340–358, https://doi.org/10.1093/applin/amv 030.

Canagarajah, Suresh (ed.) (2017): The Routledge handbook of migration and language. Oxon: Routledge.

Canagarajah, Suresh/Wurr, Adrian J. (2011): Multilingual Communication and Language Acquisition: New Research Directions. In: The Reading Matrix 11, no. 1, p. 1–15.

Carling, Jørgen (2002): Migration in the age of involuntary immobility: theoretical reflections and Cape Verdean experiences. In: Journal of Ethnic and Migration Studies 28, no. 1, p. 5–42, https://doi.org/10.1080/13691830120103912.

Carling, Jørgen/Collins, Francis (2018): Aspiration, desire and drivers of migration. In: Journal of Ethnic and Migration Studies 44, no. 6, p. 909–926, https://doi.org/10.1080/1369183X.2017.1384134.

Creese, Angela/Blackledge, Adrian (2010): Translanguaging in the Bilingual Classroom. A Pedagogy for Learning and Teaching. In: The Modern Language Journal 94, no. 1, p. 103–115, https://doi.org/10.1111/j.1540-4781.2009.00986.x.

de Bres, Julia (2014): Competing language ideologies about societal multilingualism among cross-border workers in Luxembourg. In: International Journal of the Sociology of Language, no. 227, p. 119–137, https://doi.org/10.1515/ijsl-2013-0091.

de Fina, Anna/Tseng, Amelia (2017): Narrative in the study of migrants. In: Canagarajah, S. (ed.): The Routledge handbook of migration and language. Oxon: Routledge, p. 381–396.

Duchêne, Alexandre/Heller, Monica (eds.) (2012): Language in Late Capitalism: Pride and Profit. New York: Routledge.

Ehrhart, Sabine/Fehlen, Fernand (2011): Luxembourgish: A Success Story? A Small National Language in a Multilingual Country. In: Fishman, J. A./García, O. (eds.): Handbook of Language and Ethnic Identity: the success-failure continuum in language and ethnic identity efforts. Oxford: Oxford University Press, p. 285–298.

Faist, Thomas (2013): The mobility turn: a new paradigm for the social sciences? In: Ethnic and Racial Studies 36, no. 11, p. 1637–1646, https://doi.org/10.1080/01419870.2013.812229.

Franziskus, Anne (2016): 'One does not say Moien, one has to say Bonjour': Expressing Language Ideologies through Shifting Stances in Spontaneous Workplace Interactions in Luxembourg. In: Journal of Linguistic Anthropology 26, no. 2, p. 204–221, https://doi.org/10.1111/jola.12124.

Franziskus, Anne/Gilles, Peter (2012): 'Et le präis direct etikett?' Non-overlapping repertoires in workplace communication in Luxembourg. In: Sociolinguistica: Internationales Jahrbuch für Europäische Soziolinguistik, no. 26, p. 58–71.

García, Ofelia/Wei, Li (2014): Translanguaging: Language, Bilingualism and Education. Basingstoke: Palgrave.

Gogonas, Nikos/Kirsch, Claudine (2016): 'In this country my children are learning two of the most important languages in Europe': ideologies of language as a commodity among Greek migrant families in Luxembourg. In: International Journal of Bilingual Education and Bilingualism 21, no. 4, p. 426–438, https://doi.org/10.1080/13670050.2016.1181602.

Glick Schiller, Nina (2009): A Global perspective on Transnational Migration: Theorizing Migration without Methodological Nationalism. www.compas.ox.ac.uk/media/WP-2009-067-Schiller_Methodological_Nationalism_Migration.pdf, 28/4/2018.

Grzymala-Kazlowska, Aleksandra/Phillimore, Jenny (2018): Introduction: rethinking integration. New perspectives on adaptation and settlement in the era of super-diversity. In: Journal of Ethnic and Migration Studies 44, no. 2, p. 179–196, https://doi.org/10.1080/1369183X.2017.1341706.

Heller, Monica (1987): The role of language in the formation of ethnic identity. In: Phinney, J./Rotheram, M. J. (eds.): Children's Ethnic Socialisation: Pluralism and Development. Newbury Park: Sage, p. 180–200.

Heller, Monica (2010): The Commodification of Language. In: Annual Review of Anthropology, no. 39, p. 101–114.

Horner, Kristine (2004): Negotiating the language-identity link: media discourse and nation building in Luxembourg. PhD dissertation, State University of New York at Buffalo.

Horner, Kristine (2009): Regimenting language, mobility and citizenship in Luxembourg. In: Extra, G./Spotti, M./van Avermaet, P. (eds.): Language testing, migration and citizenship: cross-national perspectives on integration regimes. London: Continuum, p. 148–166.

Horner, Kristine (2017): Language regimes and acts of citizenship in multilingual Luxembourg. In: Milani, T. M. (ed.): Language and citizenship. Broadening the agenda. Amsterdam: John Benjamins, p. 41–63.

Horner, Kristine/Weber, Jean-Jacques (2008): The language situation in Luxembourg. In: Current Issues in Language Planning 9, no. 1, p. 69–128, https://doi.org/10.2167/cilp130.0.

Irvine, Judith T./Gal, Susan (2000): Language ideology and linguistic differentiation. In: Kroskrity, Paul V. (ed.): Regimes of Language: Ideologies, Polities, and Identities. Santa Fe: School of American Research Press, p. 35–84.

Jørgensen, Jens Normann/Karrebæk, Martha/Madsen, Lian Malai/Møller, Janus Spindler (2011): Polylanguaging in Superdiversity. In: Diversities 13, no. 2, p. 22–37.

Juffermans, Kasper/Tavares, Bernardino (2017): South-North trajectories and language repertoires. In: Kerfoot, C./Hyltenstam, K. (eds.): Entangled Discourses: South-North Orders of Visibility. New York: Routledge, p. 99–115.

Kalocsányiová, Erika (2017): Towards a Repertoire-Building Approach: Multilingualism in Language Classes for Refugees in Luxembourg. In: Language and Intercultural Communication 17, no. 4, p. 474–493, https://doi.org/10.1080/14708477.2017.1368149.

Kalocsányiová, Erika (2018): At the borders of languages: the role of ideologies in the integration of forced migrants in multilingual Luxembourg. In: Journal of Ethnic and Migration Studies, https://doi.org/10.1080/1369183X.2018.1510307.

Kusenbach, Margarethe (2003): Street phenomenology: the go-along as ethnographic research tool. In: Ethnography 4, no. 3, p. 455–485, https://doi.org/10.1177/146613810343007.

Lamarre, Patricia (2013): Catching 'Montréal on the Move' and Challenging the Discourse of Unilingualism in Québec. In: Anthropologica 55, no. 1, p. 41–56.

Lüdi, Georges/Py, Bernard (2009): To be or not to be … a plurilingual speaker. In: International Journal of Multilingualism 6, no. 2, p. 154–167, https://doi.org/10.1080/14790710902846715.

Newman, David (2006): The lines that continue to separate us: borders in our "borderless" world. In: Progress in Human Geography 30, no. 2, p. 143–161.

OP (Office for official publications of the European Communities) (1973): Declaration on European Identity. In: Bulletin of the European Communities, no. 12, p. 118–122.

Otsuji, Emi/Pennycook, Alastair (2010): Metrolingualism: fixity, fluidity and language in flux. In: International Journal of Multilingualism 7, no. 3, p. 240–254, https://doi.org/10.1080/14790710903414331.

Park, Joseph Sung-Yul (2014): Cartographies of language: Making sense of mobility among Korean transmigrants in Singapore. In: Language and Communication, no. 39, p. 83–91, https://doi.org/10.1016/j.langcom.2014.09.001.

Pigeron-Piroth, Isabelle/Fehlen, Fernand (2015): Les langues dans les offres d'emploi au Luxembourg (1984–2014). University of Luxembourg.

Rodgers, Graeme (2004): "Hanging Out" with Forced Migrants: Methodological and Ethical Challenges. Forced Migration Review, no. 21, p. 48–49.

Shohamy, Elana (2006): Language policy: hidden agendas and new approaches. London: Routledge.

Silverstein, Michael (2014): How Language Communities Intersect: Is "superdiversity" an incremental or transformative condition? www.tilburguniversity.edu/upload/89a37ed3-3c2d-4d2b-bfb3-e907550f38f0_TPCS_107_Silverstein.pdf, 30/04/2018.

STATEC (2018a): Etat de la population. www.statistiques.public.lu, 15/9/2018

STATEC (2018b): Emploi salarié intérieur par lieu de résidence et nationalité 1995–2018. www.statistiques.public.lu, 15/9/2018.

Stevenson, Patrick (2006): National Languages in Transnational Contexts: Language, Migration and Citizenship in Europe. In: Mar-Molinero, C./Stevenson, P. (eds.): Language Ideologies, Policies and Practices: Language and the Future of Europe. Basingstoke: Palgrave Macmillan, p. 147–161.

Stevenson, Patrick (2014): Language (hi)stories: researching migration and multilingualism in Berlin. In: Horner, K./de Saint-Georges, I./Weber, J.-J. (eds.): Multilingualism and mobility in Europe: policies and practices. Frankfurt am Main: Peter Lang, p. 265–280.

Stevenson, Patrick (2017): Language and Migration in a Multilingual Metropolis: Berlin Lives. Cham: Palgrave Macmillan, https://doi.org/10.1007/978-3-319-40606-0.

Van Avermaet, Piet (2009): Fortress Europe? Language policy regimes for immigration and citizenship. In: Hogan-Brun, G./Mar-Molinero, C./Stevenson, P. (eds.): Discourses on Language and Integration: critical perspectives on language testing regimes in Europe. Amsterdam: John Benjamins, p. 15–44.

Van Avermaet, Piet/Rocca, Lorenzo (2013): Language testing and access. Exploring language frameworks. In: Studies in Language Testing, no. 36, p. 11–44.

Vertovec, Steven (2007): Super-Diversity and its Implications. In: Ethnic and Racial Studies, 30, no. 6, p. 1024–1054, https://doi.org/10.1080/01419870701599465.

About the author

Erika Kalocsányiová | University of Luxembourg | Campus Belval, Maison des Sciences Humaines | FLSHASE – Research on Multilingualism | 11, Porte des Sciences | 4366 Esch/Alzette | Luxembourg | T +352 46 66 44 5146 | erika.kalocsanyiova@uni.lu

Sociolinguistics, doctoral researcher; research interests: multilingualism, linguistic integration and language learning in contexts of forced migration

Acknowledgements

I would like to thank the participants for sharing their time and insights with me. Thanks are extended to Sabine Ehrhart and the editors for their thoughtful comments on previous drafts. Any inaccuracies remain my sole responsibility.

Border experiences along the Portugal/Spain border: a contribution from language documentation[1]

Xosé-Afonso Álvarez Pérez

Abstract

The project *Frontera hispano-portuguesa: documentación lingüística y bibliográfica* (FRONTESPO) was born in 2015 with the aim of exploring the linguistic situation of the border between Portugal and Spain, since, in spite of its extraordinary appeal, there was no overall description of it, and most studies were outdated. One of the tools created in the framework of this project was a speech corpus, the result of interviews with 287 informants from different age groups carried out in 64 towns on both sides of the border. In addition to linguistic data, the corpus provides information on border culture and experiences; some examples will be offered in this paper.

Keywords

Language documentation, speech corpus, personal testimonies, Spanish–Portuguese border, FRONTESPO.

1. *Introduction*

The objective of this paper is to present the basic pillars of a linguistic documentation project on the border between Spain and Portugal. Moreover, we aim to demonstrate that the interest in this initiative is not of a purely linguistic or sociolinguistic nature, as it provides information on border community culture and compiles numerous personal experiences from the inhabitants of the said communities regarding several aspects related to life on the border: contraband, clandestine immigration, personal and family relationships on both sides of the *Raya* ("line"), etc.

---

1 A Ramón y Cajal Fellowship granted by the Ministry of Economy and Competitiveness (RYC-2013-12761) funds this contribution, which was also developed within the framework of the project *Frontera hispano-portuguesa: documentación lingüística y bibliográfica* (FFI2014-52156-R), for which I am lead researcher.

Section one presents some basic notes on the historical and linguistic configuration of the Spain/Portugal border for those readers who may not be familiar with it, emphasizing the intense relationship between the two sides of the political border, as well as the richness of the linguistic landscape and the variety of sociolinguistic situations that arise along its 1,200 kilometers. Finally, we provide some information on the changes that the border territory has undergone in recent decades, which have stripped it of some unique characteristics due to depopulation and a lack of generational renewal.

Section two offers an overview of the main reasons behind the creation of the *Frontera hispano-portuguesa: documentación lingüística y bibliográfica* (Spain–Portugal Border: Linguistic and Bibliographic Documentation—FRONTESPO) project, with the intention of studying the language and culture (in a broad sense) of this exceptional space. Additionally, we provide a quick presentation of the tools of interest for border researchers: the speech corpus (section 2.1) and the multidisciplinary bibliography (section 2.2).

Finally, the third section of the chapter presents the project's potential with regard to knowledge of the tangible and intangible culture of the Spanish/Portuguese border, as well as of the life experiences of its inhabitants and the sudden changes they have experienced. The exhaustive thematic classification of the audiovisual recordings in the corpus is described; this classification allows users to quickly retrieve information on different aspects of the research. Lastly, samples are provided (selected from among many other possibilities, due to space limitations) of informant testimonies on their individual and group life experiences.

1.1 Formation and cross-border mobility

The political border between Spain and Portugal is considered to be one of the oldest boundaries in the world. Certainly, such a statement, as with any historical description on this topic, must be approached with caution, since the current concept of national border is quite different from its meaning prior to the 19th century. In that era, states had not yet established effective mechanisms of oversight over their territory, so political borders were usually a diffuse reality that did not significantly impede mobility or transnational relationships (e.g. Galician monasteries that received donations from the kings of both Portugal and Spain, see Barros 2015). Even in more modern times, the mobile nature of the borders cannot be disregarded, as discussed by geographers Trillo-Santamaría/Paül (2014).

In any case, and regardless of the significance that may be attributed to this political boundary, the fact is that the border between Spain and Portugal has remained practically unaltered since the Treaty of Alcañices (1297); later, the Treaty of Lisbon (1864) drew a precise demarcation between the two countries.

A distinguishing feature of the Spanish/Portuguese border is its peripherality (Valcuende/Kavanagh/Jiménez 2018, p. 38–41). The majority of both Spanish and Portuguese border regions are poorer than the national average. Moreover, because of the stability of the frontier and the low level of conflict in the area, state administrations were largely absent from this territory, which resulted in a precarious communications network and a lack of bureaucratic, educational, and health services that still persists today.

Consequently, the inhabitants of this marginalized territory had to develop survival strategies; many such strategies consisted of transforming the border into an opportunity. Economic constraints could be solved by resorting to cross-border trading (or smuggling), which took advantage of differences in the availability of essential goods (medicines, coffee, sugar, cloth, and the like) on both sides of the border, as well as the fluctuating exchange rate between Spain and Portugal. The lack of some services (doctors, veterinarians, priests, etc.) could also be solved by visiting the neighboring country. If it was not possible to earn a livelihood in one's own country, some families could walk a few kilometers and begin a new life at the other side of the border, sometimes even founding a new town.

Thus, over the centuries, relationships between the neighboring towns on either side of the border have always been intense (Amante 2010: 102), and are usually stronger than contact with towns located further toward the interior of the same country (Beswick 2014, p. 114). As a result, many borderland communities have developed specific feelings of identity and shared identities (Medina 2006), to the extent that some authors (e.g. Uriarte 1994) argue that there is a *border culture*. Relationships are intense, but also tense, because of the duality of the inhabitants of the borderlands. They are separated by a state boundary, which has clear symbolic and identity values attached to it, but, at the same time, there is a strong feeling of belonging to a supranational community, because of the intense cross-border relationship. Dialogue between border identity and state identity is always fraught (cf. Godinho 2009). Even self-identification may be quite complicated where there is a mismatch between state bureaucracies and experiences of life. Let us take the example of a testimony collected by Uriarte (2005, p. 74 [translation ours]):

> I was born in La Tojera [Spain] and I was baptized here in La Codosera [Spain]. I went to Portugal to study... well, I only studied for three years, no more... I write in Portuguese. My mother was born in a house 8 meters from the boundary marker, on the Portuguese side, opposite La Tojera. I was raised there. My mother was Portuguese... My father, that's another story. Here in Spain he got into trouble after the Civil War because of politics, so he moved to Portugal. I was five years old, and my brother two. So, my father and my mother were admitted into Portugal, but us, as we were Spaniards, we were rejected.

1.2 Linguistic configuration of the borderland

The Spanish/Portuguese border is a complex linguistic mosaic with extremely interesting features, which are merely outlined below.

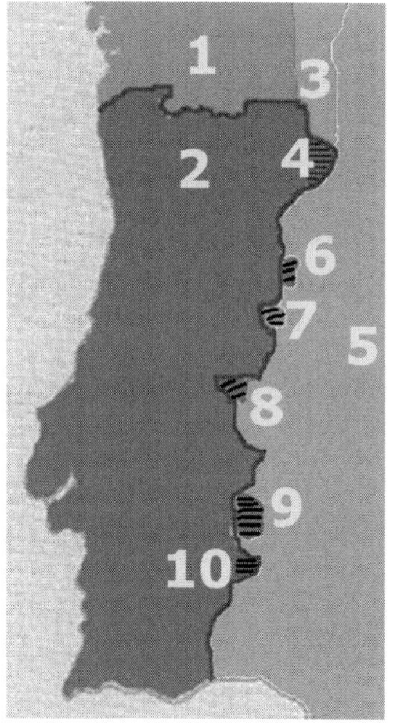

Image 1: Main linguistic areas of the Portugal/Spain border: 1. Galician, 2. Portuguese, 3. Astur-Leonese, 4. Mirandese, 5. Spanish, 6. to 9. Lusophone enclaves along the Spanish side of the border (6. La Alamedilla, 7. Valley of Jálama/ Xálima, 8. Herrera, Cedillo and strip of Alcántara, 9. Olivenza), 10. Barranquenho.

The establishment of a political border separated many territories that were quite homogeneous from a cultural and linguistic point of view. The north of the Iberian peninsula is part of the area known as the Romance continuum. Dialects spoken in that area are a direct evolution of the Latin imported into that territory two thousand years ago; therefore, there are no abrupt linguistic boundaries between adjacent towns or counties, but gradual and soft linguistic variation, with mutual understanding. The independence of Portugal (12th century) created a boundary that went through Galician–Portuguese and Astur-Leonese linguistic domains. Thus, the political border gave birth to two branches of the same linguistic system, which have evolved differently ever since, because they were under different state-sponsored languages, they had different centers of social prestige (that is, different models of educated language), and the border usually stopped the expansion of the linguistic innovations that emerged on the other side. This resulted in closely-related languages—Galician and Portuguese, Astur-Leonese, and Mirandese—that, however, have major internal differences (e.g. in terms of grammar and vocabulary) and external differences (e.g. in terms of orthography), as well as different sociolinguistic and legal statuses.

In the central and southern peninsula, linguistic transitions are sharper. Dialects spoken in that extensive area are not a natural evolution, but rather languages imported during the military conquest of the territory in the Middle Ages. Most of this expansion process took place when national frontiers were broadly defined, so linguistic areas more closely follow the limits of the political territories but, even so, there are mismatches.

Along the Spanish side of the border, there are some Portuguese-speaking localities that were the result of a variety of historical situations, such as shifts in the border, migration in different periods of history, and even military conquest (Olivenza). Until the second half of the 20th century, various Portuguese dialects were virtually the only language spoken in these areas, but they have suffered a sharp decline in recent decades, which enhances the appeal of these towns from a sociolinguistic point of view. Because of space constraints, this topic cannot be examined further here, but anyone interested in these territories, known as *linguistic enclaves*, may find a solid historical and linguistic description of the state of research in Carrasco (1996, 1997, 2007).

The aforementioned permeability and strong connection between people from both countries over the centuries have increased the appeal and complexity of this linguistic landscape. The inhabitants of both sides of the *Raya* maintain, as has been said, an intense relationship, and interpersonal contact necessarily entails contact between languages. In day-to-day interpersonal communication with their neighbors, dialect varieties are used, which can be quite different from the official language. Because of this contact situation, several processes of convergence and divergence have developed. In some cases, there is accommodation (a speaker adapts their language so their interlocutor can understand it better), as in the case of so-called *portuñol*, a mixture of Spanish and Portuguese, with interferences from the native language, which allows speakers who are not proficient in the other language to communicate with one another (Marcos-Marín 2001; Lipski 2006).

Nevertheless, the consequences of this language contact are not limited to code-switching situations. The continued cross-border relationship over the years and the relative isolation from the rest of the country have sometimes resulted in the emergence of specific linguistic varieties, such as *barranquenho*, a mixed Portuguese-based variety strongly influenced by southern Spanish dialects, spoken in the Portuguese town of Barrancos, which has close ties to the Andalusian towns of Encinasola and Rosal de la Frontera (Navas Sánchez-Élez 2011).

1.3 A changing territory

The intangible heritage of the borderland is currently undergoing an intense transformation. As happens in many rural areas, its characteristic features have been lost in recent decades, as towns have been immersed in a process of social and cultural homogenization and convergence with the rest of the territory driven by many factors. The generalization of schooling and the expansion of the mass media, especially TV, have contributed to very strong exposure to standard Spanish and Portuguese. Improvements in road infrastructure have generated a significant increase in internal mobility to county and provincial capitals (for shopping, health care, commuters, and the like). This means closer contact with the language spoken in those centers of prestige, therefore opening the way to linguistic harmonization with regional dialects. This loss of characteristic features constitutes an impoverishment of the national language as a whole. As most communities consist of rural towns that are far from prestige centers, from which innovations spread, the dialect varieties spoken there usually preserve archaic traits or specific lexical items (González Salgado 2017) that have disappeared from the rest of the linguistic domain (see an example of this process of change in section 3.2.1).

Furthermore, the traditional rural world is disappearing. Industrialization has resulted in the loss of traditional jobs and, consequently, the disappearance of the lexicon used in those crafts, as well as associated ethnographic customs. The accentuated depopulation of many towns has also led to a complete rupture with the normal life cycle of any linguistic community. Since young people emigrate to the cities or abroad, internal diversity is quite low, with only elderly people remaining, and the dialects they speak cannot be passed on to the new generations.

In addition to these issues, which are shared with rural territories, as mentioned above, factors related to the specific nature of the border area have also changed. The entry into force of the Schengen Agreement has greatly promoted mobility between Spain and Portugal; the number of cross-border commuters has risen significantly (Falagán/Carlos/Lorenzo 2013), as has cross-border mobility to make everyday purchases. Obviously, this daily human mobility means increasing exposure to the linguistic models of the other country, which may increase linguistic interference and, certainly, enhance some lines of research, such as sociolinguistics or linguistic landscape (cf. Álvarez Pérez forthcoming).

1.4 A little-known territory

Border studies is a dynamic research field that has steadily gained importance in recent times. Many works have indicated the extraordinary academic research interest in the borderlands, both inside and outside of Romance Europe, and some of these contributions have touched on linguistic aspects. In fact, in recent years, several books that include different papers with varied approaches and geographical scopes have been published, such as works by Treffers-Daller/Willemyns (2002), Filppula et al. (2005, especially part 1), and Watt/Llamas (2014).

Nevertheless, the linguistic landscape of the Spanish/Portuguese border has not received sufficient attention, despite it being extraordinarily interesting, and despite the unique nature of some of its characteristics. While research activity in the fields of anthropology, economics, and politics is quite intense—see, for example, the recent anthologies by Cairo/Godinho/Pereiro (2009), Trillo/Pires (2016), or Cairo et al. (2018)—the same cannot be said for linguistics.

Except for some short overall presentations, such as those by Maia (2001), Andrés (2007), and Gargallo (2011), there is no exhaustive study on the linguistic situation along the Spanish/Portuguese border. Although we have some dialect descriptions of areas near the Spanish/Portugal border, they are usually limited to the territory of each country: examinations from the cross-border perspective are scarce. It is true that there are some laudable exceptions, such as Santos (1967), Maia (1977), or Matias (1984); however, their contents are somewhat outdated, since the fieldwork was conducted between 1959 and 1974. The scarcity of primary data available to the research community, particularly in Portugal, must be emphasized. Neither Spain nor Portugal has an overall linguistic atlas: the *Atlas Lingüístico de España y Portugal* was abandoned, and the *Atlas Lingüístico de la Península Ibérica* and the *Atlas Linguístico-Etnográfico de Portugal e da Galiza* are still being edited today, many decades after the fieldwork was completed. In any case, as these are traditional geolinguistic works, they provide a limited typology of data: older speakers, little spontaneous speech, no publication of the recordings, and so on.

In summary, there are no comprehensive studies of the border or a significant portion thereof; in fact, the current linguistic and sociolinguistic situation of some areas and their evolution throughout history remain virtually unknown. In addition, as the main linguistic collections date back more than four decades, and most of them are unpublished or are still being edited, scholars have limited access to the primary data.

2. *A new initiative to research on the borderland: objectives and methods of the FRONTESPO project*

The FRONTESPO project began in 2015 as a sort of reaction to the state of research described under the preceding headings. Its main objective is to achieve an overarching, comprehensive study of the linguistic situation along the entire Spanish/Portuguese border, at present and historically. Accordingly, its main goals are:

a) Preservation (and promotion) of the traditional language spoken along the borderland. As explained in section 1.3, a rich cultural and linguistic heritage is disappearing at an increasing rate. It is imperative, then, to take urgent measures to document this treasure exhaustively, with scientific rigor and in a way that is open to stakeholders and scholars. We do not, however, want to restrict the perspective of the project to a "museum-like" approach. The documentation process must be the first step to show the value of cultural and linguistic diversity, with the ultimate aim of enhancing revitalization.

b) Study of the internal diversity of linguistic communities. Traditional dialectology has prioritized the language of older speakers, since it transmits a "purer" linguistic image. Without renouncing the documentation of traditional language, our project is particularly interested in younger speakers, as they exhibit extremely interesting linguistic and sociolinguistic features, because they are more exposed to standard languages via schooling and the mass media, and to regional centers of prestige, as they have greater mobility. An approach to the vision of young people is also necessary because positive attitudes of middle-aged and young speakers are essential for the survival of minority languages in bilingual areas such as Miranda do Douro, Portuguese enclaves in Spain, or the Valley of Jálama among others.

c) Exploration of sociolinguistic issues, with special attention to analysis of the linguistic identities and attitudes within border communities. The Spanish/Portuguese border is an extraordinary laboratory in which to research linguistic identities, attitudes, and even self-assessments of speakers' own dialects. Santos (1967, p. 390) gives an eloquent testimony, an ironic song collected from a Galician peasant from Entrimo (province in Ourense, Spain), where he reflects on his own dialect variety: "Eu non falo castellano | galego nin portugués: | falo *entremesellano* | que participa dos trés" ("I don't speak Castilian | or Galician or Portuguese: | I speak *entremesellano* | which takes things from those three").

However, it is not possible to study the linguistic configuration of the territory without also examining geographic and historical factors that have been key in the said configuration.

a) The first aspect that interests us is cross-border mobility. Cross-border mobility has been a constant throughout different historical periods, both openly (via migrant workers, daily purchases, intermarriage, and the like) and in clandestine contexts such as smuggling, clandestine migration, exile, and political refugees, etc. Interpersonal contact logically brings with it sporadic contact between different national and regional languages, with the consequent phenomena of interference or accommodation. However, sometimes the consequences are more structural. All along the border, there are several Portuguese-speaking enclaves in Spain that are the result of Portuguese migrations (shepherds, agricultural workers, smugglers, etc.) throughout history: Cedillo, Herrera de Alcántara, La Codosera, etc. Our aim, therefore, is to safeguard the speakers' own voices and direct experiences of cross-border mobility and their relationships with the neighboring country.

b) Another crucial aspect that interests us greatly is to highlight shared heritage and experiences. We are deeply interested in the value of unity, in what both sides of the border have in common, and in shared life experiences and memories that overcome the political boundary. In this regard, we embrace the remarks of Beswick (2014, p. 107): "exacerbated no doubt by centuries of military and political disagreement, traditional narratives concerning the nature of Spanish and Portuguese identity have generally highlighted differences rather than similarities between the two nations."

c) Finally, in the same way that we have defended the need for linguistic description not to be archaeological, we also believe that research on personal experiences should not be limited to the remote past, but rather the present must also be studied. We are also very interested in the changes in the *status quo* introduced by the Schengen Agreement. As Kavanagh noted:

> Talking not long ago with one of my friends [...] of the changes brought about at his village on the Portuguese/Spanish border by the so-called "Europe Without Borders" (or at least without internal borders), he thought for a moment and then he replied, carefully and repeating his words: "You may remove the door but the doorframe remains... You may remove the door, but the doorframe remains" (Kavanagh 2000, p. 47; cf. also Kavanagh 2011).

FRONTESPO has two tools to fulfill these objectives: a speech corpus and a multidisciplinary bibliography, which will be outlined below. We would also like to mention here our project's commitment to open access, which is essential for data to be available not only to researchers, but also to the communities being studied. It fully embraces the principles of action stated in the *Manifeste des Digital Humanities* (ThatCamp 2010), and, in order to guarantee free access to the data and the use thereof, the materials gathered or produced by FRONTESPO are available under a *Creative Commons Attribution–ShareAlike 4.0.* license.

2.1 *Speech corpus of the Portugal/Spain border (FRONTESPO-COR)*

FRONTESPO-COR (http://www.frontespo.org/en/corpus, ISSN 2605-0471) is the result of field research mostly undertaken between July 2015 and June 2016 in nine survey areas along the Spanish/Portuguese border. Sixty-four survey points make up the network. The primary criteria for the choice of the villages to be explored was that all Spanish provinces and Portuguese districts must be present and that a wide variety of linguistic and sociolinguistic situations had to be represented. Additionally, for each of the survey zones, at least one of the locations chosen in each country should have been previously explored in dialect atlases or monographs, so diachronic comparisons could be established.

Two hundred and seventeen individual and group interviews were conducted, with 287 main and secondary informants. At least three informants were interviewed at each survey point, with both sexes represented and age stratification in three ranges. As previously explained, we have not followed the *archeological perspective* of traditional dialectology; we do not neglect the transformations that are being driven by younger generations. However, we also took into account that most of the border towns are small and have an aging population, so it was not advisable to use age ranges of equal length: a) speakers over 75 years old; b) speakers between 50 and 75 years old; c) speakers under 50 years old.

The corpus consists of 290 hours of raw recordings, most of them (237 hours) on video. The fact that most of the interviews were videotaped is a strong asset in terms of both documentation and dissemination. Video recordings capture what is called the *multimodality of language*: linguistic and semantic information is not transmitted only through the voice, but also with facial gestures, eye and body movement, etc. Additionally, seeing an informant's gestures allows for a better understanding of the explanation of some concepts or activities: the shape of an object, agricultural procedures, a recipe, etc. For non-scholars, an audiovisual corpus is a friendlier format to consult and to share on social networks.

The main thematic core consists of a semi-structured conversation about several semantic fields related to the daily life of borderland communities: agricultural work, cattle, parts of the house, wildlife, winemaking, etc. There is a small questionnaire, with about a hundred concepts, which is a common basis for all the surveys, so it will be possible to establish systematic comparisons throughout the network (e.g. dialectometry or maps to explore lexical variation).

A second section explores the informants' linguistic behavior and identities, such as the (perceived) degree of divergence between their own varieties, neighbors' dialects and the standard; informants' perception of the process of linguistic change within the community; their degree of understanding of the language spoken on the other side of the border, etc.

Finally, the third block consists of a more spontaneous conversation about the informants' experiences related to the border (smuggling, migration, relationships between Portuguese people and Spaniards, and the like) and ethnographic topics (contrast between present-day life and the past, traditional procedures for making bread or cheese, etc.). Thus, we have been able to compile a large amount of material here that has a significant linguistic value, as it documents the informants' spontaneous speech and, at the same time, it can be used by researchers from a wide variety of fields.

2.2 *Multidisciplinary bibliography of the Portugal/Spain border (FRONTESPO-BIB)*

The borderland is a complex environment in which many factors (demographic, economic, historical, linguistic, political, etc.) intersect in such a way that it becomes impossible to examine certain issues without taking information from other academic fields into account. For instance, it is impossible to research the Lusophone communities in Spain without consulting literature on the historical processes of border delimitation or examining a vast number of works on cross-border migration. The need to consult the literature from several academic fields is an important handicap for border studies, since it is very difficult for scholars to keep up to date with the latest developments; in addition, some scholars are not familiar with bibliographical databases or catalogs from other academic fields. Another important issue is the existence of a significant number of little-known sources, such as articles in local journals or monographs published by the municipalities or local cultural associations, which explains their limited circulation and distribution.

FRONTESPO-BIB (http://www.frontespo.org/en/bibliografia, ISSN 2605-0498) is a user-friendly multidisciplinary database that compiles primary and secondary sources that study the border from any of its multiple perspectives (anthropology, economics, geography, literature, etc.) and enable an understanding of the linguistic situation in the region over the centuries. Currently, the site offers 1,500 records of linguistic items; we are currently working on the publication of 5,000 bibliographical sheets from other fields, but which are also relevant to linguistic studies, since we are not in a position to organize an exhaustive bibliography that covers border studies from all perspectives.

In addition to the bibliographic database, we have included several links to websites: official agencies that manage cross-border programs, studies of the area's cultural or natural heritage, pages studying the language of a particular region, geographic and historical descriptions of border towns, etc. (cf. http://www.frontespo.org/es/enlaces).

3. *Contributions to the study of border culture from a linguistic documentation project*

The main objective of our FRONTESPO project was to collect a speech corpus that would reflect the linguistic diversity within borderland communities. It is essential, for this purpose, to collect fluent and almost spontaneous speech. Informants are expected to be more relaxed when talking about topics present in their daily life, so they may be relieved of the discomfort and artificiality of the interview situation; therefore, the language they produce will be more spontaneous, and it will more closely reflect the dialect features of the linguistic variety the informant uses normally.

Besides that, we wanted to collect information that could be of interest in understanding the linguistic situation of the border: cross-border migrations, interpersonal contact and its intensity now and in past decades, language used in daily communication when the Portuguese and the Spaniards come together in the same place.

Thirdly, the surveys aimed to obtain information about traditional life in border communities that is essential to understanding the vocabulary of many semantic fields. As the *Wörter und Sachen* ("words and things") approach has demonstrated, it is not possible to separate the understanding of lexical designations from the knowledge of the artifacts they refer to. Let us illustrate this with a simple example; anyone who only thinks of modern bee hives—plastic or wood structures with sliding frames inside—will hardly understand the reasoning and etymology behind designations such as the Galician *cortizo* or Spanish *cepo*, which recall traditional constructions for apiculture, made with cork (the former) or inside a hollow tree, covered with a stone (the latter).

3.1 Subject classification of the corpus

To facilitate searching for the materials, the recordings in our corpus are organized by topic into 10 categories, with 43 topics. Below is a list of the topical categories and the most relevant topics within each one, along with descriptors or additional information, as necessary.

Cross-border relationships

- Trade and smuggling: products, means of concealment, routes, etc.
- Migrations: economic migrants, clandestine border crossings, deserters and people who avoided military service, political refugees, etc.
- Relationships with people from the other side of the border: at fairs, on pilgrimages, in stores, etc.
- Relationships with the state and its agents, especially encounters with customs officers from both sides, although other authorities are not excluded.

Historical and geographic context of border communities

- Economic and social transformations in recent decades: depopulation, aging, economic migrations, loss of traditional way of life, etc.
- The rediscovery of the *Couto Misto*, a sort of microstate that was the result of complex medieval feudal relationships. It became extinct with the Treaty of Lisbon (1864). However, in the mid-1990s, the interest in this territory re-emerged both in academic and cultural groups (see, for example, García Mañá 2000), which promoted the recognition of its unique nature and the symbolic restitution of its legal institutions.
- Testimonies on the Spanish Civil War (1936–1939), especially from the Portuguese side of the border, which was a place of refuge, albeit not always successfully (cf. Simões 2016).

Linguistic attitudes and behavior. Identity

- Linguistic situation in the community: differences between the language of older and younger people, linguistic transmission, and prospects for the future.
- Language in the neighboring places in the same country: degree of (perceived) linguistic difference from neighboring towns from Spain and Portugal.
- Language of the neighboring country and linguistic behavior with nationals from the other country: is there mutual comprehension? Must they change or adapt their language? Which country do they associate themselves with? These kinds of assessments are particularly interesting when surveying certain communities: Lusophone towns on the Spanish side of the border, people whose family history comes from the other country, etc.

Agriculture and livestock. Crafts and trades

- Horses and pack animals. Sheep and goat breeding. Pig farming. Cattle.
- Trees and forestry use.
- Gardens and fruit trees. Grains. Volunteer plants.
- Kinds of plots and agricultural operations.
- Processed products: bread, clothing and weaving, dairy products, olive oil, wine, etc.
- Tools and farm implements.

Other aspects of cultural and material reality

- Romantic relationships and family.
- Meals and parts of the day.
- Parts of the body.
- Parts of the house and related buildings. Furniture and household utensils.
- Stories and legends.
- Other ethnographic information (e.g. folk medicine).

As can be seen, this topical classification in such a large corpus will allow researchers to access extensive information on the border between Spain and Portugal from diverse perspectives, not just in the field of linguistics. This is because the corpus preserves and disseminates information and personal testimony on several subjects, especially those related to the material reality of border cultures, mobility, and interpersonal contact. In the next section, we will provide some samples as an example of the potential of this corpus.

3.2 Sample of border experiences

Due to limited space, the texts are offered directly in English (the translation is ours), except in the case of section 3.2.1., as a linguistic issue is commented on, and it is therefore important to respect the statement in the same language in which it was created. In any event, those interested may consult the original texts on the website for our speech corpus: http://www.frontespo.org/en/corpus.

3.2.1 Intergenerational dialogues with a transforming language

As has been remarked in section 1.3, the border region is undergoing a significant process of social, economic, and cultural change, of which the transformation of the language is a part. As a tangible example of the process of linguistic change, we have selected a fragment from an interview with Informant 1, born in 1952 in the town of Sela (province of Pontevedra, Spain), but who lives during the working week in the city of Vigo, fifty kilometers from there, and who is thus exposed to another Galician dialect, and, above all, to Spanish. Another inhabitant of Sela, Informant 2, 18 years older, also attended the interview, and he could not resist the temptation to correct certain answers provided during the conversation (highlighted in italics).

> INTERVIEWER: E... e cando se deixa un terreo... repousar e... non se labra dun ano para, para que despois teña máis forza?
> INFORMANT1: O barbecho. Eso era barbecho, non? Si, creo que era, si.
> *INFORMANT2: E | ou resteba.*
> INT: Resteva?
> INF1: Bueno, si, dito doutra maneira, si. E-, el [INF2] logo vaiche dar información...
> *INF2: Ermo.*
> INT: Ermo tamén?
> INF1: Si.
> *INF2: Tamén se lle dicía ermo.*
> [...]
> INF1: Esa é a naranxa.
> INT: E a árbore?
> INF1: O nara- | a naranxeira... naranxeira, laranxeira...
> INT: E cada un | E cando se quita a casca, cada unha das...?
> INF1: Gagos | ja- | ga- | jagos -como é, gajos, ou...?
> *INF2: Tetos.*
> INF1: Si.
> *INF2: Tetos.*
> INF1: Si, iso depende de... Si, cada, cada [...]
> INF1: A | cereixas, a cereixeira.
> INT: Cereixeira. | E o que....?
> *INF2: Cerdeira*
> INF1: Ou a ce- | ou cerdeira... si, si, si, si.
> *INF2: Cerdeira, cereixeira.*
> INT: E o que ten dentro, que é duro?
> INF1: Ese [sic] é a pepita.
> *INF2: Esa é a carabulla.*
> INF1: A carabuñ- | si, pepita ou carabuña, si.
> INT: Carabuña.
> INF1: Ch- | Depende...
> INT: E... aquí [fotografía]
> INF1: As castañas...
> INT: E a árbore?
> INF1: O castiñeiro.
> INF1: Ah... esas son as noces, o nogal.

INF2: *Nogueira. Nogueira*
INF1: A nogueira, si. Máis que nada nogueira.
[...]
INT: Moi ben, e... a... a parte de fóra do pan?
INF1: A f- | -do... pan? | A corteza... | a casca, a casca.
INF2: Codia...
INF1: Casca | codia, si.
INT: E o de dentro?
INF1: O de dentro é miga.
INF2: Miolo...
INF1: Bueno, miga... [Riso]
INT: [Riso] Vale, e...
INF1: É, é, é | iso vese | vai en plan de... unha década, máis ou menos, temos unha... unha visión distinta.[2]

INF1's answers are clearly influenced by Spanish (*barbecho, naranxeira, nogal, pepita, miga*) or other Galician varieties (*casca, cereixeira*), while INF2 still retains the traditional designation that was used in the town. In fact, when INF2 corrects INF1, the latter acknowledges it, and he usually agrees that the designation provided by INF2 is more genuine. That is, he retains traditional forms in his passive vocabulary, but he has lost them as active

2 To make the situation more understandable, I was compelled to provide some English synonyms that are not normally used. This is not the case in the original forms; their vitality is quite similar in current oral and popular Galician. || INT: And... when you let a field... rest and it is not plowed for a year, so it gains strength? | INF1: Fallow. It was fallow land, wasn't it? Yeah, I think so. | *INF2: And / or unplowed.* / INT: Unplowed? | INF1: Yes, well, said in other words, yes. He [INF2] will tell you later... | *INF2: Barren.* / INT: Also barren? | INF1: Yes. | *INF2: It was also called barren.* / [...] INF1: This is an orange. INT: And the tree? INF1: Oran- | orange tree... orange tree... INT: And each of them | When you remove the peel, each of the...? INF1: Pieces | Pea- | Pie – | Peace – How do you say it, pieces, or...? *INF2. Wedges*. INF1: Yes. *INF2: Wedges.* INF1: Yes, it depends on... Yes, each, each... [...] INF1: Cherries, cherry tree. INT. Cherry tree | And the...? *INF2: Prunus*. INF1: Or pru- | or prunus... yes, yes, yes, yes. *INF2. Cherry tree, prunus.* INT. And what is inside, that's hard? INF1: This is the seed. *INF2: This is the stone*. INF1: The stone | Yes, seed or stone, yes. INT: Stone. INF1. It depends... INT: And... here [looking at a photo]. INF1: Chestnuts. INT: And the tree? INF1: Ah..., these are the walnuts, the walnut tree. *INF2: Juglans. Juglans.* INF1: Juglans, yes. Above all, juglans. [...]. INT. Very good. And... and the outside part of a piece of bread? INF1: Of bread... The rind... | The peel, the peel. *INF2: Crust.* INF1: Peel, crust, yes. INT: And the inside part? INF1. Inside, it is a crumb. *INF2: Center...* INF1: Well, crumb... [he laughs]. INT [Laughs] OK, and... INF1: That shows | About a decade... more or less, we have a... a different perspective.

lexis. This concrete example is evident proof of the necessity to systematically document all the linguistic varieties spoken in the borderlands. In order to get a realistic picture, it is imperative to gather all kinds of data, and to compare the linguistic features of each age band.

3.2.2 The border as the limit of state... and clerical authority

Informant M., from the town of La Alamedilla (Salamanca, Spain), born in 1939, remembers that the town priest was very strict about prohibiting dances and parties during Lent, so the town's young people used to cross the border and dance on the hill, on the other side of the *Raya*, where the priest was powerless to do anything; his spiritual power was also limited by the confines of worldly power:

> He wouldn't let us dance here. We were little couples, already into all of that, and, of course, we wanted to dance, but since it was Lent, he wouldn't let us dance and here, since it was like that, he would follow us, the guy, if we went to dance or sing on that crest over there, he was going to catch us [...] so what did we do? [...] we went a few trees past the *Raya*, and we would go there to dance, and he was going to catch us there, the priest, he was going to catch us, but we didn't pay any attention to him, we would say to him, "Hey, man, we're in Portugal, we can dance." Some would hide, others couldn't. But we were a bit cheekier and when he said to us, "Fine, you'll have to come back down to the town eventually," we said to him, "OK, well, when we come down, you'll say something then, but now we're here in Portugal."

3.2.3 Deserters and draft dodgers during the Portuguese Colonial War

In the town of Messegães (in the local government area of Monção), we have collected detailed testimony on the heartrending consequences of the Portuguese Colonial War, a long, difficult confrontation between the Armed Forces of Portugal and different national liberation movements in the territories of Angola, Guinea-Bissau, and Mozambique between 1961 and 1974.

To avoid being drafted (or sent to Africa if they were already in the army), it was common for men of military age to try to cross the border illegally, to continue on to France or another country, where they could seek refuge. This was a very dangerous decision, as they not only had to escape Portuguese authorities, but also the Spanish Civil Guard, which would hand the fugitives over to Salazar's police, with harsh consequences for them:

- And your husband, and your husband was another one who fled... and many, many, many fled. [...] Those times were very difficult for the mothers, poor things, because it's one thing to say it and another to do it. As it happened, I, at the time, didn't have anyone; my brother was already a much older man and he already had another life. But the people who had children of military age at that time suffered a lot, a lot, a lot. And that boy, that C., had his entire family here, his mother, father, sisters, they had three sisters, he had everything; he spent years, I don't know how many, without seeing any of them. But it wasn't, it wasn't because he didn't want to come. He couldn't... if they caught him, they would arrest him. Being arrested at that time for not doing your military service was worse, it was worse, like political [prisoners], they would take them to [the penal colony of] Tarrafal. Life was very, very difficult for young men. But then the 25th of April [revolution] happened, and they came back... we were very happy. I remember that boy, when he arrived here, he visited everything, all of the houses; he seemed crazy.
- And so many, so many that left, even men who were already married and everything [...]
- They called them *carneiros* ['lambs'].
- They crossed the river here [...] they had certain places where the other smuggler who picked them up was waiting there at that place that they had agreed on, that's what they said, right? I'm not really sure. And then they went by train, but they got to a point that they had to do something, I'm not sure what, get off the train, and hide there in a place, waiting for someone to come get them, only then after the Spanish Civil Guard got them, if they got them, they came back, prison by prison, on their way to Portugal, and they suffered a lot along the way.

3.2.4 Blended identities along the Spanish bank of the Guadiana River

In the westernmost part of the province of Huelva, on the Spanish side of the Chanza/Chança and Guadiana Rivers, Portuguese speakers can be found today. They are Spanish citizens descended from miners, shepherds, or agricultural workers who crossed the border in different waves over the centuries; the most recent wave dates back to the 1920s, and the majority of the inhabitants who remain in the area are the third generation. Generally, they are bilingual speakers, who use Spanish with strangers or with the inhabitants of the municipal capitals, where many have gone to live (cf. López de Aberasturi 2016).

The informant A. G. A. was born in 1941 in El Romerano (Romerão), in the province of Huelva (Spain). His parents were also born in Spain, but three of his four grandparents were Portuguese, from the Guerreiros do Rio area, on the other side of the Guadiana, less than 1 km away. When asked by the interviewer about his self-identification in terms of nationality, he responds that he considered himself Portuguese in his town, since that language was spoken there; however, in other Spanish towns, he presented himself as "Spanish". Curiously, when he and other young people from the town made fun of the fishermen who came from Portugal, they referred to them as "Portuguese" (demonym followed by a series of imprecations).

- How did they see themselves, how do you see yourself?
- There I saw myself as Portuguese, because I spoke Portuguese, I considered myself to be Portuguese
- Even though you have a Spanish national identification document?
- Of course, we only ever talked about Portugal, because we saw ourselves as Portuguese; once you leave there, then not anymore, then you say "I'm Spanish". While I was in El Romerano, we only spoke Portuguese... Even to make fun of the fishermen, who were with, with, with their boats, to catch fish.
- With those... what did they call them, the *colher* ["spoon"]...
- *Colher*. With a *colher*. They couldn't come to Spain with the *colheres.*
- No?
- They couldn't come to Spain, because we were, we were so sick that four or five of us young guys would get together when we saw them coming, we'd take a ton of rocks, like that, we'd hide, and when they had put out their net, boom, boom, boom, boom, we'd drop the rocks, their nets were full of rocks. Of course, the nets were full of rocks so they started to go like this, to get the rocks out, because the nets were breaking. And the man started to yell, "hey, sons of bitches," and on and on, and we said to him, "go on, you Portuguese fat ass"... We were very sick, very sick.

4. Conclusion

In the preceding pages, we have attempted to demonstrate the extraordinary linguistic, cultural, and anthropological appeal of the Spain/Portugal border. Although this border space has been in the midst of a complex process of socioeconomic transformation for decades that has led to the loss of many of the traits that differentiated it from the rest of Spain and Portugal, it is still possible to document a good deal of intangible cultural heritage. Part of this legacy are the numerous personal testimonies of the community's inhabitants, which provide information on different aspects of their lives, both from a personal as well as a collective perspective: the scarcity they experienced in their youth, the emigration which emptied out towns, the new machinery that has transformed agricultural and livestock production, and, of course, numerous experiences related to living on the border, from diverse perspectives.

Therefore, undertaking a systematic process to document the intangible cultural heritage of the border is justified. In this regard, we have explained the foundations of the FRONTESPO project and its main components, and have demonstrated that, although it is a linguistic documentation initiative, it has the potential to provide results of enormous interest to researchers in other fields. The examples given in section 3.2., although scant due to space limitations, bring to light several very interesting issues for border studies, such as the linguistic transformation of communities (Sela), moving from one side of the border to the other to free oneself of the restrictions of one's own country—whether in a festive atmosphere (La Alamedilla), or in a more tragic context, that of the Portuguese Colonial War (Messegães)—, and the blended identities that result from a porous border where the political limits do not match the linguistic boundaries (El Romerano). As the distinguished writer and economist José Luis Sampedro wrote (not in reference specifically to the Spanish/Portuguese border, although this reflection fully applies):

> My borders are all transcendable, like the membrane of a cell, without whose permeability, life would not be possible; life, which is giving and receiving, exchange, crossing boundaries. And even more than transcendable, the border is provocative, erecting itself as a challenge, a loving invitation to be crossed, to be possessed, to deliver itself to give us with its defeat our triumph: that is the profound enchantment of living on the border. Enchantment comprised ambivalence, ambiguity (they are not the same), overlapping, living here and there at the same time without erasing the differences.

> Those in the center, on the other hand, experience the border in the opposite manner. That adventure repels them, or unsettles them, and they retreat from the border inwards, like the ebbing sea. They withdraw to the center of the enclosed space; they settle into black and white, fearful of the infinite, delicate grays. (Sampedro 1991, p. 16–17)

References

Álvarez Pérez, Xosé Afonso (forthcoming): Language contact on the Spanish–Portuguese border: a contribution from the linguistic landscape perspective. In: Bouzouita, M./Enghels, R.: Different perspectives on convergence and divergence in Ibero-Romance: language contact and contrasting national varieties [working title]. Berlin: De Gruyter.

Amante, Maria Fátima (2010): Local discursive strategies for the cultural construction of the border: the case of the Portuguese–Spanish border. In: Journal of Borderlands Studies 25, no. 1, p. 99–114, https://doi.org/10.1080/08865655.2010.9695754.

Andrés Díaz, Ramón de (2007): Linguistic borders of the Western Peninsula. In: International Journal of the Sociology of Language 184, p. 121–138, https://doi.org/10.1515/IJSL.2007.018.

Barros, Carlos (2015): A fronteira medieval entre Galiza e Portugal. In: Debater a História 2, no. 7, p. 27–40.

Beswick, Jaine (2005): Linguistic homogeneity in Galician and Portuguese borderland communities, In: Estudios de Sociolingüística 6, no. 1, p. 39–64.

Beswick, Jaine (2014): Borders within borders: Contexts of Language Use and Local Identity Configuration in Southern Galicia. In: Watt, D./Llamas, C. (eds.): Language, borders and identity, Edinburgh: Edinburgh University Press, p. 105–117.

Boller, Fred (1995): Die Isoglossenstaffelung in der galicisch-portugiesisch-spanischen Kontaktzone und im Lombada-Aliste-Grenzgebiet. Kiel: Westensee-Verlag.

Boller, Fred (1997): Contacto lingüístico entre el gallego-portugués y el asturianoleonés en la provincia de Zamora. ¿Frontera nítida o zona de transición? In: Lletres Asturianes 65, p. 7–31.

Cairo, Heriberto (ed.) (2018): Rayanos y forasteros. Fronterización e identidades en el límite hispano-portugués. Pozuelo de Alarcón: Plaza&Valdés.

Cairo Carou, Heriberto/Godinho, Paula/Pereiro, Xerardo (eds.) (2009): Portugal e Espanha. Entre discursos de centro e práticas de fronteira. Lisboa: Colibri.

Carrasco González, Juan M. (1996): Hablas y dialectos portugueses o galaico-portugueses en Extremadura. (Parte I: Grupos dialectales. Clasificación de las hablas de Jálama). In: Anuario de Estudios Filológicos, vol. XIX, p. 135–148.

Carrasco González, Juan M. (1997): Hablas y dialectos portugueses o galaico-portugueses en Extremadura (parte II y última: otras hablas fronterizas; conclusiones). In: Anuario de Estudios Filológicos, vol. XX, p. 61–79.

Carrasco González, Juan M. (2007): Falantes de dialectos fronteiriços da Extremadura espanhola no último século. In: Limite: Revista de Estudios Portugueses y de la Lusofonía vol. 1, p. 51–69.

Falagán Mota, Jorge/ Carlos Villamarín, Pablo de/Lorenzo Alonso, Pedro (2013): Movilidad transfronteriza de trabajadores entre Galicia y el norte de Portugal. In: Contabilidad y negocios 8, no. 15, p. 77–94, revistas.pucp.edu.pe/index.php/contabilidadyNegocios/article/view/6768, 5/14/2018.

Filppula, Markku et al. (eds.) (2005): Dialects across Borders: Selected Papers from the 11th International Conference on Methods in Dialectology. Amsterdam/Philadelphia: John Benjamins.

García Mañá, Luis Manuel (2000). Couto Mixto. Unha república esquecida. Vigo: Universidade de Vigo.

Gargallo Gil, José Enrique (2011): Fronteras romances en la Península Ibérica. In: Andrés Díaz, R. de (ed.): Lengua, ciencia y fronteras, Uviéu: Trabe, p. 35–68.

González Salgado, José Antonio (2017): El léxico portugués en las hablas dialectales de las comarcas rayanas españolas. In: Corbella, D./Fajardo, A. (eds.): Español y portugués en contacto. Préstamos léxicos e interferencias. Berlin: De Gruyter Mouton, p. 105–127.

Godinho, Paula (2009): Discursos palacianos. In: Cairo Carou, H./Godinho, P./Pereiro, X. (eds.) (2009): Portugal e Espanha. Entre discursos de centro e práticas de fronteira. Lisboa: Colibri, p. 73–91.

Kavanagh, William (2000): The Past on the Line: The Use of Oral History in the Construction of Present-day Changing Identities on the Portuguese–Spanish Border. In: Ethnologia Europaea 30, no. 2, p. 47–56.

Kavanagh, William (2011): Identidades en la frontera luso-española: permanencias y transformaciones después de Schengen. In: Geopolítica(s) 2, no. 1, p. 23–50, http://dx.doi.org/10.5209/rev_GEOP.2011.v 2.n1.37896.

Lipski, John M. (2006): Too close for comfort? The genesis of "portuñol/portunhol". In: Face, T. L./Klee, C. A. (eds.): Selected Proceedings of the 8th Hispanic Linguistics Symposium. Somerville, MA: Cascadilla Proceedings Project, p. 1–22.

López de Aberasturi, José Ignacio (2016): Dinámica sociolingüística y lenguas en contacto en la comunidad de habla de Ayamonte. PhD thesis. Granada: Universidad de Granada, digibug.ugr.es/handle/10481/46830, 9/23/2018.

Maia, Clarinda de Azevedo (1977): Os falares fronteiriços do concelho do Sabugal e da vizinha região de Xalma e Alamedilla. Coimbra: Universidade de Coimbra.

Maia, Clarinda de Azevedo (2001): Fronteras del español: aspectos históricos y sociolingüísticos del contacto con el portugués en la frontera territorial. In: II Congreso Internacional de la Lengua Española: El español en la sociedad de la información. Valladolid: Instituto Cervantes, Centro Virtual Cervantes. cvc.cervantes.es/obref/congresos/valladolid/ponencias/unidad_diversidad_del_espanol/5_espanol_y_portugues/azevedo_c.htm, 5/14/2018.

Marcos-Marín, Francisco (2001): De lenguas y fronteras: el espanglish y el portuñol. In: Nueva Revista de Política, Cultura y Arte, vol. 74, p. 70–79. www.nuevarevista.net/revista-lecturas/de-lenguas-y-fronteras-el-espanglish-y-el-portunol/, 5/14/2018.

Matias, Maria de Fátima de Rezende Fernandes (1984): Bilinguismo e níveis sociolinguísticos numa região luso-espanhola (concelhos de Alandroal, Campo Maior, Elvas e Olivença). Coimbra: Instituto de Língua e Literatura Portuguesas, Faculdade de Letras da Universidade de Coimbra.

Medina García, Eusebio (2006): Orígenes históricos y ambigüedad de la frontera hispano-lusa (La Raya). In: Revista de Estudios Extremeños 62, no. 2, p. 713–724.

Navas Sánchez-Élez, María Victoria (2011): El barranqueño: un modelo de lenguas en contacto. Madrid: Universidad Complutense.

Ossenkop, Christina (2013): Spanisch-portugiesischer Sprachkontakt in der Extremadura am Beispiel der Gemeinden Cedillo, Valencia de Alcántara und La Codosera. Wilhelmsfeld: Gottfried Egert Verlag.

Sampedro Sáez, José Luis (1991): Desde la frontera. Discurso leído el día 2 de junio de 1991, en su recepción pública, por el Excmo. Sr. Don José Luis Sampedro Sáez y contestación del Excmo. Sr. Don Gregorio Salvador Caja. Madrid: Real Academia Española. www.rae.es/sites/default/files/Discurso_Ingreso_Jose_Luis_Sampedro.pdf, 9/28/2018.

Simões, Dulce (2016): A guerra de Espanha na Raia luso-espanhola. Resistências, solidariedades e usos da memória. Lisboa: Colibri.

Santos, María José de Moura (1967): Os falares fronteiriços de Trás-os-Montes. Coimbra: Universidade de Coimbra.

ThatCamp (2010): Manifeste des Digital Humanities. https://tcp.hypotheses.org/318, 16/04/2019.

Treffers-Daller, Jeanine/Willemyns, Roland (eds.) (2002): Language Contact at the Romance-Germanic Language Border. Clevedon; Buffalo: Multilingual Matters.

Trillo-Santamaría, Juan-Manuel/Paül, Valerià (2014): The Oldest Boundary in Europe? A Critical Approach to the Spanish-Portuguese Border: The 'Raia' Between Galicia and Portugal. In: Geopolitics 19, no. 1, p. 161–181, https://doi.org/10.1080/14650045.2013.803191.

Trillo Santamaría, Juan Manuel/Pires, Iva (eds.) (2016): Fronteras en la investigación peninsular: temáticas y enfoques contemporáneos. Santiago de Compostela: USC.

Uriarte López, Luis M. (1994): La Codosera: culturas de frontera y fronteras culturales en la raya luso-extremeña. Mérida: Asamblea de Extremadura.

Uriarte López, Luis M. (2005): Culturas de frontera y fronteras culturales: la raya hispano-lusa y peruano-ecuatoriana. In: Arquivo de Beja, série III, tomo I, p. 73–84.

Valcuende, José María/Kavanagh, William/Jiménez, Juan Carlos (2018): Rasgos principales de la frontera hispano-portuguesa. In: Cairo, H. (ed.): Rayanos y forasteros. Fronterización e identidades en el límite hispano-portugués. Pozuelo de Alarcón: Plaza y Valdés, p. 37–49.

Watt, Dominic/Llamas, Carmen (eds.) (2014): Language, Borders and Identity. Edinburgh: Edinburgh University Press.

About the author

Xosé-Afonso Álvarez Pérez | Universidad de Alcalá | Departamento de Filología, Comunicación y Documentación | 3, Trinidad | 28801 Alcalá de Henares | Spain | xoseafonso.alvarez@gmail.com

Ph.D. in Linguistics (2008), BA in Romance Language Philology (2003) and Galician Philology (2005). *Ramón y Cajal* researcher at the University of Alcalá (Spain); his main lines of research include dialectology, geolinguistics, Romance linguistics, and minority languages. Further information is available on his personal website: www.geolinguistica.org/cv